M000093196

"A bold and compelling exploration of how power works in the context of today's social, political and environmental crises – looking beyond the usual political economy and behaviourist lenses – and offering fresh ideas and reflections from activism on how theory and practice can be joined up to strengthen movements for justice and human rights."

—*Andrea Cornwall, Professor at SOAS, University of London, UK*

"Like power itself, ideas about power are contested terrain. This timely collection effectively bridges theory and practice to inform a much-needed rethink of relevant conceptual frameworks, grounded in the authors' extensive hands-on experience with action-research, popular education and frontline empirical research."

—*Jonathan Fox, Professor at the Accountability Research Center, American University, USA*

"Through a range of chapters, *Power, Empowerment and Social Change* examines the nature and effect of the arbitrary use of power in contemporary democracies. The book draws upon a dialectic of practice and theory that helps dissect and expose the manipulation of democracy by ruling elites. More importantly, the essays acknowledge and illustrate the inherent power and creativity in people's struggles for justice and equality. Without these principles, there is no future."

—*Aruna Roy and Nikhil Dey, MKSS (Mazdoor Kisan Shakti Sangathan), India*

"This book is an exciting collection of chapters, which draws together theoretical and empirical work on power. The overall theoretical approach is grounded in a sophisticated understanding of the multi-dimensional nature of power relations. I highly recommend this collection to anyone who wishes to understand the complex relationship between power as domination and power as empowerment. It is ideal for both social scientists and social activists."

—*Mark Haugaard, Professor at the School of Political Science and Sociology, National University of Ireland, Galway*

POWER, EMPOWERMENT AND SOCIAL CHANGE

This book uncovers how power operates around the world, and how it can be resisted or transformed through empowered collective action and social leadership. The stakes have never been higher. Recent years have seen a rapid escalation of inequalities, the rise of new global powers and corporate interests, increasing impunity of human rights violations, suppression of civil society, and a re-shaping of democratic processes by post-truth, populist and nationalist politics.

Rather than looking at power through the lenses of agency or structure alone, this book views power and empowerment as complex and multidimensional societal processes, defined by pervasive social norms, conditions, constraints and opportunities. Bridging theory and practice, the book explores real-world applications using a selection of frameworks, tools, case studies, examples, resources and reflections from experience to support actors to analyse their positioning and align themselves with progressive social forces.

Compiled with social change practitioners, students and scholars in mind, *Power, Empowerment and Social Change* is the perfect volume for anyone involved in politics, international development, sociology, human rights and environmental justice who is looking for fresh insights for transforming power in favour of relatively less powerful people.

Rosemary McGee is a Senior Research Fellow in the Power and Popular Politics Cluster, Institute of Development Studies, University of Sussex, UK.

Jethro Pettit is a freelance consultant, facilitator and former Director of Teaching and Learning at the Institute of Development Studies at the University of Sussex, UK.

RETHINKING DEVELOPMENT

Rethinking Development offers accessible and thought-provoking overviews of contemporary topics in international development and aid. Providing original empirical and analytical insights, the books in this series push thinking in new directions by challenging current conceptualizations and developing new ones.

This is a dynamic and inspiring series for all those engaged with today's debates surrounding development issues, whether they be students, scholars, policy makers and practitioners internationally. These interdisciplinary books provide an invaluable resource for discussion in advanced undergraduate and postgraduate courses in development studies as well as in anthropology, economics, politics, geography, media studies and sociology.

Communication in International Development
Doing Good or Looking Good?
Edited by Florencia Enghel and Jessica Noske-Turner

Epistemic Freedom in Africa
Deprovincialization and Decolonization
Sabelo J. Ndlovu-Gatsheni

Foreign Aid in the Age of Populism
Political Economy Analysis from Washington to Beijing
Viktor Jakupec and Max Kelly

Researching South–South Development Cooperation
The Politics of Knowledge Production
Elsje Fourie, Emma Mawdsley and Wiebe Nauta

Aid Power and Politics
Edited by Iliana Olivié and Aitor Pérez

Participatory Arts in International Development
Edited by Paul Cooke and Inés Soria-Donlan

Energy and Development
Frauke Urban

Power, Empowerment and Social Change
Edited by Rosemary McGee and Jethro Pettit

POWER, EMPOWERMENT AND SOCIAL CHANGE

Edited by Rosemary McGee and Jethro Pettit

Routledge
Taylor & Francis Group

LONDON AND NEW YORK

First published 2020
by Routledge
2 Park Square, Milton Park, Abingdon, Oxon OX14 4RN

and by Routledge
52 Vanderbilt Avenue, New York, NY 10017

Routledge is an imprint of the Taylor & Francis Group, an informa business

© 2020 selection and editorial matter, Rosemary McGee and Jethro Pettit; individual chapters, the contributors

The right of Rosemary McGee and Jethro Pettit to be identified as the authors of the editorial material, and of the authors for their individual chapters, has been asserted in accordance with sections 77 and 78 of the Copyright, Designs and Patents Act 1988.

All rights reserved. No part of this book may be reprinted or reproduced or utilised in any form or by any electronic, mechanical, or other means, now known or hereafter invented, including photocopying and recording, or in any information storage or retrieval system, without permission in writing from the publishers.

Trademark notice: Product or corporate names may be trademarks or registered trademarks, and are used only for identification and explanation without intent to infringe.

British Library Cataloguing in Publication Data
A catalogue record for this book is available from the British Library

Library of Congress Cataloging-in-Publication Data
Names: McGee, Rosemary, editor. | Pettit, Jethro, editor.
Title: Power, empowerment and social change / edited by Rosemary McGee and Jethro Pettit.
Description: New York : Routledge, 2020.
Identifiers: LCCN 2019029840| ISBN 9781138575301 (Hardback) | ISBN 9781138575318 (Paperback) | ISBN 9781351272322 (eBook)
Subjects: LCSH: Power (Social sciences) | Equality. | Social change.
Classification: LCC HN49.P6 P687 2020 | DDC 303.3--dc23
LC record available at https://lccn.loc.gov/2019029840

ISBN: 978-1-138-57530-1 (hbk)
ISBN: 978-1-138-57531-8 (pbk)
ISBN: 978-1-351-27232-2 (ebk)

Typeset in Bembo
by Taylor & Francis Books

We dedicate this book to the courageous human rights defenders and environmental activists around the world who have lost their lives through contesting power. And to the Highlander Center, a social justice leadership training school in Appalachia, USA, that has shaped the careers of so many social justice activists, including several contributors to this book, and that suffered a devastating fire while we were compiling this volume.

CONTENTS

ILLUSTRATIONS

Figures

Tables

Boxes

CONTRIBUTORS

Mariela Arce Andrade brings a depth of experience to her work as a feminist popular educator. In Panama, she began her career as an economist, and became a founder and ongoing leader of the women's movement. She has served as the coordinator of Alforja, a network of Central American and Mexican popular educators; programme director of CEASPA, a Panamanian centre for adult education and social action; an advisor to UNICEF; and founding member of the Just Associates Mesoamerican team, where she has been a lead designer and facilitator of Just Associates (JASS) feminist leadership development schools and movement building initiatives.

Alexa Bradley has worked as an organiser, facilitator, organisational strategist and popular educator for over 25 years, with a particular focus on linking community organising to broader social movement strategies. She works with Just Associates (JASS), an international network dedicated to strengthening the voice, visibility and collective organising power of women to create a just, sustainable world for all. As JASS's Knowledge Development Director she supports the network and its partners in distilling learning from their work and sharing insights with a broad global audience. Previously she founded and directed Milwaukee Water Commons, an environmental justice organisation, and was a senior partner at both On the Commons and the Grassroots Policy Project, providing tools and training to community change organisations. Alexa lives in New York, USA.

Nandini Chami is deputy director at IT for Change (ITfC). Nandini explores the intersections of digital policy, development justice and gender equality in her research, and contributes to ITfC's policy advocacy efforts on digital rights and data governance frameworks. She also provides strategic support to ITfC's field centre – Prakriye, India – in the design of digitally enabled learning dialogues for the empowerment of rural women's collectives and adolescent girls.

With a doctorate in social anthropology, **Rosalind Eyben** has been successively a field worker for various development agencies, Chief Social Development Adviser at the United Kingdom Department for International Development and a Professorial Fellow at the Institute of Development Studies, from where she retired in 2013 to become an Emeritus Fellow. She has published extensively about power and relations in international development aid, including her reflexive memoir, *International Aid and the Making of a Better World*.

Walter Flores is the director of the Center for the Study of Equity and Governance in Health Systems (CEGSS), a Guatemalan civil society organisation (CSO) specialising in applied research, capacity building and advocacy around issues affecting indigenous population rights. He is also a steering committee member of the Community of Practitioners on Accountability and Social Action in Health (COPASAH), a global network of CSOs working towards improving healthcare services for marginalised populations through human rights, accountability and social mobilisation. He holds a PhD and an MCommH from the Liverpool School of Tropical Medicine, UK.

John Gaventa is a Professor and Director of Research at the Institute of Development Studies (IDS) at the University of Sussex, UK, having been a Research Fellow there since 1996. Linking research and practice in his own career, he has written and worked extensively on issues of citizenship and citizen action, power and participation, governance and accountability, and participatory forms of research. He is author of the award-winning book *Power and Powerlessness: Quiescence and Rebellion in an Appalachian Valley*, and with others developed what is known as the 'powercube' approach to analysing power relations (www.powercube.net).

Anita Gurumurthy is a founding member and executive director of IT for Change (ITfC), where she leads research on emerging issues in the digital context, with a focus on themes such as political economy, data governance, democracy and gender justice. She also directs ITfC's field resource centre, which works with grassroots rural communities on 'technology for social change' models. Anita actively engages in national and international advocacy on digital rights, representing southern perspectives, and contributes regularly to academic and media spaces. She is the principal investigator of ITfC's multi-country policy research project on platform governance to develop policies and laws for the digital economy. Her current research also explores gender-based violence online.

Fran Lambrick is a researcher and campaigner who has worked in Cambodia focusing on community environmental protection and activism for the last ten years. She studied for her DPhil at Oxford, using mixed methods to examine the function and impact of community forestry in Prey Lang. During this time, she met and filmed with environmental activist Chut Wutty and, after his death in 2012, continued to create the documentary *I Am Chut Wutty*, which was banned in 2016 by the Cambodian government. Fran is a co-founder of campaign group Not1More, working with at-risk activists, and organiser of the Forest Defenders Conference series.

Rosemary McGee is an interdisciplinary social scientist with an MA (Econ) and PhD in Development Studies, and a Certified Teacher in Higher Education. Her work focuses on accountability, power relations and citizen engagement, particularly on supporting people, organisations and movements to hold states and private sector actors accountable. Rosie has been a Fellow at the UK's Institute of Development Studies since 1999, interspersed with periods of international NGO advocacy and programme management, including six years in Colombia. An experienced designer and facilitator of reflective and action-oriented learning processes with students, development aid professionals and social change practitioners, she teaches on IDS's MA in Power, Participation and Social Change.

A co-founder of Just Associates (JASS), **Valerie Miller**'s experience in feminist popular education draws on many years of collaboration with colleagues around the world – from work with grassroots movements, international NGOs, UN agencies and universities to women's rights programmes, community organising efforts, and solidarity and literacy campaigns. As a designer, facilitator and evaluator of popular education programmes, she has written extensively on politics, power and educational methods aimed at developing ever stronger social movements and new generations of feminist leaders. Currently she is a senior advisor to JASS, collaborating on materials development and providing support to the Southeast Asia team.

Marjoke Oosterom (PhD) is a Research Fellow at the Institute of Development Studies, University of Sussex. Her research focuses on the impact of specific experiences of violence and conflict on forms of power and agency, citizenship and identity, and popular politics. Marjoke's specific expertise is in youth politics and young people's political and economic strategies in response to insecurity in Africa. With a background in comparative politics and development studies, she contributes to debates on political socialisation and everyday forms of politics in violent settings.

Jethro Pettit is a facilitator of reflective learning with practitioners and policymakers concerned with issues of power, civic and political participation, social movements, governance, gender, race, human rights and the environment. He designs and leads courses, workshops, research and evaluations for CSOs, donor agencies, foundations and universities around the world. Jethro is an Emeritus Fellow of the Institute of Development Studies, University of Sussex, where he previously served as a Research Officer, Research Fellow and Director of Teaching and Learning. Prior to joining IDS, he spent two decades working with and supporting civil society and community development organisations in Latin America, Asia, Africa, the US and the UK. Jethro is a Certified Teacher in Higher Education and holds a BA in Social Anthropology, an MPhil in Development Studies and a PhD in Action Research.

Aruna Rao is the co-founder and was for 15 years the Executive Director of Gender at Work (www.genderatwork.org), an international feminist network committed to ending discrimination against women and advancing cultures of equality. She has over 35 years' experience in pioneering new approaches and developing conceptual tools to advance gender equality and institutional change, and in advancing feminist leadership. Aruna has published widely; among her most recent publications are *Gender at Work: New Rules for 21st Century Organizations* (Routledge, 2016) and *Advancing Gender Equality in Bangladesh* (Routledge, 2017). She holds a PhD in Educational Administration from Columbia University, New York.

Jo Rowlands has worked for Oxfam GB since 2001, and is currently senior Governance Adviser, supporting country teams and others on design and delivery of programmes that address and attempt to shift power relations in favour of those who are usually excluded from formal power. She studied issues of power and the concept of 'empowerment', based on community-level field research in Honduras, resulting in a PhD from Durham University (UK), where she also worked for a while as a lecturer. The resulting book, *Questioning Empowerment* (1997), is a core text in many Masters programmes.

Joanne Sandler has been working to strengthen women's rights and organisational change strategies for 40 years. She is a Senior Associate of Gender at Work. She co-authored *Gender at Work: Theory and Practice for 21st Century Organizations* (Routledge, 2015) and writes for online and print journals and anthologies. From 2001 to 2010, Joanne was Deputy Executive Director of the UN Development Fund for Women (UNIFEM), and was part of the transition team for the establishment of UN Women (2011). Joanne facilitates strategic learning and planning processes for diverse social justice groups, philanthropies and multilateral organisations, and co-hosts the podcast *Two Old Bitches*.

Patta Scott-Villiers is a Senior Research Fellow at the Institute of Development Studies, University of Sussex, and holds a PhD in the philosophy of understanding in social development. Her research focuses on the political subjectivity of people on the margins and their actions, interactions and protests about threats to the essentials of life: food, environment, health, work and care. She uses an action research approach, cooperating in enquiries that aim to inform local action while generating theoretical, methodological and empirical advances in sociology. She also brings her philosophical point of view to large-scale qualitative participatory work, creating dialogues between local and global and between one continent and another.

Lisa VeneKlasen is the founding Executive Director of Just Associates (JASS), the multiregional feminist network in Mesoamerica, Southern Africa and Southeast Asia. A lifelong social justice and feminist activist, popular educator and organisation builder, she has focused on community-organising approaches to global change, bridging divides and borders, and liberation education. Through her involvement in anti-imperialist, international solidarity and human rights, she lived and worked in Central America and Zimbabwe. Her writing and practical tools on power, organising and social change – initially published in her book *A New Weave of Power, People and Politics* (2002) – has been adapted and translated by numerous NGOs and academic institutions.

Fiammetta Wegner is an action-researcher and development practitioner specialising in the design and facilitation of participatory processes. Her work focuses on organisational learning, youth leadership, power analysis and social accountability. She works as an independent researcher, trainer and facilitator. She is also part of a global community of young researchers and social innovators called Recrear, working to integrate young people more holistically in development, academic and community processes through participatory action research. In her work she likes to use experiential and creative methodologies to open spaces for individual, group and organisational learning. Fiammetta is also a dancer, and is increasingly exploring how to integrate movement in her work.

Raúl Zibechi is a journalist, popular educator and social militant born in Uruguay. He has written 19 books on popular, indigenous and black movements in Latin America, and hundreds of articles in newspapers, specialist journals and magazines. His work critiques the concept of social movements, considering it Eurocentric in origin, and proposes the idea of societies or peoples in movement, mobilising heterogeneous social relations rather than hegemonic ones. Raúl received the José Martí Prize (Cuba) in 2001 for his coverage of Argentinian movements, and was awarded an Honorary Doctorate from the Universidad Mayor de San Andrés (La Paz, Bolivia).

PART 1

Introduction

1

INTRODUCTION: POWER, EMPOWERMENT AND SOCIAL CHANGE

Jethro Pettit and Rosemary McGee

Rethinking power in critical times

We live in contentious and critical times. While humanity has made enormous progress on many fronts – from health and wellbeing, to educational opportunities, to economic prosperity, to functional government, to scientific and technical innovations – efforts to secure the equitable distribution and sustainability of these achievements are failing, putting our societies and the planet itself in peril. Struggles for justice, basic rights and the environment have become inseparable from the struggle for the survival of all. Yet, rather than uniting around common interests, societies seem more divided by powerful political, economic and religious forces. Deepening inequalities which could inspire greater collective action for change are exploited by populist narratives that pitch the poor against the poor. Political mobilisation for progressive change is suppressed, while space for civil society is constrained by politicised regulation, funding strictures, state surveillance and the criminalisation of protest. Human rights and environmental defenders, particularly among indigenous peoples, are killed with impunity under the naked collusion of governments, extractive corporations, organised criminals and security forces. Hard-won rights for women, people of colour, religious groups, LGBTQ and other discriminated-against people are being rolled back in many places. Efforts to report facts and scientific evidence are weakened by the ideological fragmentation of 'post-truth politics', facilitated by a growing dependence on the internet and social media.

In the face of these challenges, there are many starting points for analysis and action. One is to deepen our understanding of *power* – what it is, how it works and what can be done about it. The study of power has been around for decades, centuries, even millennia, and much can be applied from this scholarship and philosophy to present-day power dynamics. Some would argue that there is nothing new under the sun, just age-old human patterns of domination, control and resistance surfacing in new ways.

Yet the complex and disturbing crises we face call not for fatalism, but for a sharp reappraisal of how power operates in and around people's struggles for equity, dignity and survival. The academic literature on power often neglects the experiences, insights and theories of those working for social change, and the practical implications of power theory. While appreciating existing wisdom about power, there is a need to revisit concepts, to break out of disciplinary silos and debates, to intersect theories and to identify the strategic implications of power analyses.

This book was conceived as a resource that might help make sense of power and empowerment in present-day processes of social change, and to put this understanding to use. The authors explore the multiple dimensions of power and empowerment at play in their practices related to organising, movement-building, citizen voice and state accountability, women's empowerment, human rights, indigenous peoples' autonomy, conflict transformation, digital activism, organisational learning and popular education, among others. Interpreting these experiences with ideas from power literature, and bringing their experiences to bear on those ideas, the authors bridge theory and practice with critical and reflexive analyses of the practical uses of conceptual frameworks, methods and approaches. Through micro-level, ethnographic, inductive and reflective accounts of experience, the chapters explore what people think and do about power and empowerment, not only what is written about it. Focusing on multiple and intersecting power dynamics generally less explored in mainstream power literature – despite their significant practical import – the authors translate fresh insights into approaches for shifting power relations in favour of relatively less powerful people.

In the realm of politics, the conventional view of power as agency based on liberal, pluralist and political economy framings conceived citizens as free agents. People will inform themselves of their options, form alliances and engage civilly with political parties and leaders to secure rights, entitlements and accountability. Such a view is not sufficient on its own; nor is it suitable for all contexts. While useful for identifying the power of agents, their interests, intentions and alliances in more visible political processes, this lens can obscure the way power is embedded in socialised norms, beliefs and behaviour, shaping the boundaries of what is considered politically possible. On the other hand, with a purely discursive and structural view of power as reproduced through hegemonic norms and narratives, the scope for individual and collective agency is seen as very limited – even while structure, as the ordering of society, can enable actors to act collaboratively (Haugaard 2003). In this book, power is treated as iterative, intersectional and multidimensional, departing from the dualist 'agency vs structure' lenses that tend to prevail in theoretical debates, and avoiding the rational or causal determinism of these two perspectives. While considering actors, their drivers and motives as well as the institutions and structures that uphold inequalities, the authors draw attention to the ways in which socialised norms, constraints and opportunities for agency are actually experienced, formally and less visibly, and how moments of power can be resisted or transformed through social action and leadership.

Venturing into the terrain of 'unruly politics', for example, the book sheds light on the ways that subalterns create, take and wield power as collective resistance, often in unexpected ways that make gains by undermining received truths and power/knowledge complexes. In feminist movement-building efforts, authors explore the power of mobilising alternative visions and values within society, going beyond conventional approaches to campaigning. The power of indigenous movements for autonomy, health and natural resource rights is shown to be grounded in life-worlds incompatible with colonial logics of individualism, ownership and authority. Authors also explore the ways in which change agents can learn and unlearn power, reflectively analysing their own relative positioning to align themselves with progressive forces. With this approach, the scholarship on power is rebalanced by articulating a more practical understanding about 'agency-based' and 'structural' forms of power and their intersections; about the processes that reproduce or shift these complex dimensions of power; and about how to apply these appreciations of power in the context of social change activism.

Power debates, frameworks and concepts

There are contending approaches to understanding power in society and politics, and no agreed definitions, famously making power an 'essentially contested concept' (Lukes 1974/2005: 14). Yet the various dimensions of power that have been theorised, even where incongruent, are all worthy of inquiry. As we have seen, power is often regarded as a form of agency – whether the ability of some to dominate others against their interests, the ability to set agendas and to influence values and beliefs, or the ability to resist and act according to perceived self-interests despite pressures to the contrary. Here power is understood as capabilities exercised by particular individuals or groups, whether to coerce and control, to shape norms and narratives (as a more subtle but enduring means of control), or to resist domination and claim entitlements. Alternatively, power is conceived as a theory of social order – as prevailing norms or structures which generate social hierarchies, attitudes and behaviours of habitual compliance that serve to include or exclude. Power circulates everywhere, and there is no conspiracy, no agent at fault for power asymmetries and 'nobody to shoot' (Hayward and Lukes 2008). Oppression and discrimination – whether on the basis of gender, class, race, ethnicity, disability, sexuality or age – are internalised by the oppressed and the oppressors alike, as everyone conforms with or falls short of challenging what is 'normal'.

With the lens of agency, the powerful are seen as mobilising oppressive values intentionally (e.g. with propaganda, education, the media or religious doctrine) in order to reinforce desired behaviour. Using the lens of structure, the scope for exercising will or resistance can seem fixed and limited, leaving agents all but powerless. With a multidimensional power lens, as broadly applied by the authors of this book, the conspiratorial intentions of powerful agents may or may not be obvious, but political responsibility can be found and resisted (Hayward and Lukes 2008: 11; see McGee this volume); and it is also possible to identify the underlying values these actors seek to amplify, and to develop effective forms of resistance and alternatives to these norms. Structures are not deterministic, inscribing themselves on subjects, nor are subjects free from the constraints of their social context. Forms of agency and structure continually interact, or indeed work holistically to sustain or subvert systems of power; and power can be destabilised or created anew through collective awareness and through the articulation and enactment of alternatives. Social change in this view is a long-term, incremental and strategic process for activists and movements, reaching beyond episodic protest and advocacy, though it can also be marked by highly visible and unruly moments of rupture.

These views of power as 'constitutive of society' (Clegg and Haugaard 2009: 3), transcending structure and agency, can be described as post-structural. Analysts of civic and political power often downplay or disregard these dimensions of power, except insofar as they are acknowledged as part of the cultural or institutional backdrop. Analysis focuses on what can be seen: agents, their stated or imputed interests, and their alliances and conflicts as they compete for influence and power – the actors, political processes and institutions 'above the waterline' (Pettit and Mejía Acosta 2014). Lenses of political economy are well suited for this kind of analysis, yet tend to relegate the socialised dimensions of power to 'informal institutions' or 'ideology' rather than examining how beliefs and behaviour are shaped, how fields of possibility evolve historically and how agency can be both present and pre-constrained by structure, rolled into one performance (Butler 1990). More behaviourist versions of political economy assume that actors make informed and calculated decisions in accord with their interests, without taking into account the normative pressures or negative consequences that may shape their perception of those interests and options. These approaches also fail to factor in the embodied dispositions that underlie decisions and behaviour, as increasingly recognised in psychology and cognitive science (see Pettit, this volume).

These lenses on power yield quite different understandings of 'empowerment'. With an agency view, empowerment is often reduced to the personal acquisition of skills, abilities and resources, usually by a disadvantaged individual on an otherwise level playing field. A purely structural view implies no theory of empowerment, except perhaps a revolutionary one led by an enlightened vanguard and ideology and facilitated by the scope for shared meaning – and hence communication – inherent in social structures and systems. Seen from a post-structural and multidimensional angle, empowerment involves gaining critical awareness of structural inequalities and abilities to create, articulate and enact alternatives, usually on a collective basis (Sardenberg 2009). Given these divergent definitions, and the widespread use of empowerment to describe more instrumental approaches used by international development agencies, the authors in this volume do not always refer to the processes of transformation they describe as 'empowerment'. We have nonetheless chosen to affirm the more collective and emancipatory meaning of empowerment in this book.

Bridging theories and practices of power

The chapters that follow are presented in four sections. Part 2 emphasises theoretical and conceptual interpretations of power in the light of current contexts and crises. The authors in Part 3 introduce key frameworks and approaches to power analysis, reflecting on their application and evolution. Part 4 explores illustrative examples of agency, resistance and social action to shift power in diverse contexts. Finally, Part 5 presents approaches to facilitating learning and unlearning for reflective social action.

Part 2 – Conceptual and theoretical groundings and debates

This offers a critical review of concepts and theories used to analyse and explain power and empowerment, many of which are referred to and applied in the chapters that follow. Lisa VeneKlasen (Chapter 2.1) vividly depicts people and systems currently locked in simultaneous and frenetic dynamics of both destructive extinction and con- structive, progressive eruption, against an age-old backcloth of entrenched structural injustices. She seeks 'rearview innovations' in her historical review of experience of feminist organisers and movement-builders, setting out how the 'invited spaces' for democratic engagement in policy processes in the 1990s and 2000s diverted activists from their claimed and autonomous spaces of protest, and depoliticised their reper- toires. More recently, as corporate capitalism and patriarchy have dug in, extractivism has hollowed out livelihoods and violence and crisis have become normalised, acti- vists – among them VeneKlasen's own organisation, Just Associates (JASS) – have regrouped and focused on movement-building. JASS always focused on building women's *power within* and *power with* in personal and intimate spaces to engage in 'power for' in more public and overtly political arenas. The foremost challenge JASS activists confront today is the way hidden and shadow powers – private corporate interests, organised crime, fundamentalist groups and others – wield growing, unac- countable and illegitimate influence over public institutions and resources, with states' open collusion. As power complexifies and democratic spaces close in on even main- stream and technocratic social actors, women are often publicly leading the charge against right-wing reactionary and populist political regimes. Part of JASS's own reflective and empowering practice is to name these trends, pinpoint the contra- dictions of power and redouble its historic attention to exposing narratives of dom- ination and constructing critical and transformative counter-narratives.

Patta Scott-Villiers (Chapter 2.2) continues the theme of the colonisation by the market, as well as the totalising power of commodification and bureaucratisation. She points to the ways in which the competitive and divisive influence of competitive individualism is reshaping agency and our understandings of it, creating political sub- jects through what Foucault (2007) calls discipline and governmentality, and Haugaard (2012) calls the fourth dimension of power. As an antidote, Scott-Villiers explores *communitas*, a generic, culturally transcendental and unstructured form of human bonding between equals that underpins experiences of resistance and unruly politics, flying in the face of individualisms and nationalisms. *Communitas*, she argues, is an under-explored field of power which can help renew contemporary social rebuilding. Unruliness is a particular approach to unsettling normal power and freeing the 'negative communities' of despairing individuals trapped in it. Protests and aesthetic ruptures, prominent in unruly repertoires, are ephemeral, disruptive and often ecstatic in quality, yet powerful. In fleeting liminal states in which social order is undone by people letting go of it, communities of people grow and learn, and when the moment passes those who felt it are left with the enduring experience of *communitas*. If sustained in political action that is faithful to the momentary event and bonds of *communitas*, these experiences can be transformative. While everything and everyone is caught up in the global web of tech-led cultural reconfiguration that is termed 'digimodernism', the power of *communitas* also shapes it. As resistance emerges in event after event of political truth around the world, *communitas* offers new ways to understand how transformative political power can work towards a common good.

Unruliness can be seen as breaking those 'networks of social boundaries' that are power in Hayward (1998)'s post-structural sense. In Chapter 2.3 Rosemary McGee engages with this perspective in applying a power lens to the claiming of accountability for rights and entitlements. Her starting position is that we need to understand power so as to exact accountability, and the project of exacting accountability is a project of transforming power: their relationship is key in the quest for more effective ways of holding power to account. The chapter discusses different versions of accountability-claiming, using a range of theoretical standpoints. Those based on first- and second-dimensional, agency-focused understandings of power seek out the culpable agents and provide the accountability-seekers with information as a panacea for adjusting the power equation in the latter's favour, or to uncover and adjust practices of elite capture in public programmes. Those that have deep and long-term effects, however, are based on third- and fourth-dimensional understandings. These adopt multifaceted strategies to tackle, over years and decades, oppressive social structures and norms, discourses and beliefs which normalise cultures of non-accountability to the poor and marginalised. This chapter, like others in the book, shows how 'practical power theory', built of struggles for justice and accountability, can both illuminate practice and enrich scholarly theory.

There is little disagreement that power in the form of socialised norms and beliefs has effects on people's civic and political agency, enabling or constraining their ability to speak or act against the structural grain. Yet how this power operates and changes is less evident, even if popular education, critical consciousness-raising and 'changing the narrative' are seen as effective steps toward transformation. Jethro Pettit (Chapter 2.4) suggests that norms and conduct of power are internalised not just in the conceptual domains of cognition but in embodied habits and dispositions. Most post-structural and multidimensional theories of power offer some explanation of embodied power, from Foucault's 'discipline' (1991) to Bourdieu's 'habitus' (1980) to Butler's 'performativity' (1990). Pettit compares these perspectives and explores their alignment with emerging theories of 'embodied cognition' from psychology and cognitive science, finding that gaining critical awareness may be insufficient to catalyse agency without integrating creative and embodied practices of learning. Drawing on his teaching and action research experience with methods of body sculpting, role play and theatre exercises inspired by Augusto Boal (1979/2000), Pettit concludes that enabling civic and political agency requires a 'pedagogy for the embodied mind' that combines critical consciousness with embodied learning and action.

If embodiment is one under-explored dimension of power and empowerment, another is the way technology and connection are reshaping both agency and structure in a digital era – the subject of Anita Gurumurthy and Nandini Chami's Chapter 2.5. In a digital era, social and political configurations and spaces are only fully understood if seen as assemblages of the material, technological and biological. In the political space, humans and institutions are now joined by digital things. Through them power circulates, not only in relationships among actors but also in the digital infrastructures, data, affects, knowledge, values, contestations and bodies therein. This has implications for empowerment. Feminists have always argued that liberal visions of empowerment as individualist change processes miss out the essential element of political community. The authors give voice to feminist activists from the global South who signal both the new possibilities for constructing community in a digital age and new dangers in the internet's entanglement in contemporary power structures – an emerging digital colonialism. Citizens must push back, they argue, with transnational change strategies in which local movements built on respect for identities and solidarities contest big tech and big finance and their accomplice, the informational state.

Part 3 – Analysing power and empowerment: frameworks and approaches

This introduces some key analytical frameworks, tools and methods used by this book's authors and others to better understand power, to support empowerment and to develop strategies for social change. These frameworks and methods serve as bridges, helping to translate theories of power into practical use and to draw lessons from experience back into the advancement of theory. In several cases, methods inspired by concepts from the power literature have since metamorphosed into lenses of power analysis that enhance the original theories. This section is recommended as a starting point for readers less familiar with the power concepts and terminology used in this book. In each chapter the evolution and key elements of the frameworks are explained, illustrated with cases or examples of how they have been used, and reflected upon to draw out lessons for improving their use, or indeed for revisiting the power theories that initially inspired them.

Alexa Bradley (Chapter 3.1) opens the section with a comprehensive review of the power frameworks that have been developed and used for nearly two decades by the feminist movement-building collective JASS, which has adapted, created and popularised methods of power analysis for citizen action in many regions of the world (VeneKlasen and Miller 2002; Miller et al. 2006). In the context of a growing backlash against women, feminism and other social justice movements, Bradley provides a welcome and critical update of JASS's power frameworks. Recognising the personal as both political and intersectional, JASS engages with power from an appreciation of its *visible, hidden* and *invisible* dimensions (roughly corresponding to Lukes's three dimensions, 1974/2005). In current times the *hidden power* of behind-the-scenes actors has become bolder and more visible, while the growing collusion between state and often illegal and violent non-state actors has led JASS to incorporate a new analytical category of *shadow power*. Closer attention is also given to how *invisible power* operates through narratives, such as populist and nationalist ideologies mobilized to activate prejudices and fears. In response to these forms of power, JASS offers a framework for building 'transformative power' based on dignity, equity, inclusion, liberation and democratic leadership. Reinforcing the long-applied constructs of *power within, power to* and *power with* in processes of empowerment, JASS now includes *power for* – the vision, values and demands that orient struggles for change. With these framings, Bradley offers insights into strategies for both resisting 'power over' and building 'transformative power' in processes of movement-building.

Combining the lenses of *visible, hidden and invisible* power with the various kinds of *spaces* and *levels* in which power operates, the 'powercube' is an analytical approach widely used around the world to examine the multiple dimensions of power, particularly in processes of citizen engagement and state accountability. John Gaventa (Chapter 3.2) recounts its evolution, explains its dimensions and their interactions, and critically reviews the many ways it has been put to use by practitioners and academics in diverse settings – for purposes ranging from issue and context analysis, to education and awareness building, to programme and strategy development, to monitoring and evaluation. The *visible, hidden* and *invisible* forms of power are taken into a three-dimensional lens for analysis, allowing one to examine how they operate in *spaces* of civic and political engagement that may be *closed, invited* or *claimed*, and at different *levels* – from the household to the local, regional, national and global. Gaventa suggests that each of these aspects (power, spaces and levels) reflects a spectrum of possibilities that interact with one another, opening and closing entry points for influence and change. One implication is that efforts to shift power that focus on only one element or dimension may end up reinforcing power in another. Transformative change happens when social actors, organisations and movements work across all aspects of the cube, through coalitions and networks and using both insider and outsider strategies. Gaventa concludes with eight lessons for analysing power relations and developing strategies for change using the powercube.

Another method widely used around the world is the Gender at Work Framework, introduced in this volume by Aruna Rao and Joanne Sandler (Chapter 3.3) of the eponymous organisation. Their approach explores dimensions and intersections of power in four 'quadrants', ranging from experiences of power at the individual to the systemic level, and from the informal to the formal spheres of life. At the individual level, the informal concerns personal consciousness and capabilities of women (akin to *power to* and *power within*), while the formal concerns women's access to resources. At the systemic level, the informal focuses on deep structures and norms (akin to *invisible power*), while the formal is about the power of rules, policies and procedures. In their chapter, Rao and Sandler apply the framework, and others, to making sense of what drives the 'toxic alchemy of institutional power' that among other things permits a culture of silence and collusion around persistent patterns of gender discrimination and sexual harassment in workplaces. The framework is used here to identify the influences of patriarchal norms in organisations, and the lack of accountability mechanisms. This analysis emphasises the systemic changes needed to secure women's rights and gender equality, with a focus on discriminatory norms and deep structures of institutional power.

The challenges of bringing these and other lenses and methods of power analysis into the everyday work of development and civil society organisations is explored by Jo Rowlands in Chapter 3.4. Often the practice of power analysis remains implicit and intuitive rather than deliberate. Drawing on her experience as a governance adviser with Oxfam, Rowlands explores the steps that can be taken to embed capacities for more intentional and nuanced analysis of power by staff and organisations to better inform their actions. She identifies three interconnected elements for more effective power analysis: having good frameworks and approaches that can identify multiple dynamics of power and their interactions; combining these with theories of change so that power can be navigated; and having tools to support the building of bottom-up, countervailing power. Key frameworks and approaches to facilitation are presented along with Rowlands's personal reflections on process, and examples of putting the methods into practice with Oxfam partners in Tanzania, Myanmar and Peru. Rowlands draws attention to the need to base power analysis on explicit values and intentions, rather than treating it as a technical exercise, and the importance of continuous practice of power analysis, rather than one-off exercises.

Part 4 – Understanding agency: social action for shifting power

This is a selection of case studies from diverse contexts and around the world, most of them characterised to some degree by conflict or post-conflict power dynamics. The chapters explore experiences of action for social change that demonstrate what concepts of power, empowerment, agency and resistance mean in practice. In Chapter 4.1, Marjoke Oosterom asks how people's experiences of violent conflict affect their sense of agency and power in relationships, and identifies potential avenues for their regaining this. Links between power, agency and violence are explored through her research in conflict areas of Uganda, South Sudan and Zimbabwe, where some people have managed to overcome fear, help others and reduce the impact of violence in their lives. While acknowledging the difficulty of scaling up these experiences to resolve the underlying causes of conflict, lessons are drawn about the effects and mitigation of violent conflict on agency. People try to shape their lives to the best of their abilities, she finds, but may not think of their agency as empowering or effecting wider change. This makes it difficult to go beyond 'coping agency' to the kinds of 'citizen agency' that enable one to engage with powerful local actors. Past experiences of violence also constitute an embodied dimension of invisible power, which intensifies the socialising effects of norms and beliefs. Oosterom also explores the methodological challenges of doing research on power in violent contexts.

In the context of Guatemala, Walter Flores (Chapter 4.2) recounts experiences of power analysis with rural indigenous communities which have been profoundly excluded and marginalised. The country's Center for the Study of Equity and Governance in Health Systems (CEGSS) is a civic association which supports a large network of volunteer community health defenders, with the aim of reducing social exclusion and inequality in health care provision in indigenous communities. Flores's team initially used a range of participatory methods and visual tools to analyse asymmetrical power relations within and between community organisations and government authorities – techniques such as card-games, stakeholder mapping, scoring and ranking. But, in an interesting shift of approach, these methods were replaced by a process of facilitating 'generative conversations' about power. Questions were developed to guide interviews and deepen discussion of dimensions of power and influence, and to develop ideas of how to resist and transform power. Building upon these generative conversations, the team and communities also developed their own concepts of 'micro-power' to inform their health care service delivery strategies.

Power relations permeate the struggles of rural and indigenous communities worldwide to protect their natural resources, as vividly demonstrated by Fran Lambrick in Chapter 4.3. Environmental defenders are being killed, criminalised, attacked and threatened as a result of the destruction and appropriation of territories, forests, waterways, lands and seas – with profound consequences for communities and movements. Lambrick focuses on the effects of violence against environmental defenders, and how dimensions of power constrain and enable their resistance She draws on experiences, writings and interviews with defenders from Cambodia and Honduras, including her accompaniment and documentation of frontline resistance in the face of violence in Cambodia over ten years. Lambrick explores the power dynamics of fear and courage, noting the role of territory, place and identity in strengthening the determination of defenders. The chapter explores strategies for countering the negative narratives that pave the way for violent attacks, and for creating new narratives of solidarity and collective power. The life and assassination of Cambodian forest defender Chut Wutty is recounted, the subject of a documentary film by the author as is the experience of Honduran indigenous leader Laura Zúñiga Cáceres, whose mother, Bertha Cáceres, was killed by Honduran security forces for protesting against a hydro project on indigenous lands.

Indigenous communities in rural Chiapas, Mexico, that have created the Zapatista movement are the subject of Raul Zibechi's Chapter 4.4. The Zapatistas gained global attention in 1994 when thousands of armed indigenous people took control of the principal towns in Chiapas, seeking respect and recognition of their rights. They repossessed ancestral lands usurped by landowners, and declared their own form of self-government and territorial autonomy. Zibechi visited Zapatista communities and experienced day-to-day life with the people through an immersion 'school'. His chapter explores the characteristics of the movement he observed, focusing on the three levels of Zapatista autonomy: the community, the municipality and the region – including an extensive health system run largely by women promoters. Zibechi describes how the movement is organised and functions, and also how it portrays itself in alignment with indigenous rather than Western culture and norms. This involves a rotating system of self-government independent of the Mexican state, and high levels of participation by young people and women in leadership and decision-making. The Zapatista approach to community-based decision-making, autonomy and power-sharing defies the usual ways of describing movements, organisations or governments.

Part 5 – Learning and unlearning power for reflective social action

This presents experiences of processes of learning and reflection for social change practitioners interested in power and empowerment. The authors, all concerned with how people become reflective, power-aware social change actors, emphasise pedagogical approaches used in movement, organisation and formal education contexts.

McGee, Pettit and Wegner (Chapter 5.1) give an account of an innovative programme at the UK Institute of Development Studies – the MA in Power, Participation and Social Change (MAP) – in which they have been personally involved. Launched in 2004, MAP responded to a lack of applied, experiential and reflective learning opportunities for activists and development workers, and a need for more critical, power-conscious approaches to civic and political participation. The authors reflect on MAP's student body, its pedagogy and curriculum content, and alumni perspectives on the programme. They contextualise this against a decade of shifts in the UK university context and the development aid arena which are not conducive to experiential, collaborative and constructivist learning. Today MAP feels like a distinctly counter-current but much-needed response to the contemporary global configurations of power and politics discussed in Part 2 of this book. The counter-current practitioner-learners it attracts continue to find it a transformative experience of questioning dominant norms and assumptions, learning new ways of seeing and doing things, and repositioning themselves as agents in struggles for social justice.

Outside higher education, many organisations and practitioners have also brought methods of transformative and reflective learning into their workplaces, including techniques for developing self-awareness and reflexivity in relation to power. Rosalind Eyben (Chapter 5.2) suggests that reflexivity is the ability to recognise that what we consider 'normal' in our lives and work is profoundly shaped by power, through socialisation processes that shape beliefs and behaviour. Her chapter invites practitioners in the field of international development cooperation to adopt methods of reflexivity so as to scrutinise their beliefs, words, actions and relationships, and to enquire whether and how these are supporting or undermining social justice. Eyben reflects on ethical dilemmas arising from her participation in an immersion visit to a West African village, capturing how power operates in fluid rather than fixed ways in aid relationships. When complex power dynamics are at work, power only becomes visible and possible to shift when a sufficient number of people start talking about it, recognising how it is constructed through social interaction and changing their interaction in the moment rather than reflecting after the fact.

Shifting to the context of social movement learning, Arce Andrade and Miller (Chapter 5.3) explore the evolution of popular and feminist popular education and methods of consciousness-raising, offering lessons from their own creative practices as facilitators in Latin America. The authors explore how popular education can contribute to deeper understanding and support learners to create both personal and collective power for social action and transformation. Methods are described in detail, drawn from the 'Self-Diagnosis of Reality' learning process and other workshops developed by JASS and its regional networks for women leaders in Mesoamerica. Feminist popular education is shown to be a transformative process not just for women but for all, regardless of gender, race, class, sexuality or age. Focused on individual and collective reflection, knowledge and action, it draws on synergies created by a new appreciation of identities and the connections between hearts, minds and bodies, while critically challenging what is taken as truth about oneself and society.

Conclusion

In these critical times, the authors in this volume explore creative and positive pathways to understanding and action. Taking a fresh look at power is one important part of what is needed for supporting social change. These chapters demonstrate that power and empowerment are best understood as they intersect with real issues and struggles, rather than as a stand-alone field of theory or inquiry. Neither is power analysis the exclusive concern of any particular discipline, but rather a set of perspectives and approaches that are applicable to many issues and sectors. There are rich veins of theory to draw upon – from conceptualisations of power as agency, as structure or as post-structural and multidimensional – and good theory will seek to bridge these, to connect them with practice, and vice versa. We hold to the view that 'there is nothing so practical as a good theory' (Lewin 1943), recognising that ideas can sharpen practice, and reflection on experience can improve theory.

The authors bring decades of experience and scholarship to their writing. The social and political philosophies that underpin this book include contributions from critical, feminist, race, sexuality and intersectional scholarship which have revolutionised power thinking and practice – even as these perspectives are marginalised in some areas of power scholarship. These influences converge around the idea that power is both personal and political, and to separate these or objectify power as something 'out there' – removed from the subjectivity, experience and positionality of the analyst – is dangerous. This poses epistemological and methodological challenges for some disciplines, and aligns the power analysis approaches shared here with constructivist, participatory and action research approaches to creating knowledge. There are also therefore risks in outsourcing power analysis to 'experts' by leaders, managers and technicians who think they are too busy or unqualified to build it into their lives and work. We suggest that power analysis is integral to good practice, and is best undertaken as a reflective and reflexive process by practitioners, teams, groups and communities, through dialogue and facilitation – and, as many authors have demonstrated, not as a one-off exercise but as a continuous and evolving practice

A vital part of the book's purpose is to enable people and groups to assume their political responsibility as power becomes ever more complex and its hidden and invisible dimensions more influential. With unprecedented threats to the peaceful coexistence of people on the planet, it has never been more important not only to understand power in its multiple dimensions, but also to transform it through conscious, strategic and embodied action.

References

Boal, A., 1979/2000. *Theatre of the oppressed*. London: Pluto.
Bourdieu, P., 1980. *The logic of practice*. Stanford: Stanford University Press.
Butler, J., 1990. *Gender trouble*. London: Routledge.
Clegg, S. and Haugaard, M., eds, 2009. *The Sage handbook of power*. London: Sage.
Foucault, M., 1991. *Discipline and punish: the birth of a prison*. London: Penguin.
Foucault, M., 2007. *Security, territory, population (Michel Foucault: lectures at the Collège de France)* (G. Burchell, trans.). London: Palgrave Macmillan.
Haugaard, M., 2003. Reflections on seven ways of creating power. *European Journal of Social Theory*, 6(1), 87–113.
Haugaard, M., 2012. Rethinking the four dimensions of power: domination and empowerment. *Journal of Political Power*, 5(1), 33–54.
Hayward, C., 1998. De-facing power. *Polity*, 31(1), 1–22.
Hayward, C. and Lukes, S., 2008. Nobody to shoot? Power, structure, and agency: a dialogue. *Journal of Power*, 1, 15–20.
Lewin, K., 1943. Psychology and the process of group living, *Journal of Social Psychology*, 17, 113–131. Reprinted in *The complete social scientist: a Kurt Lewin reader* (M. Gold, ed.). Washington DC: American Psychological Association, 1999, pp. 333–345.
Lukes, S., 1974/2005. *Power: a radical view*. London: Macmillan.
Miller, V., VeneKlasen, L., Reilly, M. and Clark, C., 2006. *Making change happen 3: power. Concepts for revisioning power for justice, equality and peace*. Washington DC: Just Associates.
Sardenberg, C., 2009. Liberal vs liberating empowerment: conceptualising women's empowerment from a Latin American feminist perspective, Pathways Working Paper No. 7. Brighton: Institute of Development Studies.
VeneKlasen, L. and Miller, V., 2002. *A new weave of power, people and politics: the action guide for advocacy and citizen participation*. Oklahoma City: World Neighbors.

PART 2

Conceptual and theoretical groundings and debates

2.1

PLUS ÇA CHANGE? SHIFTING POWER IN A DISORIENTING MOMENT

Lisa VeneKlasen

Overview

Some days it feels like the tectonic plates of power are shifting so dramatically that the world will catch fire. According to climate scientists and communities confronting water crises, it is. Unregulated surveillance capitalism and right-wing authoritarianism on the one hand and unprecedented people's mobilisations against greed and injustice on the other are generating new challenges and opportunities to up-end the forces of inequality. In this 'movement moment' for democratising democracy, new actors are energising the streets and social media to confront corruption, land grabs, repression, racism and misogyny. News of resistance and activism features surprisingly in the mainstream media. The sense of possibility is palpable. Yet, with even more news of corruption, autocracy and violence against activists, women, migrants and black and indigenous people, it feels like just a new chapter in the old story of imperialism, military dictatorships and resistance, like 'the more things change, the more they stay the same.'

Politics everywhere has become agitated, polarised and chock full of paradoxes. The usual definitions of left and right are in upheaval. Low-wage workers and poor people align with right-wing populists, oligarchs and religious fanatics. Motivated by precarity and fear, citizens elect former military dictators and 'strongmen'. Erstwhile leftist liberation heroes kill and detain young protesters while quietly aligning with global capital and conservative religious hierarchies. Nike, a sportswear company with a sketchy labour rights record, emerges as a powerful voice for racial justice. A favourite outreach tool for all political sides – Facebook – is also one of the largest unregulated monopolies in modern history, trading our privacy for profit. Even the word 'democracy' is in crisis.

As a worldwide wave of justice activism explodes, dissent could not be more dangerous. Widespread repression clamps down on those fighting for rights, survival and the planet. Surveillance and misinformation have become central to our lives and politics; competing narratives divide, confuse and silence us.

A profound rethink about how to build social, political and economic democratic alternatives – long overdue – is underway. As a new generation struggles to invigorate inclusive agendas, we grapple with age-old questions: How to confront and transform the systems and beliefs that underpin inequality and violence? How to find common ground across differences? How to respond to diverse peoples' needs with bold, just solutions?

As a long-time social justice and feminist organiser, I believe that looking back through history for less-known lessons and tested strategies may offer useful 'rearview innovations' (Sax 2018). The often invisible experiences and ideas of feminist organisers – particularly in the global South – are rich with clues. As long-time colleague Everjoice Win noted, 'the #MeToo movement is the waking up of Western countries […] about something we've been fighting about in the global South for the last 50 years' (Gutiérrez 2018, my translation).

This chapter shares my political reflections from working alongside some less-known grassroots leaders and women human rights defenders in Mesoamerica, Southern Africa and Southeast Asia. My observations centre on the work of Just Associates (JASS), a multi-regional network of activists, researchers and popular educators that I co-founded. From 2006, we redirected our energies to the growing backlash against women and women's rights due to the rise of religious fundamentalisms by investing in 'back-to-basics' popular political education and cross-movement organising with women activists. At that time, community-driven solutions and grassroots empowerment had lost lustre among the international human rights and development community, replaced by 'expert' technical solutions, policy advocacy and campaigns. Trends emphasised top-down scalable solutions, and community-based efforts were increasingly defunded and devalued. JASS's strategic antidote to this one-size-fits-all approach was to build power from the 'ground up' rather than starting at policy prescriptions, legislatures and the United Nations (UN). We invested in political dialogues to enable women to analyse power in their lives and contexts to build shared agendas through a mix of conscientisation and under-the-radar organising: our attempt to 'put the power back into empowerment' (Batliwala 2007).

Today, our power analysis and feminist movement-building strategies (Miller et al. 2006; Bradley, this volume) seem prescient. The backlash against women and women's freedoms – low on the civil society agenda a decade ago – may have been the canary in the coal mine for today's 'closing civic space' and crises of rights and democracy. Women are at the forefront of political mobilisations against rising right-wing politics. Once again, sexism and racism expose the deep structural fault lines in society – the explicit misogyny, racism and gender-based violence that sustain destructive, failed economic models and fuel nationalist politics – and remind us of the unfinished work of economic and political democracy.

Drawing on JASS's locally led political accompaniment of diverse women activists and their organisations in some of the most violent and unequal contexts, the chapter offers reflections structured as follows:

- *Canaries in the coal mine* examines how economic and political dynamics of the late 1990s and 2000s shifted civil society trends, fed a backlash against women and presaged the 'closing democratic space' that came next.
- *Back to the future* gives a snapshot of current contexts and new configurations of power from the perspective of women activists in Mesoamerica, Southern Africa and Southeast Asia.
- *Power and change in disorienting times* provides suggestions for tools and strategies for dissecting new concentrations of economic and political power, and democratising our practice, formations and future agenda.

Canaries in the coal mine

Over the past few years, a mix of seemingly new threats and challenges facing social justice and human rights groups has provoked many to question their approaches (Moyn 2018). The threats include: legal and financial restrictions on international and national non-governmental organisations (INGOs and NGOs); alarming attacks on and criminalisation of human rights defenders and agendas; and the dismantling of mechanisms for accountability and redress. The hope that global policy processes would address mounting economic inequality, climate change and authoritarianism is fading as the global North enters its own series of political crises. Among many shifts underway, some INGOs have taken steps toward 'localisation', to get closer to the people they serve and to support frontline movements and activists.

Closing democratic space is not new to women and LGBTQ activists or to minority, poor, migrant and indigenous communities. Neither are the risks and violence they face for defending their territories, rights, bodies and survival. Important advances have been achieved by international civil society actors; but an over-emphasis on issue-focused advocacy and technical measures and their disconnect from their 'beneficiaries' may have obscured how deeply ingrained social norms shaped by gender, race, class and sexuality serve as the foundation of inequality, violence and political extremism, and require a wider range of change strategies.

In the late 1990s and early 2000s, a handful of critical scholars and practitioners – including many in the JASS network – pointed out the risks of an over-reliance on state-centric, individualised and technical approaches. We stressed the need to address ideological, normative and hidden power (non-state actors such as corporations, religious groups and drug cartels) if policy and legal advances are to result in the practical enjoyment of rights (see Action Aid et al. 2002, JASS et al. 2006, Miller et al. 2006). We used the image of the iceberg (Figure 2.1.1) to illustrate that solely engaging the visible aspects of a problem without dealing with the underlying forces was insufficient; any change at the tip (e.g. policy) could easily be reversed by the larger forces under the water line. We argued that discourse, ideas and social norms (or 'narratives') shaping the public view of what and who matters is a critical battleground, while opportunities to participate in [or engage in, or influence] policy making (invited

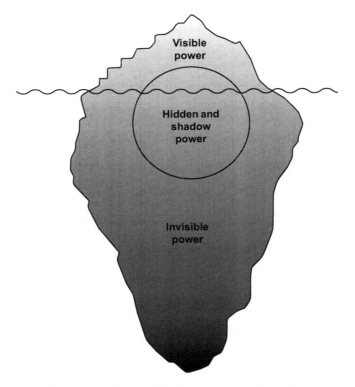

FIGURE 2.1.1 Visible power, hidden and shadow power and invisible power
Source: Author's elaboration

spaces) can be a distraction from critical contestations underway, (e.g. investing in the Millennium Development Goals vs confronting Big Pharma on HIV/AIDs).

Between 2002 and 2006, JASS and the Institute for Development Studies (IDS) regularly convened activists, practitioners and researchers – staff from human rights and development INGOs, and movement leaders from unions, economic justice and land alliances, and women's groups – to understand the changing dynamics of inequality (Action Aid et al. 2002, JASS et al. 2006, Miller et al. 2006). Applying and adapting the powercube (Gaventa this volume), we reflected on the new threats to democratic agendas, and the possibilities of meaningful people-led change.

Deepening economic insecurity and inequality

Between the 1980s and 2000s, the global embrace of neoliberalism and market economics altered the role and priorities of states, the discourse of social change, political culture and people's lives. Structural adjustment policies privatised or eviscerated basic safety nets in many parts of the world. The debt crises of the 1980s gave way to more austerity, currency devaluations and financial crises, along with deregulation and new global trade rules privileging corporate interests and the concentration of wealth in the 0.01 per cent. During this restructuring from the 1990s, the role of states gradually shifted from that of regulator and protector to one of facilitating capital and absorbing its excesses, and eventually to that of collaborator, for instance through public–private partnerships (PPPs). Market economics permeated discourse as citizens became 'consumers' and 'clients' (Cornwall 2000, VeneKlasen and Miller 2002). Transnational corporations and banks shaped policies to serve their interests – from intellectual property laws and patents on medicines to wages. By the early 2000s, the absence of a social safety net and lack of economic options were felt most deeply by women, a phenomenon described as the 'feminization of poverty' (Pearce 1978). The destabilising effects and resentments generated by these dramatic economic changes fed into rising nationalism, religious fundamentalisms and right-wing extremism (Emerson and Hartman 2006, Balchin 2011).

Religious fundamentalisms and backlash

By the early 2000s, religious fundamentalisms were resurgent worldwide. The West focused attention on Islamic versions in the Middle East and Afghanistan; Hindu and Christian varieties expanded their political and social influence elsewhere. Backlash against women's rights ranged from subtle re-prioritisation of motherhood in public policy to violent attacks. Burgeoning evangelical churches in East and Southern Africa sought to bolster their version of 'African tradition', nationhood and motherhood against the emerging rights of women. Once financed covertly by the Reagan administration as part of fighting communism, evangelical Christianity also surged in the Americas (Didion 1987), while in Southeast Asia increasing religious conservatism policed women's attire and restricted their mobility. More brutal forms included 'curative rape' of lesbians; blaming HIV-positive women for the spread of the epidemic; blaming women for sexual assault; and demonising feminists and women's rights activists as Western agitators and man-haters (Imam et al. 2016, Okech 2017).

The threat of violence and the shaming of women who spoke out or transgressed traditional roles had a chilling effect on women's activism and governments' receptivity to the women's rights agenda. Leveraging religion and nationalism, powerful actors tapped into the insidious ways that gender oppression operates, using shame to threaten women's core sense of belonging in families and communities if they did not conform (VeneKlasen and Miller 2002). Focusing increasingly on women's reproductive autonomy, the Christian right's influence over the political process in the Americas led to bans on abortion in El Salvador in 1998 and Nicaragua in 2006, and abortion as a defining agenda in US politics (DiBranco 2018).

Several of the early builders of JASS participated in local-to-global activism for women's economic development and 'women's rights as human rights' between 1985 and 2000 that planted the seeds of backlash. Multi-country mobilisations, particularly in the global South, gave birth to dynamic cross-border networks of diverse women and energised feminist movements around pivotal UN conferences: the Vienna Human Rights Conference (1993), the Cairo International Conference on Population and Development (1994) and the 4th UN Conference on Women in Beijing (1995). The Beijing Platform for Action's bold aspirations for women are hard to imagine as policy in today's regressive politics; but many governments did sign on to them, and they served – for a time – as potent tools for women activists to push their governments toward implementing equal rights in law if not practice.

The response of the religious right was swift. By the mid-2000s, expert lobbying teams – representing the Vatican, evangelical churches and the Muslim Brotherhood – filled UN conferences, joining forces to reverse women's rights gains. Meanwhile, after an initial phase of grassroots legal literacy and network-building around women's rights, focus shifted to policy work – which made sense at the time – and eventually led to defunding and devaluing critical grassroots organising and empowerment strategies, leaving women leaders at the community level ill-prepared for navigating backlash. Zimbabwean feminist Everjoice Win pointed out in 2008 that 'all these templates, checklists and talking points are not helping us deal with the pastors, chiefs, headmen and generals who want women to stay home, cook and pray' (pers. comm.; see also Win 2013). We have all have been battling reversals of women's rights gains – particularly reproductive and sexual rights – ever since.

De-politicised advocacy

By the 1990s, human rights strategies became increasingly about policy and less about people. Efforts focused more on specific issues and advocacy (*visible power*) 'on behalf of' but often disconnected from organised voices and the demands of constituencies directly impacted (Miller et al. 2005). From public services to legal rights, technical, individualised solutions failed to address the deeper dynamics of inequality. At the time, a popular gender-oriented planning framework that distinguished between 'strategic and practical' interests had the unintended effect of prioritising policy advocacy over strategies to address to basic needs (Miller et al. 2006). Presenting to the UN General Assembly in 2007, Indian feminist Srilatha Batliwala (2007) described how funding trends drove this shift:

> Donors [are] increasingly abandoning the kind of empowerment processes that feminists developed in the 1980s [... and] enthusiastically championing large-scale micro-finance programmes as the quickest route to [...] overall economic development. [...] Meanwhile, in keeping with the insidious dominance of the neo-liberal ideology and its consumerist core, we see the transition of empowerment out of the realm of societal and systemic change and into the individual.

Securitisation and militarisation

The tragic attacks of 11 September 2001 set in motion military interventions that have destabilised many parts of the world. Financed by public funds, the multi-trillion dollar corporate–government industry of surveillance and security has created an international web of paramilitary and privatised security groups that is impossible to trace or hold to account. 'Fighting terrorism' became a justification for governments everywhere to abandon human rights and focus instead on 'security', a convenient pretext to legislate more controls and surveil or jail opponents. In many countries, we witnessed how political leaders stoked fear as a powerful and paralysing political ideology combined with 'othering' that tapped into racism and xenophobia.

Militarisation and violence in Mesoamerica and Colombia were reinforced by the blowback from earlier US Cold War policy and interventions (Nicaragua, Guatemala, El Salvador, Panama), and by the 'War on Drugs' since the early 1990s in Colombia. Spreading to Mexico in 2006, US policy has fuelled the growth of organised crime and violence there, and in Guatemala, Honduras and El Salvador (Tseng-Putterman 2018).

In the mid-2000s, these global dynamics slowed the 'wave of democratisation' promised after the fall of the Berlin Wall. By 2006, a 'democratic deficit' persisted, along with multiple crises – economic, financial, environmental and health (Gaventa 2006a). Well-financed civil society organisations (CSOs) professionalised and institutionalised social change to ensure 'expert issue-focused interventions', a process over-generalised as 'NGO-isation'. Although effective for accessing media and global circles of power, these developments tended to concentrate resources, fragment change efforts and exacerbate disconnects between advocates and their constituencies (Chandhoke 2005, Edwards 2004, Lewis 2002).

Civic participation processes – popular then with institutions such as the World Bank and the International Monetary Fund (IMF) – were criticised as 'rubber-stamping' existing neoliberal economic agendas rather than allowing people to shape their own development (Cooke and Kothari 2001, Hickey and Mohan 2004). For Indonesian organiser Nani Zulminarni, the increasing government and NGO emphasis on expert-driven approaches to decentralisation, for example, devalued community-based approaches, ignored issues of power within women's realities and thus failed to bring democracy closer to people (Clark et al. 2006, Davis and Dibly 2018).

What about the women?

Many of the African, Southeast Asian and Latin American feminists with JASS hailed from an earlier era of grassroots organising, and, in some cases, liberation struggles and internationalism. Our perspectives led the JASS network to shift direction, and in 2006 we launched *Imagining and Building Women's Movements of the Future*, which reorganised our focus and regionalised our network. Driven by frontline women activists and movements, JASS deliberately shifted the entry point of strategy from policy to women. Guided by feminist popular education principles that put women and their lives (private and public) at the centre of their own transformation, we created safe spaces for structured political dialogue among diverse, mostly grassroots women activists (urban, rural, indigenous, LBTQ, young). They traced the dynamics of power in their mindsets, lives, communities and histories as the basis for emergent strategies that dealt explicitly with conflicts and built *power to, power with, power within* and, ultimately, the transformational demands we refer to as *power for* (see Bradley, this volume).

Though hard to measure in the conventional sense, this intersectional organising nurtured trust and hope that created an urgently needed sense of mutual solidarity, belonging and possibility in the midst of forces that stigmatised women who spoke out, promoting fear and isolation. The shared critical analysis produced facilitated new agendas, multiple forms of collective leadership and formations as the basis for joint action and collective self-defence.

In each of the regions where JASS works – Mesoamerica, Southeast Asia and Southern Africa – our approach evolved in different ways, developing principles and methodologies, rather than a specific plan. The non-linear decentralised process has given birth to cross-movement networks and agendas, combining the ideas and struggles of indigenous, queer, feminist and other activists, enabling thousands of grassroots women leaders in and outside feminist movements, and producing tangible (though less visible) impacts. Diverse women have practised and promoted radical democratic organisation and collective leadership, resisted dominant ideologies and created informal communities of mutual support and belonging in contexts where the social fabric is shredded and backlash is alive. As action strategies moved forward, we built alliances with mixed and male-led organisations, including from faith-based groups, to find ways to engage with people's beliefs and hearts. Despite initial reluctance to openly centre feminism in our practice because it seemed to confuse and close more doors than it opened, by 2009 it was clear that explicit feminist ideas and practice offered an alternative set of values and way of being that women longed for. Despite their challenges, these kinds of political processes are rich with untapped learning for the present.

Back to the future

The multiple crises that concerned us in 2006 have morphed and intensified. The increased influence and reach of organised crime and paramilitaries have added the concept of 'shadow power' to our analysis of the forces we face. Driven by non-state actors, hidden and shadow power have captured or colluded with the state to define policy and implementation, from healthcare to energy. Land grabs that displace indigenous and rural communities are the product of the complicities combining oligarchs, politicians, corporations and investors, enforced by police and armies, and a narrative that criminalises indigenous peoples as terrorists preventing economic prosperity. In Mesoamerica, organised crime has penetrated state structures and local economies, a trend that is globalising. Watching US news in 2017, a Honduran colleague noted that the same Humvees from the Gulf War used against US protesters in Ferguson, St. Louis were in the streets of Tegucigalpa.

Despite dramatic shifts in power, many CSOs still use an outdated playbook that relies on the state and campaigning to confront abuses of power. In 2016, we adapted the three faces of power (visible, hidden and invisible) to help activists question those assumptions about the nature of the state, and to rethink strategy to take into account the role of non-state actors in shaping policy, politics and discourse (see Figure 2.1.2).

Assumptions & Reality

Rights framework

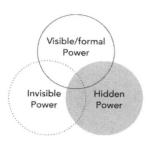

States as regulators, redistributors,
safety net providers and human
rights enforcers

Reality

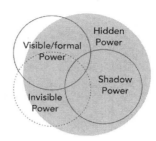

States as subsidisers, investors – facilitators and
enforcers for corporate interests and extremists;
Hidden power actors occupy policy space and
control narrative
Normalised exclusion and violence

FIGURE 2.1.2 Assumptions and reality
Source: Author's elaboration

Many activists – especially those directly confronting mining companies, droughts and violence – have pushed INGOs for greater care with global campaigning that puts them at risk of attack and divides communities. Many are increasingly critical of splashy INGO events that bring in decision-makers and invite frontline activists but rarely challenge the roots of power. In 2018, some participating activists described the extravagant events in Paris to mark the 20th Anniversary of the UN Declaration of Human Rights Defenders as irrelevant and 'human rights washing' (Enebral 2018). As one seasoned former global advocate commented in a personal communication:

> I'm sceptical and tired of these big international short-burst campaigns that are just fuelling the whole NGO–government merry-go-round with little to show for it. Even after the big showy commitment on Ending Sexual Violence in Conflict [...] few governments have actually put in the promised or requisite funding or taken much action. Do they actually change things on the ground for people? Or are they in fact playing us from both ends – benefitting from the international credibility of being active in these spaces while cracking down on us at home?

JASS activists and allies working with JASS in Mesoamerica, Southern Africa and Southeast Asia use the following expressions and terminology to explain what they are navigating.

Capitalism and patriarchy on steroids

Unchecked corporate power, often with government collusion, drives obscenely low wages, privatised costly public services, illegal land and water grabs, displacement, surveillance for profit, and attacks on communities and women activists defending rights and justice. Political forces driving authoritarianism explicitly promote a racist, gendered – sometimes anti-feminist – narrative and agenda that implicitly sanctions violence against women, 'deviants' and outsiders, including immigrants, LGBTIQ and indigenous peoples. Blatant greed and increasing attention to the rigged system that produces extreme inequality have finally put capitalism on the political agenda in some countries.

Extractivism

Patterns of collusion between government authorities, international finance capital, corporations and local oligarchs in mining, logging and energy projects deploy police, military and private security to silence opposition and local defenders. For women, the term includes the devaluation of women's labour and caregiving as essential ingredients of unequal and exploitative economies (Sweetman and Ezpeleta 2017).

Mafiocracy

This describes the infiltration by organised crime and drug cartels into state structures and 'legal' business ventures, in Mesoamerica and beyond. Affected communities must develop survival, protection and change strategies that extend beyond the state, and a heightened understanding of power and risk.

Violence (and the threat of violence) as standard operating procedure

The rise of gangs and organised crime is a problem, but governments are often the primary perpetrators of violence against defenders. From a feminist perspective, this cycle of violence extends from the public into the private realm and is debilitating to women. Continued tolerance of misogyny and gender-based violence within movements, organisations and families undermines the collective capacity of people to advance justice, and makes organisations vulnerable to divisive sexist, racist and homophobic tactics.

Elections but no democracy

Coined to describe Zimbabwe's first post-Mugabe elections, the failure of elections to deliver acceptable outcomes is common to both the global North and the South. Using the tools and pretence of democracy to consolidate executive power, reduce oversight and create new security restrictions has become a template for 'democratic' governments that are increasingly autocratic (Van Reybrouck 2016).

Disaster as the 'new normal'

Extreme weather and climate change have overwhelmed poor communities, and facilitate a command-and-control politics. Disasters are also spawning new kinds of cross-movement, multi-issue organising that increasingly recognises the leadership of indigenous and rural communities, and women as first responders (Klein 2007, Klein 2014).

Mobilisations in search of movement

From #BlackLivesMatter and #MeTo to #FeesMustFall in South Africa, #NotHim in Brazil and #BabaeAko (I am woman) in the Philippines, coordinated mobilisations have broken the silence and shifted the public agenda. Transforming potent social media bursts into organised movements demands strategies beyond social media: sustained political education and dialogue to build common values and agendas; and building new, more democratic leadership and organisational forms (see Figure 2.1.3).

Power and change in disorienting times

While democracy and human rights are under siege, new and smaller-scale inclusive politics shines bright with possibility. From energised informal worker networks (e.g. domestic workers) and a fierce new generation of 'climate justice warriors' to green alternatives, unusual allies and ideas are converging from the edges to confront interconnected crises, the concentration of economic and political power, and polarised politics. Amidst a powerful sense that 'time's up', new alliances are mobilising, driven by younger generations and women, LGBTQ and indigenous peoples, racial and ethnic minorities, and immigrants. The global mobilisation of millions of women has begun to centre women and feminists on the agendas of both the left and the right.

Overlapping power over & Change strategies

Visible: formal policies and policy agendas, decisionmaking structures, courts, legislatures, elected/appointed, budgets, boards of directors, etc.

"Inside" strategies: Lobbying, advocacy and reforming political institutions, court cases, electoral campaigns, and evidence-research.

Hidden (and shadow): actors operating behind the scenes (increasingly overt) to control public agendas, define policy; use resources to profit; use misinformation, obfuscation and narratives to delegitimize opposing views and realities

"Outside" and collective power-building strategies: Organizing, communication/information and direct action that exposes, names and shames, educates, inspires (music, art); builds common ground through engagement; mobilizes united action to pressure power; builds constituencies; resistance-propositional.

Essential deep change strategies: political popular education, critical awareness about internalized and systemic power to identify common problems-solutions (e.g. agendas); creating alternative narratives that create belonging and affirm values of dignity, equality, democracy; organize to create community and networks for shared values-mutual support; self-expression and cultural creation; mutual support.

Invisible: normalizing and socialization of what's normal, who and what counts shaped by narratives, fear, beliefs, values, ideologies – e.g. individualism, consumerism, sexism, racism.

FIGURE 2.1.3 Overlapping *power over* and change strategies
Source: Author's adaptation from Miller et al. (2006, p. 11)

To strengthen and weave connections between these distinct and sometimes small-scale transformations underway, it's vital to understand the changing terrain and shift the logic of dominant civil society organising. 'Frontline' communities know their fight directly. To connect and build on these, they need resources and multidisciplinary action research at the service of local activism that puts 'branding' and institutional turf aside and values lived experience and practical knowledge. Below are a few specific ways to refresh our tried and true power tools to support the rethinking underway:

Clarify and refresh our terminology

Words are political and can easily be co-opted and lose their meaning, particularly in a moment where the dictates of consumer capitalisms have corporations adopting an activist justice stance while paying little or no tax and minimal wages. Not everything that goes viral on twitter or gathers NGOs is 'a movement'. Buzzwords can obfuscate, as with the term 'participation' in the early 2000s (Cornwall 2007). Some of what claims to be a 'movement' is essentially a rebranding strategy for business as usual. Fuzziness about the meaning of 'movement' contributes to superficial initiatives, political confusion and the failure to invest in open-ended, long-term building. 'Movements' and 'activism' also pertain to the right wing, as Evelina Dagnino (2007) points out with her concept of 'perverse confluence'. Simple distinctions between left and right 'movements' are no longer clear, particularly when Nike, Brexiteers and Occupy Wall Street are all 'movements' (VeneKlasen 2012), and both fail to centre gender justice. Technology is a game-changer for exposing abuses, influencing agendas and connecting people; but movement-building requires a variety of collective processes, strategies, organising forms and knowledge to resist the politics of fear and scarcity, and build alternatives (McGee, this volume).

Reclaim and deepen (economic and political) democracy

Scholars have long sought to redefine and radicalise 'citizen' and 'democracy' (Gaventa 2006b, Alvarez et al. 1998). In an anti-immigrant era, reclaiming and redefining a visionary, inclusive concept of a borderless citizen made possible by a digitised, inter-connected world could give shape to a forward-looking agenda that again works to shift citizenship from 'users and choosers to makers and shapers' (Cornwall and Gaventa 2001, p. 1). Embracing economic and environmental citizenship and democracy extends the idea of 'civic participation' to endorse people's potential collective economic power as activist consumers, workers (informal and formal), shareholders and investors.

Centre intersectional analysis and feminisms

Faced by a wave of anti-feminist and misogynist politics from coordinated right-wing forces on the one hand to massive women's mobilisations on the other, gender justice is increasingly coming to the centre of politics. Feminisms offer a movement history, a framework for analysis and an alternative way of organising society and the future. Understanding patriarchy exposes how misogyny is central to the dominant–subordinate logic at the heart of authoritarianism and other exploitative, extractive systems. Feminist practice centres care, cooperation and reciprocity, and seeks to dismantle internalised oppression that feeds backlash. At its best, feminist practice offers an alternative to the competitive individualism and hierarchies that ultimately undermine democracy. As the experiences of global South feminists illustrate, in the absence of intersectional feminist analysis and organising, neither our practice nor our demands will be fundamentally democratic and transformative.

Invest in popular political education and educators

In this political moment where narratives, fear and hate are the epicentre of a polarised politics, the interconnected processes of organising and popular education could not be more important. Like feminist practice, popular education validates the dignity of each person, and emphasises political conversations at the starting and checkpoint of building transformative power. Influenced by decades of top-down solutions and an inflated sense of expertise, many NGOs start with policy or facts, and then ask: 'What do you think?' Starting from people's sense of their reality involves listening and finding connections; it's both open-ended and structured around questioning power and imagining our common goals and future.

Let's renovate the old idea of critical and collective consciousness – the focus of popular education – as an essential step in resisting backlash and building movements. The process of upending the unconscious mindsets reinforced by toxic narratives requires space for critical questioning, and tough conversations that both recognise our differences and seed trust and common struggles for the way forward. A steady diet of competitive individualism and consumerism embedded in our digital, economic and political life – complete with racism, sexism and other forms of 'othering' that blur or erase our interconnections every day – shapes how we see ourselves in the world and our politics. South Korean scholar Byung-Chul Han (2015) argues that neoliberalism is so 'seductive' that 'every individual is master and slave in one. [...] Today, anyone who fails to succeed blames themselves and feels ashamed.' This internalised blame and shame – well known by feminists and anti-racism activists – is central to the self-policing that sustains unequal economic and social systems.

Deepen and sharpen analysis of power

Many advocates still hold a narrow conception of power as policy and institutionalised politics rather than a system. The power concepts and tools discussed in this book support a timely shift back to the kind of systemic analysis that is essential for deeper holistic strategies that connect the dots between changing people and changing institutions. The following are some ways to revive and refocus these tools for new demands:

Assume and understand violence

Many civil society actors are still unprepared for the conflict provoked by their strategies that challenge dominant worldviews and expose abuses of power. Many NGOs' strategies aim to avoid conflict with those in power, and ignore the conflict and violence that exists in organisations, communities and homes. Violence and the threat of violence are central to the logic of unequal systems, reinforced in both the public and the private realms (McGee 2017). Women know that transgressing traditional roles opens them up to attacks as bad mothers, sluts and outcasts. A new era demands simple tools for understanding and navigating how change generates conflict. Backlash is an inevitable byproduct of even the most positive forms of transformation.

With a better understanding of violence and risk – inside and outside their organisations – activists organise and strategise differently. We examine and take on power and privilege within organisations, consider the long term and a wider range of smart tactics when direct action or social media are too risky. Examining violence in our politics, organisations and families helps us recognise the roots of a top-down law and order mindset in our own lives as well as in the public arena. Fear and violence take their toll on activists' bodies and minds; but much practice about activist wellbeing remains individualised, and lacks any connection to power and movements. We can learn about building collective self-defence and navigating dictatorships from indigenous communities and the history of liberation struggles, an archive yet to be adequately documented from the perspective of power and security (Fund for Global Human Rights and Just Associates 2017, Okeowo 2017, Lambrick this volume).

Name the confluences and contradictions of power

Confluences and collusion between international capital, multinational corporations, governments and political-religious extremists are tangled and contradictory, but powerful actors are politically coordinated across borders in ways that activists are not (Ardon 2017). Identifying the intersecting people, interests and webs of economic and political influence – essential for exposing corruption, narrowing strategic choices and moving new agendas when opportunities arise – demands more and better activist–researcher collaborations. Structures of power – corporate boards, governmental bodies, PPPs, philanthropic endeavours – are rife with contradictions that create opportunities for change. An old activist adage says 'no permanent friends, no permanent enemies', and examples abound that present possibilities for change. Nicaraguan feminists, for example, find themselves allied with Catholic Church leaders who are, simultaneously, direct enemies on reproductive rights and potential brokers of an end to repression.

Go beyond the soundbite

Modern-day manifestations of invisible power shaped by a steady unacknowledged diet of consumerism and individualism co-opt our agendas, and limit our ability to imagine and build collective political capacities and prioritise the developing of ideas as central to our change strategies. The incessant heroic saviour story to 'sell' social change to the unconvinced is one of many thin 'feel-good' narratives that undermine coming together and prevent deeper political change. I am conflicted about the new energy across the INGO sector about engaging with dominant 'narratives' in response to the strategies used to isolate, polarise and delegitimise activists and transformative agendas. While this is an opportunity to contextualise communication strategies in specific dynamics of power and privilege, the pressure to deliver new framing and messaging from apolitical marketing experts is bearing down. To generate counter-narratives we must make the local and shared values that centre human dignity and empathy in all our cultures alive in our political work through creative, artistic and political forms of communicating, bridging and weaving.

Look backward as well as forward

Lessons from history have informed many generations of activists (including our back-to-basics approach as JASS). Can we inform today's approaches with better understanding of experiences of fighting dictatorships and of liberation and solidarity? Some dynamics of power, such as the use of misinformation to confuse and divide, are not new. Younger activists are eager for stories about safe houses and underground strategies of liberation struggles. An invitation to a recent Women in Resistance gathering embodied this thirst by highlighting that 'there is a need for the revival of the resistance memory of women' (ANF News 2018).

Conclusion

In the era of the app as solution, there is nevertheless a growing rediscovery that people's feelings and perceptions are central to resisting anti-democratic forces and building inclusive communities and sustainable futures. People perpetually on the margins of the democratic project and bearing the brunt of economic inequality – women, indigenous and rural people, black and ethnic minorities, LGBTQ people – are (re-)asserting their claims and leading a fragile wave of deeper democratisation. Dismissing this as 'identity politics' – a trap even progressives fall into – fails to recognise the class and economic dimensions of so-called 'identity' groups (Younge 2018) and the intersectionality of exclusion. Writing about a counter-force to right-wing populism in Europe, Chantal Mouffe (2018) proposes that we build a left populism, 'establishing a bond between social movements and a new type of party to create a "people" fighting for equality and social justice'.

As we rethink and seek innovation, let's consider again the potential of old-fashioned, slow processes of political education and organising that allow us to quietly unlearn and relearn about power to imagine and build a multiracial, democratic and sustainable future. Building broad constituencies takes face-to-face organising, using the skill of listening and recognising that people are experts about their own problems (Rozworsky 2015). Shifting the balance to people as the starting point may require skill-building and experimentation for a generation that have relied on policy and technical frameworks to guide their way. As Everjoice Win said about younger activists in Southern and East Africa:

> We've lost a generation of community participation types. The new generation is much better educated than in the 1980s. They know a lot about gender policy but haven't worked alongside rural women. They have no idea how to facilitate and raise awareness as opposed to a presenting a power point of facts and policy frameworks. (pers. comm.)

We have many reasons to be optimistic about the future. Global climate justice mobilisation is one. An extraordinary multi-country, multi-perspective feminist civics lesson is unfolding across social media and in the streets in the form of #TotalShutDown or #MeToo. It presents a new opportunity to deepen the democratic agenda and make rights meaningful in a world of dislocation, one in which we thirst for a sense of belonging and reason to be hopeful. As a Kenyan activist told me, with a laugh: 'There are no simple answers to the question of freedom and dignity.' Refreshing our understanding of power and movement strategies, and excavating more hidden stories of resistance and incomplete liberation from the past, may yield useful clues.

References

Action Aid, Institute of Development Studies and Just Associates, 2002. *Making change happen 1: advocacy and citizen participation*. Washington DC: Just Associates.

Alvarez, S., Dagnino, E. and Escobar, A., eds, 1998. *Cultures of politics, politics of culture: re-visioning Latin American social movements*. Boulder: Westview.

ANF News, 2018. International women's conference in Frankfurt taking shape [online]. Amsterdam, ANF News. Available from: https://anfenglishmobile.com/women/international-women-conference-in-frankfurt-taking-shape-29588 [Accessed 5 April 2019].

Ardon, P., 2017. Guatemala: the democratic challenge [online]. London: OpenDemocracy. Available from: https://justassociates.org/en/article/guatemala-democratic-challenge [Accessed 5 April 2019].

Balchin, C., 2011. *Towards a future without fundamentalisms: analyzing religious fundamentalist strategies and feminist responses*. Toronto: Association for Women's Rights in Development.

Batliwala, S., 2007. Putting power back into empowerment [online]. London: OpenDemocracy. Available from: https://www.opendemocracy.net/en/putting_power_back_into_empowerment_0/ [Accessed 5 April 2019].

Chandhoke, N., 2005. What the hell is civil society? [online]. London: OpenDemocracy. https://www.opendemocracy.net/en/article_2375jsp/ [Accessed 5 April 2019].

Clark, C., Holmes, A., VeneKlasen, L. and Win, E., eds, 2006. *Women navigate power: stories about claiming our rights*. Washington DC: Just Associates.

Cooke, B. and Kothari, U., eds, 2001. *Participation: the new tyranny?* London: Zed Books.

Cornwall, A., 2000. *Beneficiary, consumer, citizen: perspectives on participation for poverty reduction*. Sida Studies 2. Stockholm: Swedish Agency for International Development.

Cornwall, A., 2007. Buzzwords and fuzzwords: deconstructing development discourse. *Development in Practice*, 17(4/5), 471–484.

Cornwall, A. and Gaventa, J., 2001. From users and choosers to makers and shapers: repositioning participation in social policy. IDS Working Paper, 127. Brighton: Institute of Development Studies.

Dagnino, E., 2007. Citizenship: a perverse confluence. *Development in Practice*, 17(4–5), 549–556.

Davis, B. and Dibley, T., 2018. Making women visible: interview with Nani Zulminarni. Jakarta: Inside Indonesia.

DiBranco, A., 2018. Before the alt right: Anita Hill and the growth of the misogynist ideology. *Public Eye*, Summer.

Didion, J., 1987. Washington in Miami [online]. *New York Review of Books*. Available from: https://www.nybooks.com/articles/1987/07/16/washington-in-miami/ [Accessed 5 April 2019].

Edwards, M., 2004. *Civil society*. Cambridge: Cambridge University Press.

Emerson, M. and Hartman, D., 2006. The rise of religious fundamentalism. *Annual Review of Sociology*, 32(1), 127–144.

Enebral, V., 2018. Llamémosle '(human)rightswashing' [online]. *Pikara Online Magazine*, 28 November. Available from: https://www.pikaramagazine.com/2018/11/llamemosle-humanrightswashing [Accessed 5 April 2019].

Fund for Global Human Rights and Just Associates, 2017. Interview with Abel Barrera Hernández, Mexico [online]. Washington DC: Fund for Global Human Rights. Available from: https://globalhumanrights.org/protecting-against-threats-abel/ [Accessed 5 April 2019].

Gaventa, J., 2006a. Finding the spaces for change: a power analysis. *IDS Bulletin*, 37(6), 23–33.

Gaventa, J., 2006b. Triumph, deficit or contestation? Deepening the 'deepening democracy' debate. IDS Working Paper, 264. Brighton: Institute of Development Studies.

Gutiérrez, I., 2018. Las mujeres africanas hemos tenido un 'Me too' durante 50 años, era el mundo occidental el que necesitaba despertar [We African women have been having a 'Me too' moment for 50 years, it was the Western world that needed to wake up], interview with Everjoice Win, feminist activist [online]. *El Diario*, 31 December. Available from: https://www.eldiario.es/desalambre/Africa-mujeres-occidental-necesitaba-despertar_0_841315895.html [Accessed 5 April 2019].

Han, B.-C., 2015. Why revolution is no longer possible [online]. London: OpenDemocracy. Available from: https://www.opendemocracy.net/transformation/byung-chul-han/why-revolution-is-no-longer-possible [Accessed 5 April 2019].

Hickey, S. and Mohan, G., eds. 2004. *Participation: from tyranny to transformation?* London: Zed Books.

Imam, A., Marler, I. and Malik, L., 2016. *The devil is in the details: at the nexus of development, women's rights and religious fundamentalisms*. Toronto: Association for Women's Rights and Development.

Just Associates, Institute of Development Studies and Action Aid, 2006. *Making change happen 2: citizen engagement and global economic power*. Washington DC: Just Associates.

Klein, N., 2007. *Shock doctrine: the rise of disaster capitalism*. New York: Metropolitan Books/ Henry Holt.

Klein, N., 2014. *This changes everything*. London: Penguin.

Lewis, D., 2002. Civil society in African contests: reflections on the usefulness of a concept. *Development and Change*, 33(4), 569–586.

McGee, R., 2017. Invisible power and visible everyday resistance in the violent Colombian Pacific. *Peacebuilding*, 5(2), 170–185.

Miller, V., VeneKlasen, L. and Clark, C., 2005. Rights based development: linking rights and participation: challenges in thinking and action. *IDS Bulletin*, 36(1), 31–40.

Miller, V., VeneKlasen, L., Reilly, M. and Clark, C., 2006. *Making change happen 3: power. Concepts for revisioning power for justice, equality and peace*. Washington DC: Just Associates.

Mouffe, C., 2018. Populists are on the rise, but this can be a moment for progressives too [online]. *The Guardian*, 10 September. Available from: https://www.theguardian.com/comm entisfree/2018/sep/10/populists-rise-progressives-radical-right [Accessed 5 April 2019].

Moyn, S., 2018. *Not enough: human rights in an unequal world*. Cambridge, MA: Harvard University Press.

Okech, A., 2017. On feminist futures and movement imperatives. *Development*, 60(1), 12–17.

Okeowo, A., 2017. A Mexican town wages its own war on drugs. *New Yorker*, 27 November.

Pearce, D., 1978. The feminization of poverty: women, work, and welfare. *Urban and Social Change Review*, 11(1), 28–36.

Rozworski, M., 2015. Having the hard conversations: interview with Jane McElvy. *Jacobin Magazine*. Available from: https://www.jacobinmag.com/2015/10/strike-chicago-teacher s-union-public-private-sector/ [Accessed 5 April 2019].

Sax, D., 2018. End the innovation obsession. *New York Times*, 7 December.

Sweetman, C. and Ezpeleta, M., 2017. Introduction: natural resource justice. *Gender and Development*, 25(3), 353–366.

Tseng-Putterman, M., 2018. A century of U.S. intervention created the immigration crisis [online]. *Medium*, 20 June. Available from: https://medium.com/s/story/timeline-u s-intervention-central-america-a9bea9ebc148 [Accessed 5 April 2019].

Van Reybrouck, D., 2016. Why elections are bad for democracy. *The Guardian*, 26 June.

VeneKlasen, L., 2012. Citizen action and the perverse confluence of opposing agendas. *Development*, 55(2), 158–161.

VeneKlasen, L. and Miller, V., 2002. *A new weave of power, people and politics: the action guide for citizen participation and advocacy*. Rugby: Practical Action.

Win, E., 2013. *Between Jesus, the generals and the invisibles: mapping the terrain for feminist movement building and organizing for women's human rights*. Cape Town: Just Associates Southern Africa.

Younge, G., 2018. It comes as no shock that the powerful hate identity politics [online]. *The Guardian*, 5 October. Available from: https://www.theguardian.com/commentisfree/ 2018/oct/05/no-shock-powerful-hate-identity-politics [Accessed 5 April 2019].

2.2

FINDING COMMUNITY: THE POWER OF UNRULINESS

Patta Scott-Villiers

Introduction

In the first decades of the twenty-first century, it seems as if commodification and administration have totalised their influence over all nature, including humanity, north, south, east and west. These processes have generated inequality: environmental damage, insecurity and political alienation. Rampant colonisation of the lifeworld by markets appears not unconnected to new and rising turbulence in environmental, political and social realms. What should this mean for our understanding of political power, the power by which all beings come to agreement?

In *The Theory of Communicative Action* Jürgen Habermas observes that contemporary societies have been overtaken by systems; as the lifeworld, the lived realm of informal, culturally grounded understandings and accommodations, has been colonised by the autonomous instrumentalism of the market and bureaucratic administrations. He argues that 'steering media', such as money and institutional power, bypass consensus-oriented communication with a 'symbolic generalisation of rewards and punishments' leading us to accept their rules (Habermas (1984, p. 183). The rules of these systems impose themselves on our lives and connections. We lose our sense of being part of, and responsible to, the world and society; and the heart is ripped out of social discourse. Complex differentiation between one group, technology or system and another occurs at an ever-faster rate, but at the cost of social pathologies.

Inevitably, a countermove emerges among those who sense the loss, who value communication for inquiry and consensus over communication for money and interest. To many people, given the influence of enlightened 'I think therefore I am' sensibilities, political power to rebuild fairness may seem to emanate from individuals, their contentions and their institutions. It is their capabilities to collaborate, argue, impose, impress or avoid that preoccupy our understanding of tactics and strategies, even as we recognise the role of social structures such as classes and genders, and of norms such as earning money or knowing western science, in defining desirable thought and action. Not limited to single human beings, individualism also applies to our understanding of institutions as collective units acting in competition or collaboration with one another, as countries or companies do. But another perspective reveals power's locus in the indivisibility of being: the lifeworld as a whole. The lifeworld is life as it is experienced not by each individual dissected from the rest, but, as Husserl put it, as 'the we-subjectivity' and the dynamic horizon in which we live (Husserl 1970, pp. 138–39).

Breaking the rules of dominant divisive systems reveals the lifeworld still at work as *communitas*. In this chapter, I propose to explore a contemporary understanding of *communitas*, an ontological reality that reveals itself in resistance and unruliness. The anthropologist Victor Turner described *communitas* as a generic human bond underlying or transcending all particular cultural definitions (1996, p. 68). *Communitas* is a state of being together in unstructured equal community. It has been variously understood as anti-structure, a liminal, in-between time and space in which normal social structures are abandoned and defied (Turner 1996), or as a void that underlies social interaction, arising from our realisation that we each owe a foundational debt to all others in the world (Esposito 2009).

Communitas shows itself mostly momentarily and often ecstatically. It emerges, for instance in the wild abandon of youth, the resistance of protestors and excluded people, the raptures of artists and audiences, and in the unmeasured kindnesses of care. It is a less-explored field of power, appearing invalid under modern political rules and the prevailing science used to explain politics, but one that could help renew understanding of important contemporary phenomena of resistance and social rebuilding.

I aim to show here that although individualism and identitarianism (such as nationalism) have obscured the truth of our being part of a living singularity, *communitas* is alive and well and is repairing the world (whether fast enough to oppose the fragmenting and unequalising tendencies is another matter). I argue that *communitas* offers a different view of the foundations of political power and informs action in these times of turbulent fragmentation. It explains the vagueness and emptiness of contemporary anomie (loss of belief, lassitude) among the unemployed, the precarious and the unsuccessful, and gives resistance a shape not defined only by that which it resists. I show that it is in unruliness, when we counteract, ignore or play with the divisive rules of markets and administrations, that the truth of *communitas* is glimpsed and revalidated and the potential emerges for alternative directions.

I hope this chapter will be part of that which binds individual fragmentary subjectivities back into the wholeness of our world.

I first explore the problem of political subjectivity when it is considered as a property of individuals in markets. I identify how this perspective has caused multiplying fractured selves to be set adrift from one another, even as they are enmeshed in systems of material difference and normativity. I note how the analysis of power and identity has been perforce bound up in and limited by fascination with the individual. This leads me to touch on how individualistic subjectivity creates negative communities, recognisable today in contemporary despair.

I then define *communitas* as a foundational and continuous power that resists despair, and I explore how its power comes to light at times when order is suspended. This leads me to recast political subjectivity as a phenomenon of openness and possibility, using a form suggested by feminist theorist Claudia Leeb.

Demonstrating how *communitas* and open subjectivity are revealed in unruly politics, I look at two of its many manifestations: protest and aesthetic ruptures. I ask how and whether the powerful but seemingly ephemeral qualities of unruly moments are sustained in political action, in what philosopher Alain Badiou calls 'fidelity to the event' (2012b, p. 69).

The chapter ends by proposing that the workings of *communitas* offer new analytical tools for clarifying the operations of political power, informing strategies and integrating tactics towards a truly common good.

Individual political subjectivity

With the rise of neo-liberalism and individualism in the late twentieth century it was vital to an emancipatory agenda to understand how political power drove the treatment of individuals, groups and societies. Steven Lukes's (1974/2005) breakthrough with the three dimensions of power showed decision-making, agenda-setting and ideology-forming as creating a field of power in which people were enabled and constrained as persons. This was deepened by John Gaventa to show the mechanisms by which these 'faces of power' operated, not only in public contests in multiple spaces of interaction but also in ways of mobilising bias and in transforming issues such as gender into non-issues (Gaventa 1982, Gaventa 2006). The rules that conferred the different forms of power worked through and on individuals and collectives to create hierarchies and discriminations. The usefulness of these insights allowed people who felt powerless, and their supporters, to understand the invisible and hidden processes that drove their situation and to bring into question what had been hitherto taken for granted as natural superiorities and inferiorities. Later, Clarissa Hayward (1998, p. 12) broke new ground by showing how a field of power sets boundaries rather than giving specific powers to individuals, limiting everybody's freedom but in differential ways and leaving space for boundary-breaking. Hayward drew on Foucault (1995), who had given us insight into how we self-discipline ourselves and build disciplinary administrations under which we volunteer to restrict ourselves, out of fear of the consequences of breaking the rules or a need to conform and belong, even when these rules undermine equality in the life-world. Foucault's (2007) notion of 'governmentality' – by which administrable populations are created, categorised and made subject to policy – showed how the rules multiplied and enmeshed people in ever-more complex systems of assent. In all these theories, power is suffused throughout a system, but the political subject is individual. She is watched in the panopticon; she is a member of a rights-claiming population; she is a child whose room for manoeuvre is defined by her race; or she is simply a person subordinated to others. It is not the we, but the I.

The I is also paramount in concurrent understandings of identity that weave through understandings of power. Each cross-cutting intersectional status of wealth, class, race, gender, sex and body gives birth to a new identity to compete with other identities for recognition, resources and empowerment (Crenshaw 1989). Despite Nancy Fraser's eloquent critique of Habermas's idealised public sphere as a space in which actually only the urban male white elite is free to communicate, she does not free us from the tyranny of the I. Her focus on recognition, representation and redistribution nuances the detail of who can get in and who cannot, and suggests equal identification of the individual (Fraser 1999). Even as she problematises recognition of identity where it exacerbates economic inequality or promotes separatisms, Fraser's answer, in recognising social subordination rather than identity subordination, rests on individualism (Fraser 2000). While countering unfair treatment of individuals and groups is undoubtedly crucial to struggles *within* a liberal system that identifies and specifies, the effort does not do away with the fact that individualism itself is a tool by which people and groups are subordinated. The master's tools are unlikely to dismantle the master's house (Lorde 2007 [1984]).[1]

The intense modern focus on the indivisible I is not a matter of chance, but arises from the structures of modernity and its politics of liberalism. Althusser's story of the policeman calling out 'Hey you there!' and someone turning, believing himself to be the one who has been hailed, and responding, 'Who me?' illustrates the problem of the political subject (Althusser 2001, p. 118). The citizen who responds has become the subject of what Althusser names 'interpellation'. By answering the call the citizen has been made to agree to be subject to the law that identifies and disciplines him. What is called is neither his body (although it is also present and needed for the scenario) nor his autonomous being, but the individualised political subject that he has become by answering the call.

Judith Butler's take on interpellation of the new-born, 'it's a boy/girl', likewise focuses on the tyranny of imposed identity called out by society to every member, this time at a group level (Butler 1990). The way that this identity is performed over time and space entraps it in a web from which it is hard to escape. Similarly, Adorno (2001) speaks of the colonisation of modern self through interpellation by 'the culture industry', a profit-making, advertising-saturated version of popular culture. It creates a permanent state of desire to be included, to be someone other than who we are and to have more stuff than we currently have (see also Cook 1996). By insisting on an illusory sense of individual freedom to choose goods, it perpetuates capitalist power over the subject. Today, the political subject lives in constant movement between ever more spectacles (phones, purchases, offices, social media, shops, TV programmes, investments and entertainments, to name but a few). Guy Debord 1995 [1967]) adds that capitalism in its final form presents itself as an immense accumulation of spectacles in which all that is lived is now only a reflection of the real. Since Debord was writing, new networks have overlain but not diminished his insight on how the individual has become reduced to

---

1   'The master's tools will never dismantle the master's house. They may allow us to temporarily beat him at his own game, but they will never enable us to bring about genuine change' (Lorde 2007, p. 112).

an audience of the spectacle. Most cogently, Alan Kirby (2009) has named our era the time of 'digimodernism', in which individuals live in almost complete displacement from the real, navigating the nets of communication technology.

Negative communities

The vast penetration of digimodernism and its effects may lead us to believe that *communitas* is no longer a power of much significance. On the contrary: it is still operating; but, rather than being a place of happy collaboration, it has become a limbo-like place. When each form of solidity – of law, language or body – has been hollowed out in spectacular society; when populism has overtaken formal politics because opinions are being fed on a rich diet of fake news and algorithms, community still remains.

From within the spectacle, a new form of life emerges. 'The coming being is whatever being', says Agamben (1993, p. 2), suggesting that when the spectacular has hollowed everything, then every entity will matter equally, simply as a non-entity, a unit of data perhaps. The coming community will be a limbo from which no one will be excluded. It will be singular *communitas* and leave no one behind. It will not be like community as we think we know it – designated as black or white, Lithuanian or First Nations, having this or that special characteristic. Jessica Whyte (2010) is not so sure, pointing out that even as this coming community of 'whatever-being' continues its vacuous rise, identities will continue to be caught up in more or less reactionary or emancipatory political projects. Old forms of exploitation and discrimination will find space to revive themselves, she claims. While Agamben suggests that the commoditisation of identity will nullify all identities into a single petty bourgeoisie (1993, p. 63), Whyte argues that it will continue 'to produce massive poverty, forced labor, and politicized identities'. She calls for a new political analysis that recognises that capitalism does not have a *telos*, a pre-defined end towards which it relentlessly moves, but a capacity to adapt and absorb, 'reducing life worlds to debris'. If either of them is right, the future of community based on individualism and spectacle is hardly a pretty one.

Jason Kemp Winfree also explores negative communities in which *communitas* could be said to be operating. He quotes a story from Maurice Blanchot about people gathering at the site of police killings at the entrance to a Metro station. 'Community happens anonymously, unorganized and unannounced', he observes. It dissipates and 'bears witness to human finitude'. He follows this with Jean-Luc Nancy's prescient idea that the weak kindred spirit felt by the mass of people most betrayed by liberalism will create a community of 'unemployed negativity' (*negativité sans emploi*) (Winfree 2011, pp. 80, 91). Agamben's version of community is, by contrast, a little more positive. It at least appropriates dispossession and builds a singularity based on *being* as such, suggesting that however atomised we become, *communitas* is still the foundational power. It behoves us to focus on building on *communitas* in other ways.

Communitas

A contemporary meaning of power can be built from a base in the culturally plural concept of *communitas*. Rather than deploying community as a set of rules and boundaries that categorise the rights, responsibilities and norms of people, groups, companies and territories, and rather than instructing members through interpellation, we can reframe community as a *power in itself, prior to other powers*. It is not a community with edges that exclude, but a whole that includes all that are outside. It includes those who are excluded by sovereign states, the perpetuation of which requires that they can declare states of exception (Guantanamo Bay, the Manus Regional Processing Centre, extraordinary rendition, states of emergency), the right to kill or let live, and the authority to imprison or ennoble (Agamben 1998). True politics is not in the struggles to influence the sovereign but in the struggles for those left out to come in, not as subordinates but as equals (Badiou 2005).

Since *communitas* includes everyone, it is the power from which individual belonging, capability and association must be emerging, and from which are drawn norms, solidarities, identities and sovereignties. It must be the active constant while all of the individualised and bounded powers ebb and flow. It becomes visible when these lesser powers are destabilised. Understanding *communitas* should help us work with forces of interpellation, spectacle and identity proliferation. *Communitas* gives resistance a sense of direction.

A group of young boys in Portugal in the 1970s tear around their neighbourhood in a way that is both out of control and contained by their own made-up rules. They run along walls, through yards and across rooftops, fearful and exhilarated. Back in the schoolyard, they boast to one another of their exploits. Anthropologist Julio Alves (1993) catches their words and actions and finds in them the essential elements of liminality – the experience of *communitas*, when the boys are together and quite different from everyone else – and then a coming of age, readiness to take a part in their society. Perhaps having known freedom and used it to define their part in the future society, they are grateful to put it aside. Most of us will have had some version of this experience in our youth. Turner (1982), who coined the use of the Latin *communitas* to describe this state that youth reach in rites of passage, calls it a time of humility and modelessness, which allows recognition of an essential human bond. The seeming necessity and universality of rites of passage across cultures indicates that something important is wrapped up in these liminal states. If social order acts as a restraint that conserves, protects and limits community, then periods of 'anti-structure' during which people let go of the norms that have constrained them seem to be essential to allow communities to learn and grow (Turner 1982, p. 244). Hedged by rites of separation and reintegration, initiates not only pass across a threshold of in-betweenness but also feel a sense of togetherness. In these times, the 'former rules no longer apply, and new ones remain in abeyance, a state at once liberating and terrifying' (ibid., p. 251). Liminality's communal nature offers 'a counterstroke of simultaneity, spontaneity and infinity' against limitation and inadequacy (ibid., p. 265). This power is visible, or more correctly sensible, in these wild times, but it does not go away when those who felt it move back into orderly society. *Communitas* informs their ways of being together, caring for one another, having ideas of a better world.

Political subjectivity beyond identification

This continued state of *communitas* is merely unrecognised and unnoticed. Claudia Leeb demonstrates that there is more to an individual in society than the idea of individualism has so far credited. The individual is neither a purely autonomous selfish agent nor only subject to the authority of community systems and norms. She sustains critical action as *a* being in relation to other beings who can never be entirely in the thrall of imposed identity and authority. In what Leeb calls 'a politics beyond identification', she develops the idea of the political subject as a 'subject-in-outline' (2017, p. 165). There are spaces in her/their agency-subjection that offer the possibility of something more and something together. There is room for fusion with any others (people, things, ideas) – and subjectivity is open to any sort of articulation in the world. Consider the young person who dresses up as a Goth, creates a group online who share music together, is beaten by skinheads in a UK park, is saved by an old person brandishing a walking stick, and patched up by migrants working as nurses at the local hospital who then become her friends. Her subjectivity is under constant stimulation as well as limitation.

Leeb suggests that these spaces in the political subject are 'a break in the socio-symbolic order', when a person or group acts not as she/they are bound to by identity, norms or rules, but in *whatever* way (2017, p. 22). Leeb deploys the thinking of Lacan and Adorno to clarify what is at stake. Lacan argues that spaces in the political subject are an expression of 'the real', as opposed to behaviour constructed through accepted norms. The Goth girl finds capacity for transformative agency in each of her encounters precisely because she is not precisely a Goth and not precisely a girl. Adorno calls it 'non-identity', referring to the way in which the culture that suffuses our world is never able to colonise the whole of it. The uncolonised space is *communitas*. The individual may be labelled and pinned down by signifiers, such as poor, female and black; and although she acts from where she finds herself, she also acts with creativity, perhaps as an angry person who does not need to be poor. According to Lacan, the moment of her noticing her pain and realising that she is not entirely as she has been labelled is the moment when she touches on the real (Leeb 2017, p. 25). This hole in the labelled self is not entirely comfortable, as Žižek suggests, and society and she both want to patch it with more labels or fill it with desirable normalising commodities (perhaps clothes and music), primed to give her a comforting sense of who she is, or to numb her discomfort (Žižek 1989, p. 122). But she also somehow remembers that labels and desires are always incomplete. The pain of the 'poor, black woman' in being signified or mediated into being inferior is not, or not only, individual. Her pain is part of skeins of friendship, family, history, sense, place and space, any and all of which are happening through and with her, and all of which are part of the transformation she is already contributing to. The label of poor, black woman is a social label, but her anger is also part of something common.

We hold certain ethics almost without thought, based on being together in the world, recognising not a need to conform but a simple state of being part. Emmanuel Lévinas (1969) identified the face-to-face encounter as primary in generating ethics, and argued that people labour not to have mastery over one another, but to make spaces to welcome the other. This *communitas* is the true source of transcendent (rather than simply reformist) social movement, such as those that aim to eradicate norms of racism, environmental damage, gender violence or economic exploitation. Movements such as the children's mobilisation to stop climate change that emerged in Europe in early 2019, the alter-globalisation movement that spread across the world in the early 2000s, or certain contemporary religious movements are examples, some nicer than others. Those who are mobilised do not ask to be included; they seek something new. The mesh of historical norms is not close enough to bind them into good behaviour. Conversely, where extremist leaders have been voted in through democratic politics, where nations have embraced xenophobia and nationalism and rejected liberalism but not materialism, the move is anti-*communitas*.

Unruly politics

Unruly politics, explains akshay khanna (2012, p. 165), is 'simultaneously the insistence on new languages of politics, the redefinition of spaces of politics, ruptures in the aesthetic regimes of power, and the creation of imaginaries of power beyond what is already intelligible'. The most obvious new languages arrive with a plethora of protest, arising in *communitas*. Every month, all around the world, there are protests that aim to persuade those who have the rules in their hands that something needs to change.

Protest

Everyday politics (the work of parliaments and committees, TV debates and rallies) reaches such an impasse that people protest not in order to reform, but to transform. The story of the *gilets jaunes* in France is just one of the more recent examples of a mode of politics that emerges from *communitas* to show the exclusionary truth of the everyday. From late 2018 to the time of writing (April 2019), an odd mix of people from small towns and rural areas – young, old, from truck drivers to library workers – gathered each week to protest at road crossings and in city centres across France (Harding 2019). Leaderless, they said they had felt like outcasts from society, ignored by the metropoles and abandoned in the periphery. They remind those who govern and the metropolitan elites whom they believe are exploiting them that there is a moral economy, an expectation of fair relations (Thompson 1971).

Alain Badiou interrogates a similar shape of protest that took place in Egypt across several months of 2011 and again in 2013, during which protesters were once again leaderless and calling not for specific policies, but for a general transformation of politics. Many commentators wondered why the protesters aimed neither at taking political power nor at changing regulations. People in Tahrir Square said 'Egypt is here.' They posed a new idea for what it meant to have an identity, which was not centred on the individual (a liberal notion) but on a sense of *communitas*. As Badiou put it, the Egyptian revolution was a moment when, by standing in the square and saying 'Egypt is here', the protesters indicated the real existence of the people (Herrera and El-Sharnouby 2018).

In France and Egypt, and in many other similar protests, including the Occupy movement, protesters treated one another quite differently from how they might in everyday life, and by all accounts far more respectfully. This was a form of prefiguration of the world they were looking to create through their protest, a form of *communitas* (Badiou 2012b, Maeckelbergh 2011, Van De Sande 2013).

These protests have strong parallels with the revolutionary events that swept across Europe in 1848, from Portugal to Moldavia and from Norway to Sicily and Greece. Just as in the Middle East in 2011, protests sparked in one country after another – each without leaders, each borne on a tide of popular determination, and all demanding systemic rather than specific change. Historian Christopher Clark (2019) has argued that although each of the revolts was crushed, some only after many months, the events led to profound political change, generating new constitutions, parliaments, franchises and economic policies.

The language of these protests was not concerned with the sort of political bargaining by which interest or identity was defined; nor were demands made in ways intelligible to powerful institutions. Instead, new ethical logics emerged, new modes of action were generated and spaces of power were reconfigured, all drawing on the *communitas* that could bring in the excluded.

Aesthetics

Differently from protest, but no less important to the power of *communitas*, aesthetics is a realm by which *communitas* also makes itself known through rupture. Jacques Rancière (2004) explores how, in a kaleidoscopic array of different forms, the arts can disrupt the 'distribution of the sensible' – the rules as to what it is possible and impossible to see, hear, touch, smell, approve or disapprove. The artist, if not constrained by an ethical regime set by the authorities or by a representative regime set in place through the commodification of art, can make strange the normal, create ruptures in the visible and audible, and generally make play and play havoc with our expectations. Through such an aesthetic service, a bombardment of crazy ideas and strange images, we glimpse truths unnoticed and create connections and associations that had been hitherto forbidden, lost or unthought (Latour 2007). Consider buildings in middle- and upper-class areas of São Paolo, Brazil, covered in hieroglyphs unintelligible to the residents, spray-painted by young men who scramble up the outside of apartment blocks to drape the city in their own web of language. This art is called *Pixo* and it belongs to the dispossessed (Wainer and Oliveira 2010).

Fidelity to the event

Tahrir Square in 2011, according to Alain Badiou, was an event. By 'event' Badiou means it was a moment in which the truth of political reality becomes evident. People who had taken part had understood something about the politics of the real: the politics of everyone. It was a time of *communitas*. The same can be said for many of the moments of protest, aesthetic rupture or liminality we have touched on in this chapter. It is not surprising that such moments do not last long these days. The sentiments are utopian and difficult to sustain. They challenge identity and materialist politics, and their protagonists do not speak a language understood by the nominally powerful. Nonetheless, something always changes as a result of these events. Despots fall, constitutions are amended, moral economies are renewed and, more than anything else, politics is once again made cognisant of the outsider and her importance. In each case, the political subjects enact a politics beyond identification: living out Leeb's political subject-in-outline. Their position as outsiders allows them to see the administrative and corporate spectacle as it really is: a hollow backlot constructed of plywood, with big billboards advertising perfect middle-class lives, behind which live tense conglomerations of ordinary people (Boo 2012).

Badiou's critique of everyday politics – the ways in which people are represented by leaders in sovereign parliaments and the like – is based on his experience of the student uprisings of May 1969 in Paris. These events exposed, he argued, the real weakness of social bonds such as political parties or socio-economic identities. The politics of the real, as opposed to the everyday, is not about recasting identity or interest relationships, but about unbinding them (Badiou 2005). But what follows? Do they get rebound in another, better way? Once unbound, do they get taken over by opportunist rebinders – namely populists, fascists and demagogues? *Communitas* is all very exhilarating and true, but it is unstable and frightening, and many people are quick to abandon their dreams to such enticing leaders. *Communitas* is, as Agamben would have it, a matter of *whatever being*, a state whose lack of structure is profoundly disconcerting. All this notwithstanding, however nervous *communitas* may make us, the philosophers, critical theorists and anthropologists I have quoted here are all making a similar argument: that *it is only from such a point of truth about society, sovereignty and politics that any of us can do the work of rebuilding the political world*. The energy required to transform or even transcend the institutional, ideological and internalised faces of power that bind us to the ways we do things now can *only* come from the foundational power of *communitas*.

How can people ever be faithful to what they took part in? It is never easy to keep open an egalitarian political framework in the light of state power, frontiers, laws and the police – let alone the invisible norms of inequality and environmental abuse that we have all ingested. Does *communitas* extend itself, or is there a return to hierarchy and competition, interest and identity, exploitation and excuses, however new their forms? It seems that fidelity is maintained through something akin to love. Love, Badiou says, is woven from a genuine experience of otherness. While the form may vary, the ontological real remains as it ever was. Fidelity to the event, keeping the power of *communitas* directed towards better forms of community, becomes possible because love, or ethics, is given back their place. He asks:

> what kind of world does one see when one experiences it from the point of view of two and not one? What is the world like when it is experienced, developed and lived from the point of view of difference and not identity? (Badiou 2012a, p. 22)

This point of view offers a basis for the analysis of suffering and efforts to change it, asking where and how *communitas* is operating and how it can be strengthened in relation to practical politics.

Conclusion

Power seems more dispersed through technology and culture than it has ever been, and yet the effect is fragmentation of purpose. Climate perturbation, financial volatility, political extremism, social and labour insecurity and rapid bifurcations of identity are working together at scale in ways that have challenged our understanding of power and our ability to use it for building just and sustainable societies. We as political subjects cannot merely be described as law-enabled/disabled citizens or denizens of sovereign states, or as agent-victims in our geographical and social spaces. Our lives are also subject to another sovereign: a global market. Our lifeworlds have been colonised by the instrumentality of an entirely impersonal and spectacular system of money-making and spending. Most of the structures that made up what we understood as our lives – including natures, nations, organisations, families, friendships, bodies and minds – have been made available for purchase. Normative power that may once have defined moral and cognitive order is fusing into a fast-replicating global aesthetic whose primary value is economic. This globalised aesthetic defines a set of boundaries for everyone, everywhere. Where once norms fought, now they do business.

Living through these days of financial crisis, austerity and xenophobia, at least in the north, we feel a kind of vertigo, realising that we climbed up here and cannot see how to get down. Our relentless focus on the individual as powerless, self-disciplined, empowered, complicit or indeed full of power has taken us to a dead-end of infinite fragmentation, which fits quite well with a commercial outlook. Merely combining individuals together into collectives – whether organisational, social or in movements, networks and voter coalitions – does little to get us out of the fundamental disempowerment that is going on.

But there is another way of thinking about it, a new understanding of community based on a recognition that we are neither entirely subject to the structures we have built nor the individual agency we prize. Resistance is evident across the world, replicating rapidly from one event of political truth to the next. Of course, even resistance is caught in the web of commerce and profiteering from big data algorithms; but that does not stop the power of *communitas* from informing it too. Collaboration, no longer based on a simple idea of intersubjectivity, but on a new recognition of the ontological nature of *communitas*, is vital for knowing how to reconfigure our understanding of norms and sovereignties and build movements for transformative change. New analytical tools that redefine political subjectivity and give us new insights into the truth of sovereignty, exclusion and association are essential. While globally networked media expose us to new versions of being, within the liminal spaces of the same media and the same material world, a plenitude of unruliness is rising that points to a different kind of political power.

References

Adorno, T.W., 2001. *The culture industry: selected essays on mass culture*. London: Routledge.

Agamben, G., 1993. *The coming community* (M. Hardt, trans.). Minneapolis: University of Minnesota Press.

Agamben, G., 1998. *Homo sacer: sovereign power and bare life*. Stanford, CA: Stanford University Press.

Althusser, L., 2001. *Lenin and philosophy and other essays*. New York: New York University Press.

Alves, J., 1993. Transgressions and transformations: initiation rites among urban Portuguese boys. *American Anthropologist*, 95(4), 894–928.

Badiou, A., 2005. *Metapolitics* (J. Barker, trans.). London and New York: Verso.

Badiou, A., 2012a. *In praise of love*. London: Serpent's Tail.

Badiou, A., 2012b. *The rebirth of history: times of riots and uprisings* (G. Elliot, trans.). London and New York: Verso.

Boo, K., 2012. *Behind the beautiful forevers: life, death, and hope in a Mumbai undercity*. London: Portobello.

Butler, J., 1990. *Gender trouble: feminisms and subversion of identity*. London and New York: Routledge.

Clark, C., 2019. Why should we think about the Revolutions of 1848 now? *London Review of Books*, 41(5), 12–16.

Cook, D., 1996. *The culture industry revisited: Theodor W. Adorno on mass culture*. Oxford: Rowman & Littlefield.

Crenshaw, K., 1989. Demarginalizing the intersection of race and sex: a black feminist critique of antidiscrimination doctrine, feminist theory and antiracist politics. *University of Chicago Legal Forum*, 1(8), 139–167.

Debord, G., 1995 [1967]. *The society of the spectacle* (D. Nicholson-Smith, trans.). New York: Zone Books.

Esposito, R., 2009. *Communitas: the origin and destiny of community* (T. Campbell, trans.). Stanford, CA: Stanford University Press.

Foucault, M., 1995. *Discipline and punish: the birth of the prison* (A. Sheridan, trans.). 2nd ed. New York: Vintage.

Foucault, M., 2007. *Security, territory, population (Michel Foucault: lectures at the Collège de France)* (G. Burchell, trans.). London: Palgrave Macmillan.

Fraser, N., 1999. Rethinking the public sphere: a contribution to the critique of actually existing democracy. In: C. Calhoun, ed. *Habermas and the public sphere*. Cambridge, MA: MIT Press, 109–142.

Fraser, N., 2000. Rethinking recognition. *New Left Review*, 3, 107–120.

Gaventa, J., 1982. *Power and powerlessness: quiescence and rebellion in an Appalachian Valley*. Chicago: University of Illinois Press.

Gaventa, J., 2006. Finding the spaces for change: a power analysis. *IDS Bulletin*, 37(6), 23–33.

Habermas, J., 1984. *The theory of communicative action Vol II: reason and the rationalization of society*. Boston: Beacon Press.

Harding, J., 2019. Among the Gilets Jaunes. *London Review of Books*, 41(6), 3–11.

Hayward, C.R., 1998. De-facing power. *Polity*, 31(1), 1–33.

Herrera, L. and El-Sharnouby, D., 2018. Alain Badiou on the Egyptian revolution: questions of the movement and its vision [online]. Available from: https://www.opendemocracy.net/en/north-africa-west-asia/alain-badiou-on-egyptian-revolution-questions/ [Accessed 15 May 2019].

Husserl, E., 1970. *The crisis of European sciences and transcendental phenomenology: an introduction to phenomenological philosophy* (D. Carr, trans.). Evanston, IL: Northwestern University Press.

khanna, a., 2012. Seeing citizen action through an 'unruly' lens. *Development*, 55(2), 162–172.

Kirby, A., 2009. *Digimodernism: how new technologies dismantle the postmodern and reconfigure our culture*. London and New York: Continuum.

Latour, B., 2007. *Reassembling the social: an introduction to actor-network-theory*. Oxford: Oxford University Press.

Leeb, C., 2017. *Power and feminist agency in capitalism: toward a new theory of the political subject*. New York: Oxford University Press.

Lévinas, E., 1969. *Totality and infinity: an essay on exteriority*. Dordrecht: Kluwer, Martinus Nijhoff.

Lorde, A., 2007 [1984]. *Sister outsider*. Berkeley, CA: Crossing Press.

Lukes, S., 1974/2005. *Power, a radical view*. 2nd ed. London: Palgrave Macmillan.

Maeckelbergh, M., 2011. Doing is believing: prefiguration as strategic practice in the alter-globalization movement. *Social Movement Studies*, 10(1), 1–20.

Rancière, J., 2004. *The politics of aesthetics*. London: Continuum.

Thompson, E.P., 1971. The moral economy of the English crowd in the eighteenth century. *Past and Present*, 50, 76–136.

Turner, V., 1982. Images of anti-temporality: an essay in the anthropology of experience. *Harvard Theological Review*, 75(2), 243–265.

Turner, V., 1996. *Dramas, fields and metaphors: symbolic action in human society*. Ithaca, NY: Cornell University Press.

Van De Sande, M., 2013. The prefigurative politics of Tahrir Square: an alternative perspective on the 2011 revolutions. *Res Republica*, 19, 223–229.

Wainer, J. and Oliveira, R.T., dir. 2010. *PIXO*. Video [online]. Available from https://vimeo.com/29691112 [Accessed 15 May 2019].

Whyte, J., 2010. 'A new use of the self': Giorgio Agamben on the coming community. *Theory & Event*, 13(1).

Winfree, J.K., 2011. No more beautiful days. *Epoché: A Journal for the History of Philosophy*, 16(1), 79–92.

Žižek, S., 1989. *The sublime object of ideology*. London: Verso.

2.3

RETHINKING ACCOUNTABILITY: A POWER PERSPECTIVE

Rosemary McGee

What notions of power underlie accountability struggles? How do underlying conceptions of power inform the approaches or insights currently used by activists trying to hold the powerful to account? What is left out or de-emphasised? And what does this tell us about the relationship between power theory and accountability practice: what is power theory failing to pick up from accountability-claiming practice; and what aspects of power theory is accountability-claiming practice failing to make full use of? Motivated by a concern that mainstream theoretical debates about power among political scientists seem frustratingly disconnected from what we might call 'power praxis', this chapter revisits some of the latest thinking on accountability-claiming, and views it through the lenses of power theory.

'Accountability' is inscribed with a range of meanings; and, since its emergence, 'social accountability' thinking and practice have been influenced by various conceptual frames.[1] The simplest and most prevalent versions are based closely on the 'principal-agent' theory of accountability, developed for explaining market relationships rather than those between states and citizens.[2] These see the failures of public institutions to deliver to people as failures by visible, recognisable actors who can be identified and held answerable for the flaws in their performance.

---

1 'Social accountability' refers to attempts to improve the performance and responsiveness of public institutions through citizen voice and engagement with states and corporations. As it involves the relations between citizens and state, it is a political process but is termed 'social' because it rests heavily on the initiative of citizens or social actors – e.g. civil society organisations (CSOs) – and lies outside the boundaries of the formal, election-based, political accountability that characterises democratic regimes. For a thorough review of conceptual frames, see Fox (2015, pp. 347–8).
2 'Principal-agent' theory and language is not to be confused with the language of power as 'agency' used in power theory and praxis and in this chapter.

More complex versions recognise that accountability failures go beyond individual public administrators and departments, taking the form of biases in public institutions and provisioning systems that are 'captured' by elites keen to preserve their own privileges. These need to be addressed by organised citizens, mobilising demand and using evidence of gaps in provision as 'checks and balances' to limit their exclusionary effects.

More complex still are the versions that locate accountability problems in the very systems and structures of society, polity and economy, and point to long-term or permanent engagement in 'accountability politics' (Fox 2007b) to counter, override and ultimately transform behaviours, attitudes and whole cultures of governance. What relatively powerless people can expect and get is very different at the two ends of the definitional spectrum: at one end they can request answers, while at the other they have the capacity to actually produce answers in the form of sanctions and compensations that make relatively powerful actors (in Fox's case, public institutions) play their roles properly (Fox 2007a).

I learnt that accountability is all about power years ago when conducting PhD fieldwork in a marginalised, conflict-affected, remote community in the southwestern Colombian Andes, exploring poor people's experience of and interactions with the state. Later, when working with colleagues to monitor and evaluate aid projects and programmes focusing on accountability-claiming, I realised these needed to be all about transforming power.[3] We struggled to apply theory-based evaluation, to devise programme theory and causal chains that enabled us to judge whether these programmes had helped people shift power, and to understand how. Even the programmes that started from concrete, observed accountability problems tended to be driven less by a careful analysis of the concrete instance and more by a general commitment to generating transparency and expecting it to strengthen accountability, in scantily defined ways. Drawing on insights from the latest thinking about transparency and accountability, citizen engagement and citizen agency (e.g. Joshi and Houtzager 2012, Joshi 2013, Kosack and Fung 2014, Carothers and Brechenmacher 2014, Peixoto and Fox 2016), we pieced together often implicit programme theories retrospectively from 'clues' in the programmes' activities. Insofar as the parameters of particular evaluations or learning reviews allowed, we tried to devise indicators and rubrics and apply them within deep, contextualised understandings of what had changed for the better in the lives of the accountability-claimants in the course of the initiative, to which the programmes might plausibly have contributed. But to judge whether power relations were truly and sustainably transformed to the claimants' advantage would have required additional insights into their lifeworlds and their perceptions of self and other, not only then but into the future – vantage points which few evaluations afford.

In this chapter I use power theory to problematise different versions of accountability-claiming, hoping to tease out their different implications for strategy

---

3   My colleagues were Cathy Shutt, Jethro Pettit, Patta Scott-Villiers, Katy Oswald and John Gaventa.

in ways that can enhance current approaches to securing accountability. In the next section I trace the development of prominent social theories of power, highlighting the distinction between agency-based accounts and structural and post-structural accounts as an aspect particularly relevant to accountability struggles. I go on to discuss the question 'Why analyse power?', focusing particularly on why *activists* need to analyse power, and noting the relationships between different versions of power and different understandings of accountability and corresponding attempts to claim it. This helps explain the limited effectiveness of some mainstream contemporary approaches to claiming accountability, and directs attention to others which, while quite removed from the realm of academic power theory and aid agency orthodoxy, engage with power and accountability in all their complexity and make practical power theory out of their struggles.

Which version of power? Agency, structure or a post-structural view?

Two key early works in power theory are Dahl's work *Who Governs?* (1961), exploring political government decision-making from a pluralist perspective, and Bachrach and Baratz's article 'Two Faces of Power' (1962), contrasting a political science standpoint with a sociological standpoint and exploring power from a behaviourist perspective. Both works see power as agency, as consciously exercised by knowing agents.

According to Dahl's earlier work, 'A has power over B to the extent that he can get B to do something that B would not otherwise do' (1957, p. 202). He used this to develop his argument in *Who Governs?* that political power in the context of US democracy is pluralistic and exercised through representative democracy, rather than being captured by a small élite, as had been claimed by scholars on the political left. Bachrach and Baratz's critique of Dahl was that by focusing on which agents observably exercised decision-making power, his study missed a vital aspect: the 'dynamics of *nondecision-making*', which 'tend to limit the scope of actual decision-making to "safe" issues' and keep others off the table. 'Nondecision-making' arises from bias expressed in the 'dominant values, the myths and the established political procedures and rules of the game [of] the institution under scrutiny' (Bachrach and Baratz 1962, p. 952). Politics works by some issues getting organised in and others getting organised out, a process that has been referred to as 'the mobilisation of bias' (Schattschneider 1960, p. 71). Bachrach and Baratz argued that these hidden political agenda-setters, the 'second face of power', need to be counted among the powerful as well as Dahl's 'visible decision-makers'.

Building on this critique, Lukes, in *Power: A Radical View* (1974), describes power as something less tangible than Dahl's (1961) or Bachrach and Baratz's versions. Referring to Dahl's 'observable decision-making' as a 'first dimension' of power and Bachrach and Baratz's hidden agenda-setting as a 'second dimension', Lukes adds a third dimension – 'securing the consent to domination of willing subjects' (Lukes 1974/2005, p. 109). Since Bachrach and Baratz had called their theoretical contribution a second 'face' of power in relation to Dahl's, the term 'face' got applied to

Lukes's third dimension, too. Gaventa (1980), a student of Lukes, was among the first to apply Lukes's third dimension empirically, using it to study the action and inaction of relatively powerless groups in rural coal-mining communities in Appalachia, USA. In his original work (1974) Lukes defined this third dimension as intentional 'thought control' exercised by the powerful over the less powerful, describing it as 'insidious' (2005, p. 27) and 'hidden from direct observation' (Hayward and Lukes 2008, p. 6). Others re-stated its insidiousness (e.g. VeneKlasen and Miller 2002), and pointed out that it can be deeply 'internalised' (Gaventa 2006, Haugaard 2003). Following VeneKlasen and Miller (2002, see also Bradley this volume), the third 'face' has come to be known as *invisible power*, contrasted with *visible power* (first dimension) and *hidden power* (second dimension).

The above understandings are of power as a property of human agents, relational, expressed as a contest of human agency, as actors getting other actors to do things they would not otherwise do. Yet not all visions of power see it as agency. In contrast to the agential accounts of the 'Anglo-American power theorists' (Hayward and Lukes 2008) and reflecting the ongoing debates about agency vs structure that dominated the social sciences throughout the twentieth century, there are also structural and post-structural power theorists, many of them political sociologists like Gaventa. These versions define power in terms at least as invisible as Lukes's third dimension, in which agency and intentionality are highly nuanced or actually absent. In these accounts power is not about intentional 'thought control', but operates as 'self-reproducing social processes in which the thinking and behaviour of the powerful and powerless alike are conditioned by pervasive norms' (www.powercube.net).

Others have developed structuralist perspectives without reference to the Anglo-American power debates, understanding power as a property of society and social structure 'exercised through multiple, interacting, large-scale social processes' (Hayward 2018, p. 56). Post-structuralists see it as lying even deeper than social structures – in the knowledge itself which underpins social structure, constructed and propagated through discourses and norms, which help disperse power through society. Some of these structural and post-structural versions are explicitly called 'power' – for example Foucault's terms 'metapower' and 'biopower'. Others are not – for instance Gramsci's 'cultural hegemony' (1971); Foucault's 'discourse' and 'discipline' (1979) and 'regimes of truth' (Rabinow 1991); and Bourdieu's 'habitus' and 'field' (1990). They have emerged from diverse standpoints and over a long period: Gramsci's 'cultural' expansion of the 'material' Marxist notion of hegemony dates from his Prison Notebooks of the 1920s and 1930s; Foucault's and Bourdieu's work dates from the 1970s and 1980s. Altogether, these 'continental' power theorists offer quite different versions from the view of power as the consciously coercive action of one actor in relation to another which dominates in Anglo-American political science.

Bridging the structure–agency divide, there are also power theorists influenced by Giddens's 'structuration theory' (Giddens 1984), which posits that in the creation and reproduction of social systems neither structure nor agency take precedence. Active subjects engage with and constitute social structures; and structure is 'both medium and outcome' of the recurrent practices of social actors.

Some theorists, such as Haugaard and Digeser, bring Lukes into dialogue with Foucault, and argue that there are four dimensions of power – of which two are visible and two less so. Haugaard (2012, pp. 43–4) argues that the first is about direct agency and domination of A over B, whereas the second is about systems biases that benefit A over B. The third dimension concerns the tacit knowledge that frames a kind of natural attitude which makes actors see a particular social order as part of the natural order of things. Like Foucault's *epistemes*, Bourdieu's *habitus* and Giddens's 'practical consciousness', these forms of knowledge make certain ways of structuring social life appear inherently reasonable and others inherently unreasonable. Seen thus, the third dimension has both a dominating and an emancipatory aspect. It naturalises a particular order of things – which is a contingent social construction – as the only possible order of things; but also, it is emancipatory for social actors to share tacit knowledge, as it facilitates collaboration between them. The fourth dimension, discussed by Digeser (1992) and Haugaard (2012), is largely based on Foucault's account of power as forming subjects. It concerns the social construction of social subjects with certain inherent dispositions. Foucault (1979) argues that social actors internalise certain dispositions through discipline and self-surveillance. The modern state has enormous powers to shape the social ontology of social subjects (Haugaard 2012, pp. 47–50), and does so in ways that secure from them compliance based on self-restraint (ibid., p. 36) – a quality that can have both dominating and emancipatory aspects.

Less famously than Foucault or Bourdieu, and writing in direct response to Lukes's agential account and Giddens's structuration, Layder (1985) points out that although power is intrinsically about action and agency, group relations are asymmetrical, reflecting differential 'prior constraints' which are structural in nature – a point also made by Bourdieu (1990, p. 54), for whom the 'anticipations' of an individual's *habitus* 'give disproportionate weight to early experiences'. Layder argues that 'power is not only instantiated in action, but is also instantiated in structure. To view power as inherently, exclusively, and indissolubly linked to agency, is to emasculate and obviate structural forms of power' (1985, pp. 147–8). Haugaard (2003) is also influenced by structuration theory, building on it in a way I shall return to later.

Hayward, writing in the 1990s and 2000s, made it her project to 'de-face' power – that is, to strip it of the property of agency with which the Anglo-American power theorists had imbued it. Taking as her point of departure structural and Foucauldian post-structural accounts, she calls power 'a network of social boundaries' that together define fields of action for all actors. Power's mechanisms consist of 'laws, rules, norms, customs, social identities, and standards' that constrain and enable inter- and intra-subjective action (Hayward 1998, pp. 1, 12). In trying to grasp what Hayward and other associated theorists mean when they describe power from post-structural and structural perspectives, it may be useful to think of the best-known form of it: the social structure of patriarchy, which feminists understand as affecting everyone, everywhere, in every aspect of their life (see the discussion of Butler's work in Pettit, this volume).

Re-visiting *Power: A Radical View* in 2005 in the light of these and other later works, as well as the reactions to it, Lukes critiques his earlier work for focusing too exclusively on 'the *exercise* of power' and on 'the power of some *over* others' (1974/2005, p. 64). Accepting that 'power should not be conceived narrowly as requiring intention, actual foresight and positive actions', he points out that it could consist of 'the powerful [...] being *capable of* [...] affecting (negatively or positively) the (subjective and/or objective) interests of others' (my emphasis). The third dimension, then, is extended to refer not only to the intentional exercise of agency to control others' thoughts and preferences, but also to the potential to do so. Consequently, 'the powerful' 'include those who both contribute to and are in a position to reduce or remedy others' power-lessness' (Lukes 1974/2005, p. 68) – agents who act by omission as well as by commission.

But, although Lukes came to recognise power as being about both individual and collective agency, both agency and the capacity for agency, both 'social agency' (or 'social power') and decision-makers' agency or 'power as domina-tion', and both active and structured, he 'will not attribute power to structures or relations or processes that cannot be characterised as agents', and insists that 'to have power is to have power *over* another or others' (Lukes 1974/200, pp. 72, 73, emphasis in original).

Why analyse power?

In Lukes's work he affirms that the point of locating power is to 'fix responsibility for consequences held to flow from the action, or inaction, of certain specifiable agents' (1974/2005, p. 55): that is, to assign moral responsibility or liability so as to hold individual or collective agents to account by making them answer for and redress grievances they have caused. His later discussion of why it is useful to ana-lyse power is more nuanced (ibid., pp. 65–9). He draws on Peter Morriss's uniquely detailed philosophical account of why we need the concept of power. Morriss (2002) sets out three 'contexts' in which we talk of power: practical, moral and evaluative, all of them to do with the relationship between human agency and structure. The 'practical' context relates to Lukes's concern that 'we need to know our own powers and those of others in order to find our way around a world populated by human agents, individual and collective, of whose powers we need to be apprised if we are to have a chance of surviving and flourishing' (1974/2005, p. 65) – essentially, understanding power for survival. The 'moral' context refers to the tracing and attribution of outcomes impinging on the interests of human beings to the actions or omissions of politically powerful human agents – that is, under-standing power so as to apportion responsibility or blame. The 'evaluative' context is about the distribution and extent of power within a social system, which entails judgements about the capability and responsibility of actors to affect the interests of others – that is, understanding power so as to strategise (ibid., pp. 66–9).

Hayward argues, more explicitly, that the reason for studying power is 'to enable and motivate change' (2006, p. 162) – articulating the same principle that motivated the feminist movement-building collective Just Associates (JASS) to publish *A New Weave of Power, People and Politics: The Action Guide for Advocacy and Citizen Participation* (VeneKlasen and Miller 2002). For those who see power as faceless and structural, Hayward holds that the study of power should focus on 'patterned asymmetries' in the ways in which power – that is, the network of social limits which defines fields of action – shapes possibilities (1998, p. 14). Rather than asking about how power is distributed and who has power over whom, she argues, we should ask: '"How do power's mechanisms define the (im)possible, the (im)probable, the natural, the normal, what counts as a "problem"? Do fields of social possibility vary systematically, for example, among groups or across social settings?' (Hayward 1998, p. 16).

The notion of an 'A' who observably exerts power over 'B' (to use Dahl's formulation) or of hidden 'status quo-oriented persons and groups' mobilising bias in their own interests (as in Bachrach and Baratz's formulation) offers clear focuses for unmasking, mobilisation and remedial actions. In contrast, power as multiple, interrelated social processes, or as norms, culture and discourse, is harder to see than power as dominating or coercive agency: probably less amenable to the application of tools and frameworks for exploring the power problem and developing empowerment strategies, and harder to rally or mobilise dissent against. On the one hand, in the fourth dimension of power as discussed by Digeser and Haugaard, Foucault's subjectification creates social subjects with the kind of self-restraint that makes relationships of responsibility and accountability possible, assuming that the particular social order it legitimates is one which commends accountability-claiming and -giving. On the other hand, as Hayward puts it (2018, p. 56):

> It is one thing to confront a landlord who discriminates against a would-be tenant, or a boss who sexually harasses his employee, but it is quite another to redress racial inequalities that have been institutionalised over centuries, or to dismantle a system of deeply entrenched, interlocking, inegalitarian gender norms.

Although structural understandings of power do not implicate any 'specifiable agents' to be held accountable for consequences flowing from their action or inaction, Hayward argues that responsibility nonetheless exists and can be pinned on actors. It is what she calls 'shared political responsibility', drawing on Young's (2004) work on global labour justice: all who benefit from the outcomes of structural power have a political obligation to 'understand, to deliberate with one another about and to participate in the collective action oriented towards transforming the processes and the institutions through which, together, they exercise power' (Hayward 2006, p. 162). In later work Hayward (2017) reiterates what this political responsibility means for her: that there is an onus on those privileged by structural injustice and structural power to assume political responsibility for structural change.

Social accountability: 'power to the people'?[4]

If our concern is with enabling accountability claimants to shape appropriate strategies and achieve their ends, how we conceive of power matters:

- Is the understanding of 'power as agency', dominant in the social sciences and in most people's intuitive understanding, an adequate one?
- Is there always an agent on whom to pin unaccountable performance and behaviour and its problematic consequences?
- Are structural understandings of power based on norms, beliefs, ideology, discourse and habituated behaviours a better fit with some contemporary accountability struggles?
- If so, how can intuitions and understandings of the structural nature of power be translated into more effective accountability-claiming actions?

In struggles for accountability, activists are motivated and mobilised by injustices, imbalances or systematic asymmetries in terms of who can actually enjoy the rights that are ostensibly theirs, including who gets what and whose voices are heard. Some of these struggles are explicitly framed and designed as accountability initiatives or programmes – mainly those funded by European and North American official or philanthropic development aid, where accountability is often pursued in conjunction with other aid agency goals such as transparency, openness and empowerment. Beyond that tiny subset is a whole universe of activism around the globe that falls outside the aid discourse and field of vision, does not receive aid programme funding (or sometimes any systematic funding at all) and yet – insofar as it claims the realisation of rights – is fundamentally part of an accountability-claiming struggle. Taken together, these activities address a vast and diverse range of 'power problems' conceived in various ways – for example 'patriarchy', 'colonisation' or 'mental slavery'. While some are based on explicit analyses or understandings of underlying power inequalities, many make little or no explicit reference to Western academic concepts of power.

A critical review of evidence on accountability aid initiatives discerning why some efforts work better than others, and under what conditions, is a useful starting point for asking power questions of accountability struggles (Fox 2015). While Fox's review is restricted to aid-supported projects and programmes, and relatedly uses the language of 'social accountability', his analysis has broader applications to the wider world of accountability struggles beyond the borders of mainstream 'Aidland'.[5] He builds on many observations arising in the previous few years from studies on accountability

---

4   'Power to the people' has been used in titles of both accountability aid programmes – including Christian Aid's 'Power to the people: making governance work for marginalised groups' (2008–13) – and accountability research studies and impact evaluations, including 'Power to the people: evidence from a randomized field experiment on community-based monitoring in Uganda' (Björkman and Svensson 2009).

5   'Aidland' is a term 'borrowed from [development aid ethnographer] Raymond Apthorpe … to capture the aggregate effect of expert thought and planning which is the virtual world of aid professionals' (Mosse 2011, p. 7).

struggles and evaluations of accountability aid programmes, among which three are particularly central:

- The 2000s–2010s saw the fast spread of apolitical social accountability discourse and a plethora of tools such as citizen report-cards and community score-cards based on the assumption that more information about citizens' entitlement or service delivery failures would lead to change (Joshi and Houtzager 2012). Yet social activism in pursuit of accountability needs to be recognised as a highly political power struggle (Goetz and Jenkins 2005, Fox 2007a, Fox 2007b).
- As such, conflict, resistance and reprisal from vested interests in response to accountability claims need to be anticipated and met appropriately (VeneKlasen and Miller 2002, Fox 2007a, Fox 2007b). Strengthening of collective citizen agency for accountability struggles is usefully conceived of as building 'countervailing forces' vis-à-vis anti-accountability forces (Fung and Wright 2003, Fox 2007b).
- Making accountability claims or struggles succeed is more complex than it once appeared. Many aid-funded accountability programmes lack clear, underlying 'theories of change' specifying the working understanding of the problem being addressed and how the programme actions are expected to resolve it (Gaventa and McGee 2013). Context is all-important. Growing evidence on key determinants of success points to the need for an 'ecosystems approach', 'taking scale into account' and reconciling tensions between confrontational approaches and constructive engagement (Fox and Halloran 2015, Fox 2016).Yet putting these lessons into practice is proving difficult, perhaps because their operational implications are not very compatible with normal aid delivery models.

Fox critiques the key proposition in the World Bank's 2004 *World Development Report* (WDR), that there is a 'short route to accountability' by which citizens can directly exact accountability from service providers through oversight and voice mechanisms. The WDR proposes the 'short route' as preferable to the 'long' – the traditional political accountability process in which citizens choose and re-elect political representatives who stay responsive to them by governing bureaucracies properly and ensuring these hold frontline service delivery staff to account.[6] Fox draws a distinction between what he calls 'tactical' and 'strategic' approaches to claiming accountability. Tactical approaches are 'bounded interventions with citizen voice as the sole driver [which] assume that information provision alone will inspire collective action with sufficient power to influence public sector performance' – as in the 'short route' proposition – and have an 'exclusive focus on local arenas'. Strategic approaches, in contrast, have 'multiple, interconnected tactics, [foster] enabling environments

---

6   Fox locates as a key flaw in the 2004 WDR's 'short–long route model' as its adoption of 'principal-agent theory' as its theoretical premise. The principal-agent model, he argues, was extended from its origins in market relationships and applied to mainstream development thinking; and, in the process, was stretched beyond its applicability and validity.

for collective action, to reduce perceived risk [, entail] citizen voice coordinated with governmental reforms that bolster public sector responsiveness [and] scaling up [… and are] iterative, contested and therefore uneven processes' (Fox 2015, pp. 346, 352). For accountability reforms to succeed, strategic efforts need to enlist reformers within the state to work collaboratively with reformers in society in a 'sandwich strategy',[7] civil society actors need to build broad constituencies or 'scale horizontally', and pro-accountability efforts need to be interconnected up and down the whole governance system between the centre and the most decentralised levels – they must be as 'vertically integrated' as the anti-accountability forces (corruption, inefficiency, unresponsiveness) that they counter.

These insights offer clear direction for developing future accountability-claiming initiatives. They help explain the limited impact of many past and current initiatives, especially those heavily reliant on tech innovations (McGee et al. 2018, Peixoto and Fox 2016). While Fox does not explicitly unpack power much further than distinguishing citizens' power from that of state institutions, he does firmly treat 'social accountability' as the struggle to alter the power relations between citizens and public authorities. However, at the time Fox was writing, numerous aid programmes pursuing citizen voice, government responsiveness, empowerment, transparency or openness were coming on stream that failed to recognise power and engaged only superficially with the concept of accountability itself. Many of them focused narrowly on just the aspect of state–citizen relations that is most immediately important to most citizens throughout the world and especially in the global South: the state's responsibility to provide – or regulate its contractors to provide – universal basic services. And many were informed by an underlying, often highly implicit, notion of power that itself limited their effectiveness and sustainability.

Tactical accountability initiatives: targeting the agents of domination

The reading of 'the problem' underpinning many other 'Aidland' initiatives of that time was that people lacked information about their entitlements, and states and/or service providers lacked data on service inadequacies or breakdowns. This tendency was typified in many respects by the Making All Voices Count programme I worked on during this period.[8] Born in an era of tech optimism about the 'power of

---

7   This is also referred to by Borras and Franco (2009, p. 74) as the *bibingka* strategy, in which 'mobilizations "from below" meet reformist initiatives "from above"'. *Bibingka* is a term used in the Philippines to describe a rice cake baked from both above and below.

8   Making All Voices Count (2012–17) was an international initiative that aimed to harness the power of innovation and new technologies to support effective, accountable governance. Working in 12 countries across Africa and Asia, the programme funded new ideas that amplified the voices of citizens, and enabled governments to listen and respond. A significant research, evidence and learning component explored the roles technology can play in securing responsive, accountable government and building an evidence base on what works and what doesn't. See https://www.makingallvoi cescount.org/.

information', it sought to 'empower' citizens or consumers with information and tech-based feedback channels so that their 'voice' would prevail and turn non-responsive bureaucrats, technicians and service managers into responsive ones. Also typical of it are the 'citizen voice' and 'government responsiveness' ICT platforms reviewed by Peixoto and Fox (2016) and numerous others of the same period.

Slogans aside, analysis of power is strikingly absent from these solution-driven, tech-optimist narratives. If they address any 'power problem', it is power as dominating agency, or *power over*. Implicit in them is that the 'agents' – service provision managers, government bureaucrats and elected politicians – have acquired too much dominating power over the 'principals': marginalised service users and constituents. This *visible power* – vested in their official roles as the managers of public funds, technicians with technical capacity and elected representatives of citizens' interests – is legitimate only insofar as these actors fulfil their respective governance and service delivery duties. When they do not, the solution is to correct the information asymmetry between the relatively 'powerless' users, residents, citizens, constituents and the 'powerful' service providers, bureaucrats and elected representatives. The former are given more information about their entitlements and about how widespread their service delivery problems are; and the latter get information gaps filled in the data at their disposal for making planning and budgeting decisions, all under threat of evidence-based exposé if providers remain unresponsive.

Assuming the power problem is first-dimensional in nature (i.e. the principal A has power over the agent B to the extent that A can get B to do something that B would not otherwise do), and assuming B is well disposed and only lacks information in order to do it, the service user A's acquisition or mobilisation of information would change the balance of power, increasing the extent to which A can get the power-holder (B) to improve their services. But are most contemporary accountability failures as simple as that?

Peixoto and Fox tested whether platforms for user feedback on service delivery problems induced institutional responsiveness from service providers. They found that ICT-enabled citizen voice mechanisms relying on service delivery user feedback are relevant when they increase the *capacity* of policymakers to respond (i.e. by providing information they did not already know), but do not influence their *willingness* to do so: that is, they work 'when policymakers already care' (Peixoto and Fox 2016, p. 24). When the challenge is how to get policymakers to care in the first place, then the question is how ICT platforms can enable collective action to reinforce citizen voice. After all, as they point out, poor service provision is not only down to decision-makers not knowing about problems; it is 'civic engagement that generates the civic muscle necessary to hold senior policymakers and frontline service providers accountable' (ibid., p. 22).

Other initiatives to improve public services are based on more complex understandings of the underlying power problem. They address the problems of service providers failing to reach the most geographically marginalised or socially excluded of citizens, and seeking to fudge compliance with universalist provisions in the service delivery agreements they hold with governments; government functionaries

withholding information about entitlements and quality standards; elected representatives responding selectively to the priorities of different groups of citizens,
stoking élite capture and urban bias; and systematically under-representing non-
élite, non-urban voters throughout their periods of office, except at election time.
These more politically informed framings of the accountability problem all recognise second-dimension or *hidden power* at play, setting the political agenda, mobilising bias, 'organising in' certain issues and 'organising out' others.

Initiatives based on this understanding respond to *hidden power* in the form of
élite capture and bias by counter-mobilising and counter-organising. A good
example is community scorecard initiatives, multi-pronged participatory strategies
in which service users engage with providers in increasing awareness of entitlements and capacities, undertaking community monitoring of services and processes,
clarifying mutual expectations and influencing the exercise of authority (Walker
2016). In contrast to solely information-based initiatives, community scorecard
processes promote collective action to expose and contest *hidden power*, overturn
biases and 'organise in' service users' interests which otherwise tend to get 'organised out'. While the evidence on community scorecard approaches shows that
these can strengthen service provision and community–state relations, a generally
positive review of them nonetheless notes 'little evidence that the programmes
were creating fundamental changes in power dynamics or the nature of citizen-
state relationships, unsurprisingly perhaps given the limited and time-bound nature
of these interventions' (Wales and Wild 2015, p. 5).

Digging deeper, also at work is *invisible power*. Applying the lens of *invisible power* to
marginalised peoples' low expectations of their entitlements, or their apparent passivity
or apathy in the face of perpetual service deficits through the lens of invisible power,
casts a different light on service providers' neglect of would-be users in remote places,
marginalised socioeconomic classes or discriminated-against ethnic or religious minorities. These actions and omissions – whether arising from third-dimensional 'intentional acts of "thought control" by the powerful' or fourth-dimensional 'self-
reproducing social processes in which the thinking and behaviour of the powerful and
powerless alike are conditioned by pervasive norms' (www.powercube.net) – stifle or
reverse the development of a sense of entitlement, and with it the civic energy to
mobilise against them. When governments, often in the position of contractor or
regulator rather than direct provider of services, tolerate this status quo rather than
assuming the responsibility of representing their whole electorate, tax base or citizenry,
they can be seen as taking advantage of and compounding this use of *invisible power*, or
as a locus of structural power. To apply this lens to water delivery failure as an example, actual human agents – water technicians proposing budgets, parliamentarians
approving them, water technicians executing the plans and budgets – are not able to
remedy the systemic delivery failure because, in a context of finite resources for the
water department, structural power holds in place and normalises discriminatory
practices in budgeting, regulating and providing public services. Instead of recognising
and addressing this in all its complexity, funders and implementers of accountability

programmes have often simply asked all the louder such simple binary questions as 'how to close the feedback loop' and 'what works and what doesn't?'

If the underlying problem is the exercise of *hidden power* or *invisible power*, there are motivations and benefits at stake which are not touched by redressing information asymmetry. Feedback-based 'solutions' do not recognise the roots of the 'problem' in structural power and try to tackle these. Information measures are likely necessary but are not sufficient, and are quite likely to come with their own biases towards the modern and tech-based formats used by the less poor. Even when the 'solution' includes aggregating and publicising the grievances of masses of individuals all dissatisfied with service provision, it is unlikely to take effect unless this aggregated information is exchanged into a different, more political, currency. These approaches fall under Fox's definition of tactical initiatives, and are explained on one level by his and Peixoto's conclusions (Fox 2015, Peixoto and Fox 2016).

More complex, problem-driven approaches – like community scorecards that not only improve information flow but also build interfaces of contestation and constructive engagement between accountability claimants and unaccountable institutions or service providers – can address second-dimension power; but their impact is also limited, by the short-termism and project-centricity that characterises much aid practice. The limitations of such approaches are understood more deeply by reappraising them as weak responses to, or diversions from, the full complex of power – visible, hidden, invisible, structural as well as agential – that is at play in systemic non-accountability. To transform this, a different version of accountability-claiming is needed.

Strategic accountability struggles: transforming structural power

In contrast to the tactical tech 'solutions' and citizen voice projects, some initiatives stand out as quintessentially 'strategic'. An ill fit with the aid industry's repertoire of forms and formats, they have received far less attention in Aidland than the tactical initiatives.

The Workers' and Peasants' Empowerment Organisation, *Mazdoor Kisan Shakti Sangathan* (MKSS), started in 1990 in Rajasthan, India, as a campaign for administrative transparency in the management of a famine relief scheme. Corrupt and untransparent management of the scheme meant that poor people dependent on famine relief were unable to obtain the legal minimum wage for their work. Initial persistent attempts to work within the rules to ensure entitlements were upheld were stonewalled. MKSS shifted ground and diversified its tactics from a rules-based repertoire to more contentious and unruly approaches, recognising the need to pursue more accountable governance for the rural poor in more thorough-going ways than opening up bureaucratic records through securing a Right to Information (RTI). MKSS's key actors describe this as 'a breakthrough in thought and strategy leading to structural changes in modes of protest [and] the beginning of evolving structural changes in government functioning' (Roy and MKSS Collective 2018, p. 94).

MKSS's perception of the power problem developed out of the founder activists' deep immersion in the lifeworlds of the rural poor people being cheated out of fair payment for their famine relief work. The founder-leaders lived for three years in a mud hut on the social, economic, political and geographic margins of Rajasthan society before launching the organisation. From this positioning, they recognised the structural constraints that constituted both the dependence of local people on their famine relief scheme entitlements and consequent inability to challenge flagrantly corrupt scheme operators; and the unquestionability and unassailability of scheme administrators and their political accomplices. A single-stranded 'solution' based on enhancing the power-less's power through information that reduced their disadvantage vis-à-vis the powerful (the cheating rations-shopkeepers and work gangers) was not going to get far, and would fast descend into brutal violence targeted against identifiable individuals.

MKSS's response to this structural and agential reading of the power problem has itself been both structural and agential. Tactics include:

- holding massively attended public fora at which the first-dimensional *power over* of corrupt individuals is exploded and second-dimensional *hidden power* is unmasked by exposing, challenging and shaming public officials through pre-senting and debating irrefutable evidence of wide-scale corruption in the public works programme;
- slowly and patiently building and activating the countervailing agential power of individuals and their collective MKSS through rising prominence, legiti-macy and trust;
- countering the corrupt and violent *invisible power* of norms, beliefs, ideology, discourse and habituated behaviours with progressive, transformative counter-norms and alternative discourses. This is achieved through careful analysis, re-grouping and adapting strategy in the wake of violent and intimidating repri-sals, and eschewing at individual and organisational levels the behaviours and attitudes associated with the powerful – from the casually corrupt to the rou-tinely patriarchal (Roy and MKSS Collective 2018).

Fundamentally, MKSS's strategy rests on recognising, rejecting and modelling alternatives to the structural power of Indian norms of caste, gender, urban bias, lit-eracy bias and other forms of social exclusion that have made it possible for such unaccountable governance to thrive unchecked for centuries. The trust and credibility MKSS activists acquire through their *modus operandi* has enabled them to surface abu-sive norms in safe spaces, subject them to collective dialogical analysis, and demonstrate alternative norms which are eventually taken on by the movement as a whole as part of its internal culture and methods, coherent with its outward-facing claims.

Seen through Fox's (2015) lenses, MKSS is a vertically-integrated strategic initia-tive that uses grassroots pressure and engages reformers in the state. It also deploys information provision and feedback mechanisms, centrally and crucially, and today is enabled and facilitated by the use of ICT to connect its activists, process data, and publicise, mobilise and coordinate support for its work. The political nature of its struggle is sadly evident from its longevity and the fact that, by 2015, 50 RTI activists had been killed for their roles in it (Pande 2015). It is hard to imagine how MKSS might have fitted into the Aidland frame, a consideration which is instructive as to the scope for sustained, deep transformation in accountability power relations to be achieved via conventional aid projects and programmes.

Accountability as political responsibility and societal answerability

Accountability activists with an agency-based understanding of power ask 'who has too much/too little power around here?' and then take sides, giving one party enough access to information to hold the other answerable or to enforce action, as is common in 'tactical' accountability initiatives. In strategic accountability struggles, the approach of starting from users' or citizens' perspectives and working to find the funding leakages or abrogation of duty might lead to 'somebody to shoot' or sanction – like the hundreds of Indian public servants and intermediaries exposed by MKSS and sanctioned for their misdeeds.[9]

But holding individuals to account is hardly the point. When the accountability problem is perceived to be structural, systemic power that normalises institutional bias and social discrimination, institutional or individual answerability is not enough; neither is the assumption of responsibility by any identifiable actor; and, if we follow Foucault as in Digeser (1992) and Haugaard (2010, Haugaard 2012), the social subjects formed by fourth-dimensional power are probably disposed to confirm rather than counter it. Getting to the bottom of the unaccountable status quo is, for the most part, about uncovering shared political responsibility, which implicates not only the identifiable actors who enact it, but also those who don't suffer it but tolerate it – and as such play a contributory role in the bigger picture of how things are.

Embracing the fact that power is not only agency-based and is often more problematic in its other forms means not ignoring structural or post-structural power or assuming that radical changes will ensue from redress of who holds power over whom. It involves noticing whether fields of social possibility vary systematically between different groups of people or different social settings, and asking how power's mechanisms in any given situation are defining 'the (im)possible, the (im)probable, the natural, the normal, what counts as a "problem"' (Hayward 1998, pp. 15–16). It entails visibilising normalised discourses and practices by naming, describing consciously taking positions on them and building new narratives (McGee 2017, VeneKlasen and Bradley, both this volume). It means highlighting the scale of operation and efficacy of structural power at the same time as emphasising the discretion of each individual to stop acting in complicity with it.

---

9   Hayward and Lukes (2008), debating structural vs agential understandings of power, borrow the term 'nobody to shoot' from John Steinbeck's *The Grapes of Wrath* to refer to a situation in which someone seems subjected to power but there is no identifiable agent to hold to account for the constraints on them.

In short, while all social activism is agency, social activism well-honed to address structural power is agency oriented to visibilising and challenging structures, norms and dispositions, as well as bolstering the agency of those disadvantaged by the status quo. While Haugaard's (2003) theoretical work gives us a name for this – 'disconfirming structure' – the feminist movement-building collective Just Associates gives us a set of perspectives and practices with which to replace these structures with alternative ones based on different value premises: 'transformative power' (Bradley, this volume). It is society and polity that have something to answer for, not only particular institutions or individual actors.

Conclusion

Accountability is about power. Probing our understandings of power can help explain why social change efforts based on narrower versions of power and accountability have fallen short of bringing about transformational and systemic change. It can also broaden and deepen understandings of accountability, and of what strategies are necessary to achieve it.

A look at real-life practices of accountability-claiming through the lenses of agential and structural arguments in theoretical debates on power reveals that the heavily information-reliant approaches to claiming accountability common in aid programmes to date do not recognise or address the structural roots of the 'problems' to which they proffer 'solutions'. Their failure to analyse these problems as power problems constrains them from attending to structural power and injustice, and from mobilising shared political responsibility to change it.

On the other hand, identity-based struggles such as those advancing feminist or racial justice claims, or issues-based movements defending human rights, environmentalism or a living wage, are all about holding society to account. They drive transformative strategies deep into the layers of systemic and structural norms that marginalise, disempower and dispossess.

In between the power theorists, the funders and implementers of mainstream aid accountability initiatives, and the movements for rights and social justice lie differences of situation, position, discipline, profession, organisation, identity, ontology and epistemology. But they have in common an interest in enabling the relatively powerless to hold the relatively powerful to account. Power theory stands to be enriched if the theorists watch and learn more closely from the practice of social justice movements. Aid actors would achieve more lasting impact if they applied a power analysis to their accountability work, and took on board its full implications in shifting from tactical to strategic accountability programmes. More widespread engagement with power theory by social justice activists could help calibrate and fine-tune their work, as well as enable power theory to be built more systematically from practice than currently. Power theory is too important to leave to academic political science debates. There is also 'practical power theory', constructed in the everyday practice of accountability-claiming movements, that comes with all the validity of its origins in real-life power and accountability struggles.

References

Apthorpe, R., 2011. Chapter 10 coda: with Alice in Aidland: a seriously satirical allegory. In: D. Mosse, ed. *Adventures in Aidland: the anthropology of professionals in international development*. Oxford: Berghahn, 199–220.

BachrachP. and Baratz, M., 1962. Two faces of power. *American Political Science Review*, 56 (4), 947–952.

Björkman, M. and Svensson, J., 2009. Power to the people: evidence from a randomized field experiment on community-based monitoring in Uganda. *Quarterly Journal of Economics*, 124(2), 735–769.

Borras, J. and Franco, J., 2009. Redistributing land in the Philippines: social movements and state reformers. In: J. Gaventa and R. McGee, eds. *Citizen action and national policy reform: making change happen*. London: Zed Books, 69–88.

Bourdieu, P., 1990. *The logic of practice*. Cambridge: Polity Press (R. Nice, trans.). First published as *Le sens pratique*, Paris: Éditions de Minuit, 1980.

Carothers, T. and Brechenmacher, S., 2014. *Accountability, participation, and inclusion: a new development consensus?* Washington DC: Carnegie Endowment for International Peace.

Dahl, R., 1957. Decision-making in a democracy: the supreme court as a national policy-maker. *Journal of Public Law*, 6, 279–295.

Dahl, R., 1961. *Who governs? Democracy and power in an American city*. New Haven, CT: Yale University Press.

Digeser, P., 1992. The fourth face of power. *Journal of Politics*, 54(4), 977–1007.

FoucaultM., 1979. *Discipline and punish*. Harmondsworth: Penguin.

Fox, J., 2007a. The uncertain relationship between transparency and accountability. *Development in Practice*, 17(4), 663–671.

Fox, J., 2007b. *Accountability politics: power and voice in rural Mexico*. Oxford: Oxford University Press.

Fox, J., 2015. Social accountability: what does the evidence really say? *World Development*, 72, 346–361.

Fox, J., 2016. Scaling accountability through vertically integrated civil society policy monitoring and advocacy. MAVC Working Paper. Brighton: Institute of Development Studies.

Fox, J. and Halloran, B., eds. with Levy, A., Aceron, J. and van Zyl, A., 2015. *Connecting the dots for accountability: civil society policy monitoring and advocacy strategies*. Report from Open Government Hub workshop, 18–20 June 2015, Washington DC. London: Transparency and Accountability Initiative. Available from: https://www.transparency-initiative.org/wp-content/uploads/2017/04/connecting-the-dots-for-accountability.pdf [Accessed 5 June 2019].

FungA. and Wright, E.O., 2003. *Deepening democracy: institutional innovations in empowered participatory governance*. New York: Verso.

Gaventa, J., 1980. *Power and powerlessness: quiescence and rebellion in an Appalachian valley*. Urbana and Chicago: University of Illinois Press.

Gaventa, J., 2006. Finding the spaces for change: a power analysis. *IDS Bulletin*, 37(6), 23–33.

GaventaJ. and McGee, R., 2013. The impact of transparency and accountability initiatives. *Development Policy Review*, 31 (S1), 3–28.

Giddens, A., 1984. *The constitution of society: outline of the theory of structuration*. Cambridge: Polity Press.

Goetz, A. and Jenkins, R., 2005. *Reinventing accountability: making democracy work for human development*. Basingstoke: Palgrave Macmillan.

Gramsci, A., 1971. *Selections from the prison notebooks of Antonio Gramsci*. New York: International Publishers.

Haugaard, M., 2003. Reflections on seven ways of creating power. *European Journal of Social Theory*, 6(1), 87–113.

Haugaard, M., 2010. Democracy, political power, and authority. *Social Research*, 77(4), 1049–1074.

Haugaard, M., 2012. Rethinking the four dimensions of power: domination and empowerment. *Journal of Political Power*, 5(1), 33–54.

Hayward, C., 1998. De-facing power. *Polity*, 31(1), 1–22.

Hayward, C., 2006. On power and responsibility. *Political Studies Review*, 4, 156–163.

Hayward, C., 2017. Responsibility and ignorance: on dismantling structural injustice. *Journal of Politics*, 79, 396–408.

Hayward, C., 2018. On structural power. *Journal of Political Power*, 11(1), 56–67.

Hayward, C. and Lukes, S., 2008. Nobody to shoot? Power, structure, and agency: a dialogue. *Journal of Power*, 1(1), 5–20.

Joshi, A., 2013. Context matters: a causal chain approach to unpacking social accountability interventions. Work-in-Progress Paper. Brighton: IDS and South Africa: SDC.

Joshi, A. and Houtzager, P., 2012. Widgets or watchdogs? *Public Management Review*, 14(2), 145–162.

Kosack, S. and Fung, A., 2014. Does transparency improve governance? *Annual Review of Political Science*, 17, 65–87.

Layder, D., 1985. Power, structure and agency. *Journal for the Theory of Social Behaviour*, 15 (2), 131–149.

Lukes, S., 1974/2005. *Power: a radical view.* 2nd ed. London: McMillan.

McGee, R., 2017. Invisible power and visible everyday resistance in the violent Colombian Pacific. *Peacebuilding*, 5(2), 170–185.

McGeeR., Edwards, D., Anderson, C., Hudson, H. and Feruglio, F., 2018. Appropriating technology for accountability: messages from Making All Voices Count. MAVC Research Report. Brighton: Institute of Development Studies.

Morriss, P., 2002. *Power: a philosophical analysis.* Manchester: Manchester University Press.

Mosse, D., 2011. Preface and acknowledgements. In: D. Mosse, ed. *Adventures in Aidland: the anthropology of professionals in international development.* Oxford: Berghahn, vii–x.

Pande, S., 2015. *Dying for information: right to information and whistle-blower protection in India.* Bergen: Chr. Michelsen Institute.

Peixoto, T. and Fox, J., 2016. When does ICT-enabled citizen voice lead to government responsiveness? World Development Report Background Paper: Digital Dividends. Washington DC: World Bank.

Powercube, n.d. Available from: https://www.powercube.net [Accessed 5 June 2019].

Rabinow, P., ed., 1991. *The Foucault reader: an introduction to Foucault's thought.* London: Penguin.

Roy, A. and MKSS Collective, 2018. *The RTI story: power to the people.* New Delhi: Roli Books.

Schattschneider, E.E., 1960. *The semisovereign people: A realist's view of democracy in America.* Fort Worth, TX: Harcourt Brace College Publishers.

VeneKlasen, L. and Miller, V., 2002. *A new weave of power, people and politics: the action guide for advocacy and citizen participation.* Rugby: Practical Action.

Wales, J. and Wild, L., 2015. CARE's experience with community scorecards: what works and why? ODI Project Briefing. London: Overseas Development Institute. Available from: https://www.odi.org/sites/odi.org.uk/files/odi-assets/publications-opinion-files/9452.pdf [Accessed 5 June 2019].

Walker, D., 2016. How systemic inquiry releases citizen knowledge. *Systemic Practice and Action Research*, 29(4), 313–334.

Young, I.M., 2004. Responsibility and global labor justice. *Journal of Political Philosophy*, 12 (4), 365–388.

2.4

TRANSFORMING POWER WITH EMBODIED PRACTICE

Jethro Pettit

Introduction

Social activists and academics are increasingly turning their attention to the influence of socialised norms and belief systems on civic and political agency. Looking beyond the wilful exercise of power by some over others, and beyond political economy and rational choice framings of power, there is growing interest in how power is created and reproduced through dominant narratives and behaviour (Clegg and Haugaard 2009, p. 3). Much debate in this direction was sparked by Steven Lukes's *Power: A Radical View* (1974/2005), which compelled political scientists to acknowledge how people's needs and beliefs can be manipulated to secure their 'willing consent to domination'. Yet thinkers and activists from critical, constructivist, feminist, race, queer and other perspectives have long seen power as the reproduction of socialised norms – residing in the very fabric of society rather than in episodic struggles for domination or resistance. This internalised or 'invisible power' as we generally call it in this volume (after VeneKlasen and Miller 2002, Gaventa 2006) is particularly insidious and resilient, shaping the possibilities for civic and political agency.

Power conceived as 'more systemic, less agent specific [... and] more generally constitutive of reality' (Clegg and Haugaard 2009, p. 3) could imply that those who are marginalised have little scope or agency to challenge the status quo. Yet a less pessimistic view of socialised power recognises that norms are malleable, ever evolving and subject to disruption and re-creation by agents. This may happen through everyday acts of resistance (Scott 1985), through 'unruliness' (Scott-Villiers, this volume) or through moments of 'disconfirming' or 'de-structuring' established ways of seeing or doing things (Haugaard 2003, pp. 90–92, drawing on Giddens 1984). Agency is not separate from the constitution of power, in dualistic opposition to structure, but plays a central role in continuous processes of cultural signification (Butler 1990, pp. 195–8). But enacting alternative values and narratives, even in minute ways, can be instances of structural change – not only in politics but in culture, science, philosophy, art, education, the media and in everyday moments of domestic and social interaction. Of course, this proactive re-shaping of norms does not always lead to progressive outcomes; the point is that structures are not fixed, inscribing themselves on agents, but are continually affirmed or reconfigured through minute acts of compliance and resistance.

Social activists who understand power in this way tend to focus not just on winning immediate political battles, but on shaping values and beliefs, linking the personal and political, pushing back against those who propagate oppressive narratives, and articulating and enacting norms that align with their claims. This can be challenging work given our pervasive collusion with systems of power through behaviour that tacitly complies with prevailing norms. Patriarchy, racism, homophobia, xenophobia, nationalism, fascism, class and caste hierarchies, consumerism, environmental exploitation and many other forms of inequality and exclusion are all profoundly naturalised in many societies – even where their propagators and beneficiaries can be identified and challenged. An intersectional view that recognises how multiple forms of exclusion overlap and amalgamate poses further challenges for agency. We may be relatively liberated in relation to some spheres, for example gender or sexuality, but deeply implicated in others, such as class or consumerism. What scope then do we have as everyday civic and political beings to shift these embedded forms of power? How can we disrupt our own 'willing consent to domination' – or indeed our willing consent to dominate? How can we expose and transform embodied and habituated collusions with power?

Social movements and liberation struggles have often responded to invisible power with popular education activities that foster critical consciousness, such as campaigns inspired by the literacy methods of Paolo Freire's *Pedagogy of the Oppressed* (1970). Recognising and unlearning socialised beliefs and assumptions, and gaining critical objectivity on structural power, enables a shift from 'practical consciousness' to 'discursive consciousness' (Haugaard 2003, p. 100). Transformative learning usually focuses on the critique of structures of oppression, with the expectation that heightened conceptual awareness will stimulate agency for resistance. Yet habituated patterns of behaviour can be remarkably resilient to reasoned thinking. In this chapter I argue that invisible power is constituted by more than the narratives, beliefs and language held in the conceptual domains of our consciousness. It is also manifest in our individual and collective embodiment of social dispositions, such that critical consciousness alone will not catalyse civic and political agency. While oppression can be rationally exposed and analysed, 'aha moments' will not generate agency without also disrupting embodied collusion with power.

Anglo-American political science has largely failed to account for the embodied and intersectional dimensions of power and democratic citizenship (Hawkesworth 2016). Political economy analysis therefore tends to focus on agents, their interests and alliances that can be observed 'above the waterline' (Pettit and Mejía Acosta 2014; see also introduction to this volume). Yet an emerging perspective among social theorists, social activists and cognitive scientists points to more embodied and intersectional dimensions of power and exclusion – challenging liberal and rational choice assumptions about civic and political participation. Research on embodied cognition is recognising the situated, perceptual and somatic dimensions of neural processes, seeing behaviour as enactive and experiential rather than responding to central commands from the brain, or to mental representations of reality, as traditionally assumed in cognitive science.[1] Action does not necessarily follow logic, reason or choice: it can flow from a more complex processing of embodied and habituated experience of what is normally said or done, which suggests that even when conscious of oppressive power relations we tend to comply rather than resist.

As a university teacher, and a facilitator of reflective learning and action research with civil society activists and organisations, I have become more curious about the ways that power is habituated – existing not just 'out there', imposed through social and political structures and ideologies, but self-reproduced through micro-moments of speech, gesture and movement. I've been struck by how resilient internalised power can be to dialogue and analysis, and have been drawn to facilitation methods that combine critical reflection with practices of creative and embodied learning. By this I mean proactive methods and disciplines for understanding bodily powers, actions and reactions both viscerally and logically. Social mobilisation and transformative adult learning strategies often include theatre, role play, scenarios and hands-on work experience, as well as meditation, yoga, tai chi and other martial arts. Collective action in the form of protests and marches is also embodied practice, serving not only as visible displays of solidarity but as creative, bodily enactments of alternative imaginaries, values and narratives. By working with and through the body, combining embodied practices of learning and action with processes of critical awareness-raising, I have found that we can expose and transform these patterns of power.

In this chapter I begin by revisiting theories of power, asking how they account for the cognitive and embodied processes that create and reproduce power, and what possibilities or constraints are implied for civic and political agency. Next, I look at research from the field of embodied cognition, relating its theories of mind to the findings on invisible power and agency. Finally, I share insights from my experience leading embodied practices as a teacher and action-researcher, particularly enactment, body sculpting and exercises inspired by Augusto Boal's *Theatre of the Oppressed*. In the conclusion I suggest that enabling civic and political agency requires a 'pedagogy for the embodied mind' that integrates critical consciousness with embodied knowledge.

---

1   'Cognition is embodied when it is deeply dependent upon features of the physical body of an agent, that is, when aspects of the agent's body beyond the brain play a significant causal or physically constitutive role in cognitive processing. In general, dominant views in the philosophy of mind and cognitive science have considered the body as peripheral to understanding the nature of mind and cognition. Proponents of embodied cognitive science view this as a serious mistake. Sometimes the nature of the dependence of cognition on the body is quite unexpected, and suggests new ways of conceptualising and exploring the mechanics of cognitive processing' (Wilson and Foglia 2017, p. 1).

Invisible power: socialisation and embodiment[2]

Lukes (1974/2005) famously argued that power is not always observable or marked by coercion or conflict. Responding to academic debates about who wins or loses in policymaking, he distinguished three 'dimensions' of power, suggesting that identifying who prevails in observable decision-making (the first dimension) and detecting how power works behind the scenes through agenda-setting and 'mobilisation of bias' (the second dimension) don't adequately account for how people's 'willing consent to domination' is secured. For Lukes, the third and most insidious dimension of power is the manipulation of need and beliefs, normalising oppression in such a way that some conflicts and decisions never need to arise.[3] This third dimension of power, in Lukes's original formulation, is something *deliberately used* by powerful actors to manipulate others' beliefs. Power is *exercised* by those who have it over those who don't to shape their perceived interests, without coercion or force.

Inspired by Lukes, John Gaventa characterises this third dimension as socialisation in addition to wilful manipulation, seeing it as a 'form of power in which conflict is more invisible, through internalisation of powerlessness, or through dominating ideologies, values and forms of behaviour' (Gaventa 2006, p. 29). Here invisible power is not limited to the overt influencing of beliefs, but is a process by which all actors are conditioned and constrained by social norms. In the same vein, Lisa VeneKlasen and Valerie Miller define invisible power as what 'shapes the psychological and ideological boundaries of change', including 'people's beliefs, sense of self ... acceptance of the status quo [... and] sense of superiority or inferiority as "natural"' (Miller et al. 2006, p. 10, see also VeneKlasen and Miller 2002, and Bradley, this volume). Invisible power can thus be understood both as *a form of agency* – intentionally used by the powerful to manipulate the less powerful (or indeed used subversively by the less powerful to disrupt dominant and oppressive narratives) – and as *a process of socialisation* that naturalises norms and behaviour for everyone, powerful and powerless alike.

Challenging Lukes's agency-centric account, Clarissa Hayward (1998, 2000) argues that putting a 'face' on this dimension of power hides the ways in which norms and beliefs shape the boundaries of acceptable thought and self-constraint for *all actors*. The idea that ideological power is wielded by actors obscures self-reproducing forces of discourse and knowledge. Following Foucault, she locates power not in the wilful intentions of actors but in 'networks of social boundaries' that incorporate all actors into norms, rules and standards which govern their freedom:

---

2 This section is adapted from Pettit (2016a).
3 Lukes's three dimensions of power have been reformulated over the years by contributors to this volume (notably VeneKlasen and Miller 2002, Gaventa 2006) as visible power (the first dimension), hidden or shadow power (the second dimension) and invisible power (the third dimension). However, these forms of power have acquired new meanings and implications for strategy, and continue to evolve in the diverse contexts in which activists and authors are working, as evidenced in the chapters in this volume.

> Power's mechanisms are best conceived, not as instruments powerful agents use to prevent the powerless from acting freely, but rather as social boundaries that, together, define fields of action for all actors. Power defines fields of possibility. It facilitates and constrains social action. (Hayward 1998, p. 12)

Lukes later came to accept both ways of understanding this third dimension of power, while defending his focus on the intentional manipulation of beliefs in processes of political contestation.

Power viewed in this way shifts attention not only from agency to socialisation, but from reason, choice and intent to embodied dispositions and involuntary behaviour. It changes the focus from power as driven by perceived self-interests to more complex cognitive processes whereby social conduct and positioning are embodied and habituated – including in ways that may be counter to one's interests. Here invisible power recalls Foucault's (1991) 'disciplinary power' where institutions like schools and prisons need not rely on coercion or punishment to enforce behaviour; subjects discipline themselves, subjugating their bodies to what's considered acceptable or to what will not be punished. In this view of power there is no need for a prior ideology or discourse to determine action: experience itself shapes 'discursive practices' or 'bodies of knowledge' that define what is normal or deviant (ibid.). Knowledge does not determine or imprint behaviour in a causal fashion. As summarised by Haugaard (2003, p. 106):

> tacit knowledge is created by going through the motions of predictability… When actors are inculcated with routinized behaviour then the appropriate actions and reactions become virtually reflex … The physical insistence upon routine produces an actor with a particular, and desirable, practical consciousness knowledge who is unlikely to reflect.

Judith Butler similarly argues that gender identities are embodied through what she calls *performativity* – repeated, ritualised acts that constitute power while simultaneously being constrained by existing norms and discourses. For Butler, 'the body is always an embodying of possibilities both conditioned and circumscribed by historical convention. In other words, the body is … a manner of doing, dramatizing, and reproducing a historical situation' (1988, p. 521). Butler rejects the idea of the body as a 'passive medium that is signified by an inscription from a cultural source figured as "external" to the body' – departing from some readings of Foucault that there is a passive material body 'prior to discourse' (1990, pp. 175, 176). Binaries of mind/body, culture/nature and structure/agency drop away in her more iterative account, where 'what is called gender identity is a performative accomplishment compelled by social sanction and taboo' (1988, p. 521). Butler sees language and body as 'invariably related' because 'the speech act is at once performed (and thus theatrical, presented to an audience, subject to interpretation), and linguistic' because 'speech itself is a bodily act with specific linguistic consequences' (1990, p. xxvii).[4] This theatrical dimension makes performativity a collective rather than an individual process – public rituals re-enacted within and also reaffirming the boundaries of legitimised social meanings (1988, p. 527, cited Turner 1974).

This historical and embodied reproduction of power is also at work in Pierre Bourdieu's concept of *habitus* (1980). Here power is a cultural and symbolic creation, constantly reaffirmed through a subtle interplay of agency and structure. This occurs through the effects of *habitus* – the practical, learned and subjective habits or dispositions that shape our behaviour; and *field* – the norms, standards and structures that prevail in society. *Habitus* is neither a result of free will nor wholly determined by structures, but arises from a kind of interplay between them over time: dispositions are shaped by past events and structures, and at the same time shape current practices and structures, and condition our very perceptions of these (Bourdieu 1984, p. 174). We don't 'reason through our actions based on an objective assessment of the outcomes' (Bourdieu 1980, p. 54), as rational choice advocates would suggest. Rather, over time, we internalise the 'objective conditions' of structures in a subconscious and embodied way – as *habitus* – which regenerates structures. We tend to avoid doing or saying things that don't make practical 'common sense' within the confines of the field, and we rationalise our behaviour around what is allowed or not allowed. While rational-objectivists would have us experiment with *all* possible actions and outcomes, *habitus* gives 'disproportionate weight to early experiences' in life that have shaped our rationality (Bourdieu 1980, p. 54), so we are innately constrained by our own history.[5]

Despite differences among these theories of power, all of them draw attention to the role of the body, beyond logical processes of cognition, in creating and reproducing power. There is a shared implication that even with the ability to reflect critically and objectively we will not necessarily 'act' differently in relation to power. The body is a central driver in the performance and (re)production of power, tending to act in accord with historical, normative boundaries. This raises doubts about rational-objectivist notions of choice and the Cartesian ideal that reasoned thought precedes and determines action. Turning to questions of civic and political agency, this understanding of power disrupts liberal, pluralist and behaviourist assumptions that citizens rationally assess and select from political

---

4   Roman numeral citations from Butler (1990) are from her 1999 preface to the 2nd edition of *Gender Trouble*.

5   More than a set of rules we are consciously aware of, *habitus* is the internalisation of social experience, the processes by which normative responses are *physically inscribed in our bodies*. Bourdieu is not often cited for this aspect of his thinking because it is easier to grasp the idea that *habitus* reflects cognitive 'beliefs'. Yet with *habitus* social relations are 'turned into muscular patterns and bodily automatisms … a way of bearing one's body, presenting it to others, moving it, making space for it, which gives the body its social physiognomy' or 'bodily hexis'. The body acts as a 'memory-jogger' with its 'complexes of gestures, postures and words … which have only to be slipped into, like a theatrical costume, to awaken, by the evocative power of bodily mimesis, a universe of ready-made feelings and experiences' (Bourdieu 1984, p. 474).

alternatives. Choice and its aggregation (e.g. through markets or elections) lose meaning as the very field of possibilities and permissible actions within that field are constrained – the more so if there are negative consequences for transgression. Agency is constrained by what might be called *civic habitus* (Pettit 2016a, Pettit 2016b). While for Lukes the scope for agency is compromised by ideological manipulation, perpetrated by actors with capacities of coercion (even if not exercised), here agency is undermined by deeply socialised and embodied norms and boundaries. Possibilities of choice and action are shaped by prior life experience and by disciplinary norms and consequences that have been repeatedly performed and habitually embodied.

Embodied cognition

Social theories have clearly attempted to understand embodied power and its possible effects on civic and political agency. But what do cognitive scientists have to say about the habituation of norms and boundaries, and whether or how tacit compliance with power can be disrupted? If power is embodied, to what extent can newfound insight change behaviour, or non-conforming behaviour shift boundaries and norms? Is critical consciousness sufficient as an impetus for civic and political agency, or do our bodies themselves need to reconfigure internalised power? Theories of invisible power as embodied are remarkably consistent with findings from cognitive science, neurobiology, neurolinguistics, artificial intelligence, psychology and neuro-philosophy.[6] There is a growing field of 'embodied cognition' which questions computational and representational assumptions about cognition, and departs from Western philosophical binaries of mind and body, reason and feeling, structure and agency, etc. This broad field shares a common thesis that:

> Many features of cognition are embodied in that they are deeply dependent upon characteristics of the physical body of an agent, such that the agent's beyond-the-brain body plays a significant causal role, or a physically constitutive role, in that agent's cognitive processing. (Wilson and Foglia 2017, p. 1)

---

6   Some studies of embodied cognition, including those of Varela et al. (1991), like the theories of embodiment found in Bourdieu, Butler and Foucault, were influenced by the continental philosophy of phenomenology, particularly Husserl (1913) and Merleau-Ponty (1964), who was one of the first to link phenomenology with cognitive science. Varela et al. are also influenced by Buddhist philosophies of consciousness. Other foundations of embodied cognition – not covered here due to space considerations but arguably congruent with ideas of embodied power – are from neuroscience (e. g. Damasio 2000, Damasio 2006), neuro-linguistics (Johnson 1987, Lakoff and Johnson 1999), artificial intelligence (Clark 2008), psychology and neuro-philosophy (Gallagher 2005, Thompson 2007). The account of Varela et al. here is adapted from Pettit (2016b). For a good summary of the field of embodied cognition see Wilson and Foglia (2017).

The field of embodied cognition is too vast to elaborate here, but it is worth considering an early influential argument made by Francisco Varela, Evan Thompson and Eleanor Rosch in *The Embodied Mind* (1991). Contrary to traditional representational models of cognition, they maintain (like Bourdieu) that we don't rationally plan our actions by evaluating and choosing from available options. Rather, we perceive, respond and improvise in a highly flexible way according to context and history: we are '*situated* agents, continually coming up with what to do' (Varela 1999, p. 55, original emphasis). In studies of visual perception and action, Varela and his colleagues reject the 'computationalist tradition' in cognitive science, which assumes that sensory data is gathered and processed by a controlling centre somewhere in the mind, which then responds to an 'internal representation' of reality upon which it can act (1999, p. 54). Brain-imaging techniques are unable to detect any such centre of cognition; instead, there are complex multidirectional networks of activity and feedback loops through which coherence emerges (1999, p. 49). Our mind neither 'recovers' an objective outer world (realism) nor 'projects' an inner construct of the world (idealism), but instead functions via a process of 'mutual specification' which enables us to 'enact a world' (Varela et al. 1991, pp. 172, 151).

This proposal sheds light on the possible workings of both *habitus* and *performativity* – and not coincidentally, as Varela, Bourdieu and Butler were all influenced by Merleau-Ponty's studies of visual perception (1962) and by Husserl's phenomenology (1913). Yet it is significant that social theories of embodied power find support in neurobiological studies of 'enactive cognition' where '*The cognitive self is its own implementation: its history and its action are of one piece*' (Varela 1999, p. 54, original emphasis). For Bourdieu, *habitus* is what gives us 'practical sense' of 'things to be done or said, which directly govern speech and action' – what he calls 'a feel for the game' (1980, p. 66). And in Butler's performativity the body dramatises its own historical conventions (1988, p. 521). This meeting of the body and its historical and situated context, like the encounter of *habitus* and *field*, are where 'the organism both initiates and is shaped by the environment', and both are 'bound together in reciprocal specification and selection' (Varela et al. 1991, p. 174). This mutual process reflects the post-structural view that agency and structure are not in dualistic opposition, but iteratively and mutually constitute power – even perhaps as a singular embodied experience, as Butler would suggest, rather than a 'play' back and forth.

This view could be dismissed as overly deterministic, denying any possibility of autonomous free will or of mind over matter. But these accounts all acknowledge, albeit in different ways, that there is a *mutual* process at work, not a one-way inscription of the environment or social structures upon the individual (Ingold 2000, Rawnsley 2007). For Butler, 'performativity is a theory of agency', inviting us to recognise the 'delimiting power' of the field that defines gender identities and conditions the possibilities for action, and to find ways to transform it (1990, pp. xxv, xxiii) – without the illusion that agency is completely separate from and opposed to structure. The stated aim of *Gender Trouble* was precisely 'to understand what political agency might be, given that it cannot be isolated from the dynamics of power from which it is wrought' (ibid., p. xxv). For Bourdieu, *habitus* is not deterministic, but an interplay of both 'structured' and 'structuring' dispositions which 'is constituted in practice and is always oriented towards practical functions' (1980, p. 54). And for Varela et al., 'perception is not simply embedded within and constrained by the surrounding world; it also contributes to the enactment of this surrounding world' (1991, p. 174). The question is not whether we have agency, but what is the 'we' that is acting, what is it acting 'upon' and how can we become more aware of this situated, historical and enactive process.

The embodied turn in cognitive science doesn't deny possibilities of agency; but it does challenge long-held assumptions about autonomy, rationality and agency in Western thought. Rather than the Cartesian dualism of 'I think therefore I am', mind and body are integrally situated in context and experience. While not explicitly concerned with power, ideas of embodied cognition have profound implications for efforts to enhance civic and political agency. Transforming power at this level involves accessing the enactive and situated body, its senses and feelings, its collective experience and relationships, and its profound connection to the world. In my experience this reclaiming of embodied existence as a pathway to civic and political power cannot be achieved with analytical or linguistic forms of cognition alone, but calls for embodied practices of learning.

Embodied practices for transforming power

Educational theory and practice also recognise the role of the body and its senses, feelings and experience in facilitating deeper and transformative learning (see for example Gardner 2006). Yet these approaches tend to find traction in infant, primary and secondary education rather than further and higher levels. In the training courses for development workers and social activists, embodied learning exercises – if used at all – are treated as *steps toward conceptual sense-making*, as means to an end rather than being valued in themselves as methods of learning. The exploration of power through drama, movement and body is non-existent in most university-level social science courses. Learners may be taught *about habitus*, disciplinary power or performativity, and are expected to use this theoretical understanding to go out into the world and make a difference; but they are not asked to examine how power is enacted with their own bodies. Where acknowledged, embodied practices are to be used with subjects of change, but not by change agents themselves. Yet without capacities for the embodied transformation of power, change agents are likely to mirror and reinforce dominant norms and behaviour, however unwittingly.

Many methods can be used effectively to bring the body into processes of transformative learning. Here I focus on theatre techniques inspired by Boal's *Theatre of the Oppressed* (see also McCarthy 2004, Guhuthakurta 2008, Mills 2009). These approaches can range from communicating messages in dynamic ways to deeper and more participatory processes of group reflection and action. In my practice as a facilitator of learning processes with civil society organisations, and as a university teacher and researcher, I've experimented with methods of storytelling, simulation, role play, body-sculpting and Forum Theatre (Boal 1994). Here I will draw out insights from using these embodied practices to explore power, and from Boal's explanations of his methodology, and explore their relevance to ideas of invisible power, embodied cognition and civic agency.

Methods of re-enactment and role play can be excellent ways to surface the personal experience of learners as a starting point for exploring power through body and feeling, to grasp its essence *before* moving on to more abstract sense-making. This can be a sensitive process, and it is important to set boundaries of safety (such as limiting body contact); to allow participants to opt out if they wish; and to be prepared to interrupt the action if boundaries are crossed. Scenes can be developed from learners' life experiences in response to prompts such as 'a time I felt contradiction or discomfort in my work' or 'a time I felt powerful or powerless'. Creative writing or storytelling exercises can be used to develop raw material for the scenes, inviting learners to share narratives in pairs or small groups, and then to develop them into performances to share and discuss in plenary. Guidance can be given to help participants develop their performance pieces – for example using embodied symbolism, metaphor and fantasy rather than necessarily aiming for realism. This approach ensures a concrete 'showing' of power in bodily experience rather than an abstract 'telling', and surfaces forms of power that could otherwise be flattened by conceptual language.

Methods of body-sculpting can also be used individually and in pairs or groups to further explore moments and experiences of power. This can take the form, for example, of exploring two poses that represent alternate states of feeling less or more powerful in particular situations. Working in pairs, participants can take turns mirroring one another's poses, or re-sculpting each other to try out alternative poses. Reflection can be deepened by drawing the contrasting poses on paper, writing words on them and sharing these in a 'gallery walk', in addition to performing and discussing them in plenary. Learners often comment on having gained surprising new insights into themselves and their embodied behaviour, for example in how they relate to others or how they deal with conflict. Body-sculpting exercises can make us more sensitive to what we are feeling and doing in everyday situations, and to how minute differences in posture and gesture, directions or aversions of gaze and facial expressions are part of how we experience and exercise power. We can identify and practise power-shifting postures and movements, get better at 'reading' others' body language and become sensitive to how we might feel and act rather than only thinking our way out of oppressive power dynamics.

Boal's Forum Theatre method adds deeper levels of exploration to enactment and body-sculpting. Scenes are performed for an audience by a prepared cast with a protagonist who is trying to resist or change an oppressive power dynamic. The audience, or 'spectators', can stop the action and take the place of the protagonist to try out alternative strategies, while the facilitator can also freeze the action and 'dynamise' it, for example asking the actors to reveal their thoughts and feelings. The underlying power dynamic often remains unchanged, sparking discussion about structural aspects of power and the need for longer-term, systemic and collective change strategies; but the protagonist can also succeed in at least partially disrupting the power in an embodied way, offering clues to the potential forms of agency that can effect change. Forum Theatre exercises can be facilitated with participants with no theatre background at all, or they can be led by an experienced troupe.

Forum Theatre exposes power at both the level of socialised structures, narratives and beliefs and at the level of individual dispositions and actions – dimensions that are not always integrated well in critical pedagogy. It visibilises the particular and personal, in addition to the general and social, inviting embodied awareness of individual and collective agency while also critiquing the ideologies, structures and beliefs that enable or constrain that agency. For some this exploration of power at both the personal and structural levels can be uncomfortable, rubbing against ideals of what it means to gain critical consciousness. It brings in the 'non-rational' body and enlarges the personal rather than jumping to abstract and collective concepts, which can be unsettling for those used to more analytical and structural critique. Boal's methods have been criticised as 'therapy', crossing the line from social analysis to trauma healing. He was accused of 'bourgeois individualism' during his political exile from Brazil when adapting his methods to the 'new oppressions' and alienation he observed in Europe. Boal's English translator and protégé, Adrian Jackson, defends this connection between the 'socio-political' and the 'psycho-therapeutic':

> The truth of the matter is that the work ... has always had therapeutic effects, and that these effects have been as much on individuals as societies. Therapeutic is not necessarily a pseudonym for normalising ... The implantation of oppression in our heads is not nullified because we face concrete 'actual' oppressions outside – far from it: the two work inextricably together, they compound each other. (Jackson cited in Boal 1994, pp. xxi-xxii)

For Boal power is not just an objective social structure, but is lived by subjective individual beings. His ideas of 'osmosis' (how we inscribe social norms within ourselves) and 'ascesis' (making visible and understandable the general law behind a particular event) speak to the connections between the individual and wider social structures, much like discipline, *habitus* and performativity. A theory of power based on internalisation and embodiment calls for an emancipatory approach to learning that works with bodily experience. Boal saw a need to address power at the individual and embodied level as well the group and societal level, using theatre to imagine and enact new possibilities. In the context of social activism against dictatorships and structural violence in Latin America, Boal wanted to move beyond the more instrumental forms of popular theatre he had used in the past. Influenced by Freire, he sought to create 'a theatre which is not didactic, in the old sense of the word and style, but pedagogic, in the sense of a collective learning' (Boal 1994, p. 7). Much popular theatre was 'agit-prop', which at the time 'seemed right ... to exhort the oppressed to struggle against oppression. Which oppressed? All of them. The oppressed in a general sense. Too general a sense' (ibid., p. 1). Boal saw limits to 'sending messages' and giving 'solutions' to the oppressed (ibid., p. 3), and wanted a theatre that could transform real lives:

When the spectator herself comes on stage and carries out the action she has in mind, she does it in a manner which is so personal, unique and non-transferable, as she alone can do it, and as no artist can do it in her place ... I learnt to see the human being struggling with her own problems, individual problems, which though they may not concern the totality of a class, nevertheless concern the totality of life. (Boal 1994, p. 7)

While there were no dictators using violence against the poor in Europe, Boal observed 'new oppressions', 'loneliness', the 'impossibility of communicating with others' and 'fear of emptiness'. We conform to society without noticing it: 'the cops are in our heads, but their headquarters and barracks must be on the outside' (1994, p. 8). This view resonates with Hayward's idea of power as 'networks of social boundaries' that enable or constrain (2000), Bourdieu's notion of *field* (1980) and Butler's iterative and historical constraints on action (1990). Oppression doesn't just affect one part of the population, but ensnares everyone in its invisible grasp. Forum Theatre's ability to enquire into how we embody power with or without overt coercion has given it a wide appeal.

Acting in what Boal called the 'aesthetic space' of the stage also enables a deeper reflection on the phenomenon of power. The stage, even defined as a line across a room, provides for a special kind of reflexivity – the ability to see yourself 'in the act of acting, in the act of feeling, the act of thinking' (1994, p. 13). This self-awareness during the re-creation of the lived moment is not simply conceptual:

Knowledge is acquired here via the sense and not solely via the mind ... This process of knowledge ... is constituted not only of ideas but also of emotions and sensations. Theatre is a therapy into which one enters body and soul, soma and psyche. (Boal 1994, p. 28)

Forum Theatre aims not only to understand power but to change it. For Boal, theatre can 'stimulate knowledge and discovery, cognition and recognition'. It provides a kind of 'plasticity' which invites creativity, imagination, dreams and memory and 'awakes in each observer, in diverse forms and intensities, emotions, sensation and thoughts' (1994, pp. 20, 21). Reflection is done with the body, senses, creativity and imagination. This is again a challenge to the idea that pragmatic action flows from abstract conceptualisation (theorising our experience), as in the popular notion of 'learning cycles' (e.g. Kolb 1984). Agency can also flow from bodily experience and the creative exploration of alternatives with the body.

Conclusion

Our bodies understand and experience power in ways that our conscious minds do not. Somatic and emotional reflexes serve as living maps of our past experiences with power, through which we trace and re-perform habituated patterns of hierarchy and domination. It is in our bodies that agency and structure converge and construct meaning, blurring self and society, and constituting ourselves as more than an individual, rational and centrally commanding brain. The social, philosophical and biological sciences are converging around the embodiment of cognition and of invisible power. This has profound implications for social activists and professionals, and how we can effectively create and mobilise civic and political agency. Transforming invisible power requires an experiential awareness of the body, its senses, its embedded history, its ways of responding and relating to others, and its profound connection with the world.

Methods of enactment, simulation, role play, body-sculpting and Forum Theatre constitute one of several traditions of embodied practice and learning. These techniques can enable us to replay our sensory and emotional experiences, re-create physical renderings of invisible norms and boundaries, and imagine and enact changes in our habituated collusion with invisible power. Other traditions of embodied practice and learning can be equally effective and complementary. In performance art, for example, the body can be used to recognise and challenge cultural norms (e.g. De Preester 2007). There are growing communities of practice and training in techniques of embodied facilitation (e.g. Walsh n.d.; see also https://embodiedfacilitator.com/). Feminist popular education offers well-developed methods for exploring embodied experiences of patriarchy, gender and power, thereby enhancing more discursive approaches to critical pedagogy (see Arce Andrade and Miller, this volume). There are growing examples of the use of embodied learning processes in social mobilisation work, including practices of yoga, tai chi and other martial arts and energy work (see for example Friedman 2017). Like Boal's *Theatre of the Oppressed*, these methods intersect unapologetically with therapy and trauma-healing, making links between experiences of power at the personal and societal levels.

Embodied practices of learning and action need to be repositioned from their fringe status as fun or entertaining activities, or as stages *toward* critical consciousness, to the very core of what it means to generate meaningful civic and political agency. This is not to deny the vital work of political and ideational struggle in shifting invisible power, but to suggest that without complementary efforts to transform embodied power, critical and discursive initiatives will fall flat. A 'pedagogy for the embodied mind' departs from rational-objective, individual consciousness-raising and looks beyond the propagation of alternative narratives as primary drivers of change, embracing the power of embodied knowledge and stimulating civic and political agency in both mind and body.

References

Boal, A., 1979/2000. *Theatre of the oppressed*. London: Pluto.
Boal, A., 1994. *The rainbow of desire: the Boal method of theatre and therapy*. London: Routledge.
Bourdieu, P., 1980. *The logic of practice*. Stanford: Stanford University Press.
Bourdieu, P., 1984. *Distinction: a social critique of the judgement of taste*. London: Routledge.
Butler, J., 1988. Performative acts and gender constitution: an essay in phenomenology and feminist theory. *Theatre Journal*, 40(4), 519–531.

Butler, J., 1990. *Gender trouble*. London: Routledge.

Clark, A., 2008. *Supersizing the mind: embodiment, action and cognitive extension*. Oxford: Oxford University Press.

Clegg, S. and Haugaard, M., eds, 2009. *The Sage handbook of power*. London: Sage.

Damasio, A., 2000. *The feeling of what happens: body, emotion and the making of consciousness*. London: Vintage.

Damasio, A., 2006. *Descartes' error: emotion, reason and the human brain*. London: Vintage.

De Preester, H., 2007. To perform the layered body: a short exploration of the body in performance. *Janus Head*, 9(2), 349–383.

Foucault, M., 1991. *Discipline and punish: the birth of a prison*. London: Penguin.

Freire, P., 1970. *Pedagogy of the oppressed*. New York: Herder & Herder.

Friedman, M., 2017. Transforming cultures of violence: ploughing the soil, planting the seeds of new social norms [online]. Toronto: Gender at Work. Available from: https://genderatwork.org/wp-content/uploads/2018/06/Transforming-cultures-of-violence-Feb-22.pdf [Accessed 5 May 2019].

Gallagher, S., 2005. *How the body shapes the mind*. Oxford: Oxford University Press.

Gaventa, J., 2006. Finding the spaces for change: a power analysis. *IDS Bulletin*, 37(5), 22–33.

Gardner, H., 2006. *Multiple intelligences: new horizons*. New York: Basic Books.

Giddens, A., 1984. *The constitution of society*. Cambridge: Polity Press.

Guhuthakurta, M., 2008. Theatre in participatory action research: experiences from Bangladesh. In: P. Reason and H. Bradbury, eds. *The SAGE handbook on action research: participative inquiry and practice*. London: Sage, 510–521.

Haugaard, M., 2003. Reflections on seven ways of creating power. *European Journal of Social Theory*, 6(1), 87–113.

Hawkesworth, M., 2016. *Embodied power: demystifying disembodied politics*. London: Routledge.

Hayward, C., 1998. De-facing power. *Polity*, 31(1), 1–22.

Hayward, C., 2000. *De-facing power*. Cambridge: Cambridge University Press.

Husserl, E., 1913. *Ideas pertaining to a pure phenomenology and to a phenomenological philosophy. First book: general introduction to a pure phenomenology*. The Hague: Martinus Nijhoff.

Ingold, T., 2000. *The perception of the environment: essays of livelihood, dwelling and skill*. London: Routledge.

Johnson, M., 1987. *The body in the mind: the bodily basis of meaning, imagination and reason*. Chicago: University of Chicago Press.

Kolb, D., 1984. *Experiential learning: experience as the source of learning and development*. Englewood Cliffs, NJ: Prentice Hall.

Lakoff, G. and Johnson, M., 1999. *Philosophy in the flesh: the embodied mind and its challenge to Western thought*. New York: Basic Books.

Lukes, S., 1974, 2005. *Power: a radical view*. London: Macmillan.

McCarthy, J., 2004. *Enacting participatory development: theatre-based techniques*. London: Earthscan.

Merleau-Ponty, M., 1962. *The phenomenology of perception*. New York: Humanities Press.

Miller, V., VeneKlasen, L., Reilly, M. and Clark, C., 2006. *Making change happen 3: power. Concepts for revisioning power for justice, equality and peace*. Washington DC: Just Associates.

Mills, S., 2009. Theatre for transformation and empowerment: a case study of Jana Sanskriti theatre of the oppressed. *Development in Practice*, 19(4/5), 550–559.

Pettit, J. and Mejía Acosta, A., 2014. Power above and below the waterline: bridging political economy and power analysis. *IDS Bulletin*, 45(5), 9–22.

Pettit, J., 2016a. Why citizens don't engage: power, poverty and civic habitus. *IDS Bulletin*, 47(5), 89–102.

Pettit, J., 2016b. Civic habitus: toward a pedagogy for citizen engagement. In: A. Skinner, M. Baillie Smith, E. Brown and T. Roll, eds. *Education, learning and the transformation of development*. London and New York: Routledge.

Rawnsley, A.C., 2007. A situated or a metaphysical body? Problematics of body as mediation or as site of inscription. *Janus Head*, 9(2), 625–647.

Scott, J.C., 1985. *Weapons of the weak: everyday forms of resistance*. New Haven and London: Yale University Press.

Thompson, E., 2007. *Mind in life: biology, phenomenology, and the sciences of mind*. Cambridge, MA: Belknap Press of Harvard University Press.

Turner, V., 1974. *Dramas, fields, and metaphors*. Ithaca: Cornell University Press.

Varela, F.J., Thompson, E. and Rosch, E., 1991. *The embodied mind: cognitive science and human experience*. Cambridge, MA: MIT Press.

Varela, F.J., 1999. *Ethical know-how: action, wisdom and cognition*. Stanford, CA: Stanford University Press.

VeneKlasen, L. and Miller, V., 2002. *A new weave of power, people and politics: the action guide for advocacy and citizen participation*. Rugby: Practical Action.

Walsh, M., n.d. *Working with the body in training and coaching* [e-book]. Brighton: The Embodied Facilitator Course. Available from: https://embodiedfacilitator.com/wp-content/uploads/2016/10/working-with-body-e-book.pdf [Accessed 5 May 2019].

Wilson, R.A. and Foglia, L., 2017. Embodied cognition. In: E.N. Salta, ed. *Stanford Encyclopaedia of Philosophy (Spring 2017 Edition)*. Stanford, CA: Center for the Study of Language and Information. Available from: https://plato.stanford.edu/archives/spr2017/entries/embodied-cognition [Accessed 3 June 2019].

2.5

TOWARDS A POLITICAL PRACTICE OF EMPOWERMENT IN DIGITAL TIMES: A FEMINIST COMMENTARY FROM THE GLOBAL SOUTH

Anita Gurumurthy and Nandini Chami

Overview

The digital moment is exciting and exasperating in equal measure for feminists immersed in the political practice of 'empowerment'. On the one hand, internet-mediated space is synonymous with a new grammar of political performativity that links the intensely 'personal' with the 'public', 'civic' and 'political' in strikingly creative ways (Raman and Kasturi 2018). Feminist practitioners who are increasingly disenchanted with the limitations of conventional legal-institutional channels for social change have found a cornucopia in digitally mediated political action that harnesses the destabilising potential of cultural performance (Baer 2016). Just think of the countless flash mobs, Twitter storms, digital media-based street installations and meme projects organised by feminist groups in the global North and South (Baer 2016, Subramanian n.d., Vemuri 2016).

On the other hand, emerging practices of 'digital feminism' are caught in a double bind (Baer 2016). Even as they attempt to challenge existing gender and other social hierarchies, their transformative potential hinges on whether and how progressive feminist narratives catch the public eye in the unending streams of information. Also, emerging digital media cultures are characterised by a post-feminist sensibility; as funny memes become the default for attracting attention in the incessant flows of the internet, both performance and the female body become commodified. We are witness to paradoxical representations of female subjectivity in this neo-liberal context that 'promote sexual agency and abstract notions of empowerment at the expense of politics' (French 2017, p. 161). The perverse confluence in cyber-space of politically charged actions and depoliticised performance results in a farcical situation where any woman who speaks online is labelled a 'feminist' (Devika 2018).

The theoretical question that confronts us in this complex bricolage of simultaneous assimilation (into the status quo) and destabilisation (of normative gender orders) is as follows: From the standpoint of feminist politics, what does doing empowerment really mean in digital times? This is the question we take up in this chapter, weaving together insights from existing literature on empowerment, technology studies, theories on internet and society, and reflections of ten feminist activists in India from diverse age groups, gender locations and histories of activism. In a field that has limited theoretical interventions from the global South, the voices of activists grappling with practical and theoretical quandaries in their political practice, we felt, would provide a useful epistemic contribution.

Empowerment as a politics of community and reflexivity

Empowerment, simply put, is the aspirational goal of feminist political practice, and is concerned with 'changing power relations in favour of those who previously exercised little power over their own lives' (Sen 1997, p. 2). A rich body of scholarship, mainly from the South, underlines how, as a feminist ideal, empowerment may be seen as a destination (of gender-transformative change) as well as the journey to the destination (Batliwala 1993, Batliwala 2007, Kabeer 2005). It is the political aim of feminist action as it is also the political process of shifting those gender hierarchies that constrain individuals from meaningfully exercising life-choices through 'radical and collective transformation of economic, political and societal relations' (Cornwall and Anyidoho 2010, p. 145). It is concerned with promoting 'growth in self-confidence, acquisition of new capabilities and consciousness' as well as building the 'capacity to act collectively to demand rights and recognition' (Cornwall and Edwards 2010, p. 5). To put it differently, empowerment is as much about collective action for tackling deep-rooted structural inequalities as it is about transforming the lives of individuals (Batliwala 1993, Sardenberg 2008).

A praxis that focuses exclusively on economic, legal and personal change for individual gains without a concomitant investment in collective mobilisation and community building cannot further the vision of empowerment in its 'liberating' sense of 'transforming the gender order of patriarchal domination' (Sardenberg 2008, p. 19, emphasis added). This is why Southern feminists have long stressed the fostering of a political community as the core of a feminist political practice for empowerment, rather than individual-centric actions (Batliwala 1993, Sen 1997).

In this view, building a community is not an ahistorical, universalist vision of a global sisterhood of women that relies on an essentialist identity politics of sexual difference (Mohanty 2003). Rather, it calls for a situated politics of engagement that forges contingent political solidarities. For example, in post-independent India, the connections between and differences in women's experiences vary across conjunctures and give rise to specific solidarities. Women have come together and have forged communities, singularly or variously, as Muslim, Dalit, indigenous, queer, farmer, garment worker, etc. (Menon 2015); or, for instance, in the case of young women in Indonesia – rural, urban, Muslim, Christian, indigenous and lesbian, gay, bisexual, transgender and intersex (LGBTI) activists – have forged the Young Indonesian Women Activists' Forum, grounded in their shared experience of being young feminists (Pettit 2018). In this vision of concrete community building, the ethics of solidarity are, hence, rooted in a relatedness with other women, based on very specific and common concerns – reflecting 'an ontological basis' of 'mutuality and co-implication' (Mohanty 2003).

Notably, this idea is markedly different from the masculinist ideal of political communities or publics. As Braaten (2013, pp. 148, 150) argues, in the Habermassian framing, community building is conceived as the process of 'establishing an abstracted form of social relationship' that stems from a 'mutuality of shared justifications' – essentially a rational process of consensus building. This ignores the role of social embeddedness in shaping intersubjective ties. In contrast, in the feminist vision, the Habermassian framing is inverted; here, a political community/public arises out of the ties rooted in shared experiences of oppression wherein solidarity is as much the ideal as it is the means to produce the norms that make community possible.

A feminist public can serve as a safe space for political identity formation, allowing the room for individuals to free themselves of shame or stigma, find affirmation and mutuality, and become self-aware about differences of location and similarities of experience. This is akin to the Fraserian vision of 'counterpublics' – discursive arenas that enable members of subaltern groups to formulate 'oppositional interpretations of their identities, needs and interests' challenging the narrative hegemony of the mainstream (Fraser 1990, p. 67). By promoting critical consciousness-raising, agency and radical meaning-making, feminist publics serve as training grounds to develop the capacities to reflect upon the exploitative structures of patriarchy, capitalist globalisation, race, caste, heterosexism, etc., and fashion counterclaims that challenge these hegemonic structures in their specific contexts.

This recursive loop between a feminist politics of community and reflexivity and the feminist publics it forges and sustains is at the heart of a political practice of (liberating) empowerment.

How the 'space of circulation' radically restructures the political arena

We now turn to the foundational ways in which the digital has radically restructured the political arena with its constitutive relationships. In recent years, a particular branch of technology studies – posthumanism – has drawn attention to how traditional social science theories, with their human-centric bias, cannot fully explain human action. They tend to narrowly focus on human subjectivities and the socio-cultural forces of discourses and ideologies, relegating non-human entities (whether other biological forms, technological artefacts or the physical elements of the material world) to the role of passive, inert objects that human agents act upon. Posthuman scholars (Latour 2005, Braidotti 2013, Rose and Walton 2015) posit that it is important to account for the complex entanglements of human beings in highly fluid systems composed of interconnections that are not stable or fixed. Therefore, they argue that social configurations be seen for the material, technological and biological assemblages that they are.

Posthumanism underscores how objects and their actions 'should not be left out of the explanation' and we should not 'pretend that they matter and make a difference only in some instances. An entire project may rest upon whether or not an object actually does what it is supposed to do' (Dolwick 2009, cited in Rose and Walton 2015, p. 5). In other words, the agentic properties of material entities in structuring social arrangements are as important to study as the role of human subjects.

Extending a posthuman approach to the study of politics in digital spaces would involve devoting equal attention to how human actors and technological objects together make up the active elements of political configurations – that is, acknowledging the data network and its algorithms as 'things' that are inextricable from the social arrangements they co-constitute, rather than 'objects' out there. Bruno Latour (2004) uses the conceptual handle of 'things' as a framing device to emphasise the agentic properties of non-human entities. In this view, 'objects' become 'things' when matters of fact give way to their complicated entanglements and become matters of concern.

Understood this way, political space – characterised as it is by a dynamic web of dependencies between human beings and digital things – can be seen as a space of circulation. Power circulates in this space comprising the digital infrastructures, the data it carries, the affects it generates, the knowledge it legitimises, the values it embodies, the contestations it contains and the bodies it encompasses. Depending on the specific human and non-human collectivity or assemblage that makes up this space, configurations of subjectivity and inter-subjectivity, individual and collective agency, and discourses of truth and common sense arise in this space of circulation.

Feminist political actions and feminist publics are enmeshed in the space of circulation as assemblages of material, discursive and affective elements. This idea of the feminist public in digital conjuncture corresponds to Dewey's 1927 theory of 'material publics' (as cited in Marres 2010). Dewey draws attention to how things become active agents of politics, playing a material role in mediating the public's capacity for self-recognition, sustainability and holding itself together as a public. Sustainable energy campaigns, for example, rely on how material home-based practices – that is, intimate acts of 'saving energy at the household level' – become linked to the external issue of 'climate change'. Electrical gadgets such as thermostats, geysers and light bulbs function as 'devices of affectedness' (Marres 2010), enabling specific affordances to link to the discursive issue of climate change, and forging a 'public' of environmentally conscious energy consumers.

Bringing a posthuman lens to the study of feminist political practice is neither post-power nor post-political. It is not about endorsing an uncritical cyber-feminism rooted in 'hyped-up disembodiment' or 'fantasies of trans-humanist escape' (Braidotti 2013, p. 102). On the contrary, it is a call for the radical reimagining of the embodied structure of human subjectivity and relational ethics in a context where bodies have become 'techno-cultural constructs immersed in networks of complex, simultaneous and potentially conflicting power-relations' (Braidotti 2006, p. 20). Building on this notion of non-unitary subject-positions, posthumanism goes on to advocate the call for a sustainable relational ethics that is based on an enlarged sense of interconnection between self and others, including non-human others, by 'removing the obstacle of self-centred individualism' (ibid., p. 36). Though restricted by their co-option into market capitalism, digital technologies still hold enormous potential for accommodating such inter-relational visions of the self through radical re-alteration of our cosmologies and social relations (ibid.). Bringing this approach to feminist politics would mean acknowledging the importance of digitally augmented 'places' for community building that are based on the 'democratic values for a coexistence of people and planet; smart and non-smart; intelligent and affective' (Gurumurthy 2018).

A reflexive politics of empowerment in the space of circulation

A transformed space of political performance implies the need to understand how the political practice of empowerment (understood as the recursive loop between reflexive feminist political action and the creation of feminist publics) also changes in the 'space of circulation'.[7] To discuss this, we juxtapose reflections of feminist activists we interviewed with posthuman analyses of the digitally mediated political terrain.

The upside of virtualisation and deterritorialisation

The internet has heralded the emergence of loosely bounded, trans-local digital networks in which people connect with one another as individuals in ways of their choosing, rather than being tied down by geography or destiny (Castells 2000). In such 'networked individualism', individuals build selective relationships based on narrowly defined, curated versions of themselves, breaking free from the confines of ascribed identities (Castells 2000, Wellman 2001). As Respondent G, a feminist journalist, observed:

> The internet enables you to define the sub-genre of the person you are and locate (others like you) who you want to connect with. This is just not possible if you are stuck with only [face-to-face] interactions in your neighbourhood.

Expressing a similar sentiment, Respondent I, a feminist researcher and practitioner interested in student activism online, highlighted:

> The internet is a lifeline for people who feel alone and alienated in their immediate offline relationships. Take the case of youth who are trying to figure out their sexual identity. Their families don't understand them; their schools/colleges and teachers censure them; they may not be able to find friends who understand them in their day-to-day life. The freedom that digital spaces offer stands in sharp contrast to the rigidity of offline interactions.

7   We deploy the term 'politics of reflexivity' in the sense it is used in the feminist tradition: of a politics of change that is focused on a constant negotiation between the subjective aspirations of individuals and gendered structures of power that shape possibilities.

Respondent I is alluding to the possibilities of anonymity and proximity that deterritorialised digital space enables. Individuals from marginalised gender locations are able to carve out safe spaces to consolidate their incipient identities and hone their collective political subjectivities. 'Communities of fate or risk' (Fraser 2005) with similar histories of oppression, can thus be forged through a process of shared critical reflection (Thampi and Kawlra 2012, Gurumurthy and Chami 2012).

The deterritorial space of circulation also lowers the thresholds of participation. Individuals are able to belong more easily in political campaigns or forums on the 'platformised' internet. Respondent F, a practitioner working on sexual and reproductive health and rights, pointed to this:

> Today, unlike earlier times, one can know what happens somewhere without having to go there. And to support it, one doesn't necessarily have to go there physically, though that option can be exercised if necessary. It is now possible to be a part of it through the internet.

Conversely, in the space of circulation, feminist publics acquire a certain legibility, with digital platforms bringing the 'bridging capital' (Kavanaugh et al. 2005) to build new ties. Trans-local communication networks also open up new possibilities for the 'interpellation' or emergence of feminist political subjects who share an embedded vision of solidarity-building. As Respondent J – a feminist activist with over two decades of experience in movements building and popular education – remarked:

> In internet times, we are now able to mobilise globally, including people with whom perhaps one would not normally feel associated. We are able to forge cross-border, cross-issue and cross-spectrum connections. If a feminist activist in Egypt or Libya is in jail for her activism [...], sitting in India, I can lend my voice and support. Earlier, [in the days of pre-digital activism], I would not have the power to do it. I would not even know about it.

Also, the simultaneity that makes global connection possible on the internet transforms the very narrative of politics. New configurations of political action emerge in the space of circulation: flash mobs, multi-site protests, crowd-sourced petitions, meme culture, hashtag activism, etc. that reflect new modes of resistance and new subject positions. Some of these new configurations are spatially dispersed, but embedded locally in various places. As Respondent C – a feminist activist who has set up a new media platform for youth – reveals in her discussion of #Iwillgoout campaign in India:[8]

---

8   This country-wide campaign was launched in January 2017 to protest against the trivialisation of street sexual harassment by men in power. The immediate trigger was the molestation of women revellers who were part of New Year's Eve celebrations on the streets of Bengaluru.

The news of the molestations in Bengaluru came out on January 1, 2017 and this led to a lot of discussions in the media. A local politician said something along the lines of 'if there is a sugar cube in the open, ants will be attracted to it' – in a crass reference to how women going out at night were 'asking for it'. Others piled on with their sexist comments. And there was a huge Twitter discussion around this. In the online feminist forums that I am part of, there was increasingly the feeling that we should do something about this. We did not know each other personally but only through the groups. More and more people joined in and we started a WhatsApp group of all those who wanted to take some action about this. Out of our discussions, a plan took shape to organise a multi-site protest in different cities in India at 5 pm on 21 January. We picked the date since it coincided with the global Women's March against Trump. We did not have a budget or a lead organisation. It was this collective that came together online and it was all these young feminists jointly taking the lead in over 30 cities – mobilising on WhatsApp, Google Hangouts, Facebook. In Delhi alone, there were some 5000 people who attended the march. And national and international media picked it up and took note of this. I think this is certainly a great example of how the internet is changing the tools of protest.

In addition to opening up new pathways for building subjectivity, political identity and solidarity, and enabling new political 'doings', the disintermediating affordance of digital space also democratises the public, destabilising hierarchies within. Respondent H – a feminist activist working at the intersections of gender, sexuality politics and media rights – talks about how digital space:

> has enabled the formation of many amalgamations of voices, especially for the articulation of political identities that have been hitherto invisible. Take the case of disability. [Women living with] disability were completely bereft of rights, and as a group they were completely invisibilised. But they have been able to immensely benefit from [coming together online]. Similarly, look at how the internet has forced a public conversation around caste.

Reading power into the space of circulation

The space of circulation is by no means an unqualified feminist utopia. As a network of infinite platforms that mediates connections and shapes the sensibilities of our online experience, the internet is very much implicated in the contemporary structures of power. Digital corporations, almost all of which are based in the global North, control the economy and society. Over the past decade, the Big Four digital platforms – Apple, Google, Facebook and Amazon – have acquired a market capitalisation of $2.8 trillion, outstripping the gross domestic product (GDP) of many developing countries (Kiger 2018). Domestic and international laws and policies stand at an uneasy intersection as the digital paradigm disrupts institutions and demands new norms.

Economic and political power in the twenty-first century is predicated on data extractivism (Morozov 2018). All data that flows over the digital network is sought to be harvested and put to the service of algorithmic intelligence that is completely reorganising economy and society.

In the online communications sphere, digital platforms deploy algorithmic gaming tactics to privilege 'click-bait' content that attracts user traffic and facilitates targeted ad-serving through micro-profiling. Algorithms hyper-nudge every aspect of online inter-actions – from persuading you about what to add to your shopping cart, to suggesting the jobs you should apply for, recommending the news you should read and telling you which political opinions to endorse. In fact, democracy itself has been marketised, as evidenced in the Cambridge Analytica scandal where a data analytics company hired by the Trump presidential campaign in 2016 gained clandestine access to private information of more than 50 million Facebook users, exploiting the social media company's laissez-faire governance of its data-sharing partnerships with individual app developers (Granville 2018). Against this backdrop, the early promise of the internet as a new realm of human sociability founded on completely democratised, horizontalised communication seems to have withered away (Foster and McChesney 2011).

Network capitalism's connivance with the surveillance state poses serious concerns to democracy in the digital age. Governments in both developed and developing countries work closely with digital corporations to watch citizens, in a brazen undermining of human rights. The 2013 exposé by the former CIA employee Edward Snowden of the United States PRISM surveillance programme has conclusively revealed the existence of a US government back door to data held by Apple, Google, Facebook and Microsoft. Governments from developing countries have also joined the surveillance game. For instance, the Chinese government is collaborating with the Alibaba group to set up Sesame Credit, a nation-wide social credit system that will assign a trustworthiness score for all citizens based on extensive mining of behavioural and preference data.

The ideological force of class, race, gender, caste, heteronormativity, etc. per-vades the online publics, constructing a digitally mediated society in which social hierarchies of domination and exploitation are perpetuated. The whole of sub-Saharan Africa registers only 0.7 per cent of the world's domain names, a statistic that reveals the negligible impact the region has on the online geographies of information and knowledge (Ojanperä et al. 2017, Graham and Sengupta 2017). Similarly, on Wikipedia – often positioned as the encyclopedic repository of global human knowledge in digital times – over 80 per cent of the content is edited by white males from North America and Europe. Only one in ten Wiki editors self-identifies as female (McCambridge and Sengupta 2013). The internet may be rightly valorised for democratising feminist politics, but it is equally a site where sexism, misogyny and vitriolic hate speech proliferate.

Networked individualism in the digital age encourages individuals to seek out others like themselves, avoiding interaction where they are forced to confront oppo-sitional views (Vatnøy 2017). Respondent I, cited earlier, also commented on how feminist publics could become closed and exclusionary, unwilling to accommodate difference. In privileging a fragmented politics, the space of circulation allows assertions of identity to trump solidarity-building, which process may be perceived as long and fraught, and therefore avoidable:

> There are a lot of feminist groups on Facebook which accept you as a member only after you answer a few questions for them. For example, there is a certain radical feminist group which asks you the question: 'Do you believe a person born with male genitalia can ever be a woman?' They use this response to determine whether you are transphobic and against alliances with the trans-movement. There are other groups which sort members differently as they have a different view [on trans-inclusivity]. While each group will [justify such sorting] by pointing to how they cannot deal with people who drain their energies in internal discussions and want to exclude them, this exclusivity is what polarises the debate more and more. Everyone wants to find their niche and stay within it. There is no willingness to engage with difference.

Low costs of participation could imply low immersion, with possibilities for dialogue making way for a porous and fragile community that eschews reflexivity. As Respondent A, a feminist activist who is part of a student queer collective, avers, practices of feminist politics in online queer groups veer towards a cultural liberalism where the celebration of difference comfortably elides the different (non-queer) facets of social power present within:

> There are some queer support groups online which state upfront that this is not a space for asserting political opinions. To explain with an example … they would be okay if members are sending Diwali or Navarathri greetings,[9] but they will not tolerate a debate on the Hadiya case.[10] I find this hard to understand – how can you live a queer identity fully if you insist on being apolitical?

In the internet-mediated public sphere, political deliberation seems to be replaced by what is referred to as 'epideictic rhetoric', that is, the aggregation, circulation and repetition of text and images through which individuals declare their affirmation of the beliefs and values of the collective/community that they seek to belong to (Jeff 2017). The hashtag convention of Twitter exchanges, the 'forwarded as received' tendencies in WhatsApp conversations, the 'likes' protocol of Facebook

9   Popular festivals in India.
10 The Hadiya case refers to a recent controversy wherein Akhila, a 24-year-old medical student, had converted to Islam, assuming the name 'Hadiya', and married a Muslim man of her choice against the wishes of her family. Her father filed a judicial petition seeking annulment of the marriage, alleging that she been brainwashed by fundamentalist groups and was not acting of her own free will. After a protracted legal battle, the Supreme Court upheld the constitutionally guaranteed rights of an adult woman to enter into an inter-religious marriage and follow a religion of her choice. For more details, see https://en.wikipedia.org/wiki/Hadiya_court_case.

interactions – all of these are structured by the grammar of epideictic discourse in which the declaration of 'who we are as a community' is the focus, rather than reasoned debate around facts.

The filter bubbles that close off deliberation in the public arena reinforce confirmation bias, the tendency to interpret new facts one encounters to reinforce one's existing beliefs or theories. Respondent D, a queer feminist activist, spoke about how fragmented publics pave the way for a culture of intolerance and hostility, antithetical to the safe space so essential for nurturing a politics of identity and solidarity:

> On internet spaces, there seems to be no room for individuals to freely raise questions and build understanding when they are trying to engage with an issue. When you are first learning, you need room to ask politically incorrect questions. But this is not possible in the internet culture that's always focused on 'calling out'. In a group, everyone is constantly looking for what's wrong in something someone said without paying attention to the larger issue at stake.

The algorithmic architectures of the platform economy are geared towards a virality that actively promotes simplistic and ephemeral communication flows. This, as Respondent F, cited earlier, remarked, can dislodge the very processes of reflexivity and radical meaning making:

> How do you sustain interest and retain community feeling around your campaign's demands and issues in the current context where a 240-character tweet [sic] draws attention only until the next piece of content comes along?

The unholy marriage between surveillance capitalism and the informational state implies a closing in of democratic spaces. As online anonymity becomes notional, feminist practices that threaten the status quo are under siege. Respondent A analysed this:

> On the internet, you can never be completely safe. You might use filters and other strategies to keep information about you [in] separate [buckets], but there's only so much management you can do, right? How can you [trustingly] put something out there that you didn't want to be traced back to you? Earlier, [if you are a member of the queer community] you had a set of 'known enemies' to fear – let's say police officials who are patrolling 'cruising spots' in the town. But on the internet, you don't know [the reach of] the surveillance net. It is not possible to know where all your information travels to. This can make one paranoid.

The circulation logics of digital materiality seem to leave little room for a radical, transformative politics. They produce and affirm what Moawad (2017) terms 'Silicon Valley's sexual liberation politics', an electronic continuation of the offline trend of banks and credit card companies sponsoring gay pride parades, that resonates with neo-liberal capitalism's depoliticised version of freedom, choice and enterprise.

What this means is that, to gain circulation, narratives of resistance must be appetising and marketable, keeping pace with and using the logics necessary to become legible. Respondent E – a feminist researcher working at the intersections of gender, sexuality and technology – reflected on this issue by sharing the experience of the Dakota Access protests in the USA in 2016. This was a campaign led by First Nations communities who were protesting against the proposed construction of an oil pipeline that would cross Native American land.

> The social media campaign initiated by the grassroots communities spearheading the Dakota Access protests was a huge success. It had an understandable and digestible story line that foregrounded identity, race and environmental concerns. The storyline was like a rhythm – shock-worthy and wonderful, without being confused – and it brought together many individual voices from the frontlines. To produce this social media narrative, the core committee behind the protests had hired a media company.

The eyeball-grabbing narratives managed by the media company fetched the #NoDAPL hashtag of the Dakota Access pipeline protests over 4 million tweets between September and November 2016. However, this route may not be open to all groups engaged in political action, given the necessary resources and social capital required to leverage the expertise to game the algorithms of social media spaces.

It is also an open question as to whether the alienation of the First Nations communities from their land, as an inextricable theme in this narrative of corporate exploitation, could have found takers. Indeed, this erasure of a particular politics of claims-making – one that combines critiques of capitalism, colonialism and domination of all kinds – seems to be characteristic of the space of circulation: As Respondent G, cited earlier, reflected:

> I had gone to [details withheld] to be a part of the protests against the land acquisition bill. Outside the district collector's office, a whole bunch of young people had congregated. They had printed copies of the land bill with them. They laid it on the ground and pooped on the copies. Someone shot a video and posted it on YouTube. I would have thought this would go viral but it didn't … and when looking back on this, I feel that of course it didn't; its aesthetic does not fit into the 'cute-funny' fluff that is prized online.

To sum up, the digital conjuncture presents possibilities for the political practice of empowerment, with its constitutive elements of conscientisation, agency, solidarity and a radical meaning-making. But in the online circuits of the attention economy, information and communication flows on the internet often end up flattening difference by invisibilising discursive power and polarising and fragmenting publics. Whether feminist action ends up as superficial or authentic in the space of circulation depends on the extent to which the community it creates is able to demonstrate a mutual and embedded intersubjectivity, awareness about power hierarchies and reflexivity in claims-making.

Conclusion: reflections on empowerment and social transformation in the contemporary conjuncture

The discussion in this chapter, using a feminist compass, demonstrates how political practice for empowerment and social transformation must be pegged to the specifics of our posthuman condition, calibrated in relation to the complex entanglements between human actors and digital 'things', and adequate to the global frames in which power is negotiated in current conjuncture. The goal of transformative change, in terms of a shift in deep structures, must deal with the power paradox characterising posthuman society. The affordances of the digital for democratising society are constantly in struggle with the algorithmic apparatus deployed by the powerful (digital corporations and states) to discipline voice and game participation. As powerful countries and their corporations seek planetary control over data for harnessing the digital intelligence that will then allow them the remote control to take autonomy away from, and manipulate, less powerful countries and peoples, activists have noted the emergence of a digital colonialism (Pinto 2018). This should not lead us to sweeping generalisations that announce the 'death of transformative politics' or bemoan the emergence of a zombied generation of digital natives who are completely bereft of agency. The internet generation is no more or no less political than its predecessors.

The task then is to address the necessary connection between techno-materiality and power. This involves paying attention to the normative basis of democracy across scale. The shifting lines between the 'private' and 'public' in the context of the digital need to be tackled head-on. Norms are needed to reconcile the right to privacy with freedom of information; the right to control personal data with the collective right of communities to data; the right to be forgotten with the right to public knowledge; patent rights that power platform companies with society's right to scrutinise algorithms, and so on. These norms, determining the boundaries and configurations of public and private, present a highly contested terrain. The battle lines are deeply ensconced in a divide between the North and the South as exploitation in the digitally mediated global market place becomes more sophisticated, less visible and remarkably brutal (Sassen 2014). Faced with criticism from employees and the general public, the powerful digital corporations have rapidly redirected the debate, invoking the language of ethics to contain the misdeeds of algorithms and digital intelligence through self-regulation.

How the choices and freedoms of the most marginalised in the world will be promoted and nurtured for real empowerment depends on the way new global institutional frameworks can set the terms of democratic governance of digital space, and rearticulate rights and citizenship across scale. Also, to contain the excesses of power in the digital moment, the place of a radical politics of liberating empowerment cannot be overemphasised. As democratic rules, norms and institutions are redesigned in the digital age, new solidarities are needed for citizens to push back at big power; transnational strategies for change need to build critique and action from below, consciously going against the grain of the dominant digital force field. Local movement building to bring together diverse struggles is necessary to mount a challenge to the informational state in cahoots with big tech and big finance. As feminism reminds us, such a practice of empowerment must make room for articulations of identity and solidarity that strike at the heart of structures of injustice.

References

Baer, H., 2016. Redoing feminism: digital activism, body politics, and neoliberalism. *Feminist Media Studies*, 16(1), 17–34.

Batliwala, S., 1993. *Empowerment of women in South Asia: concepts and practices*. New Delhi: Asian-South Pacific Bureau of Adult Education.

Batliwala, S., 2007. Taking the power out of empowerment: an experiential account. *Development in Practice*, 17(4/5), 557–565.

Braaten, J., 2013. From communicative rationality to communicative thinking: a basis for feminist theory and practice. In: J. Meehan, ed. *Feminists read Habermas: gendering the subject of discourse*. RLE Feminist Theory. Abingdon and New York: Routledge, 155–178.

Braidotti, R., 2006. Affirming the affirmative: on nomadic affectivity. *Rhizomes*, 11/12. Available from: http://www.rhizomes.net/issue11/braidotti.html.

Braidotti, R., 2013. *The posthuman*. Cambridge: Polity Press.

Castells, M., 2000. Materials for an exploratory theory of the network society. *British Journal of Sociology*, 51(1), 5–24.

Cornwall, A. and Anyidoho, N.A., 2010. Introduction: women's empowerment: contentions and contestations. *Development*, 53(2), 144–149.

Cornwall, A. and Edwards, J., 2010. Introduction: negotiating empowerment. *IDS Bulletin*, 41(2), 1–9.

Devika, J., 2018. Women claiming the digital as 'own space': reflections on the Malayalam public sphere [online]. Lecture presented at national dialogue on gender-based cyber violence in advanced centre for women's studies, TISS, Mumbai. Available from: https://itforchange.net/e-vaw/wp-content/uploads/2018/03/Event-Report-of-National-Dialogue-on-Gender-Based-Cyber-Violence.pdf [Accessed 11 January 2019].

Dolwick, J.S., 2009. 'The social' and beyond: introducing actor-network theory. *Journal of Maritime Archaeology*, 4(1), 21–49.

Foster, J.B. and McChesney, R.W., 2011. The internet's unholy marriage to capitalism [online]. *Monthly Review*, 62(10). Available from: https://monthlyreview.org/2011/03/01/the-internets-unholy-marriage-to-capitalism/ [Accessed 11 January 2019].

Fraser, N., 1990. Rethinking the public sphere: a contribution to the critique of actually existing democracy. *Social Text*, 25/26, 56–80.

Fraser, N., 2005. Transnationalizing the public sphere [online]. *Republicart*. Available from: http://www.republicart.net/disc/publicum/fraser01_en.htm [Accessed 11 January 2019].

French, S., 2017. Neoliberal postfeminism, neo-burlesque, and the politics of affect in the performances of Moira Finucane. In: E. Diamond et al., eds. *Performance, feminism and affect in neoliberal times*. London: Palgrave Macmillan, 161–173.

Graham, M. and Sengupta, A., 2017. We're all connected now, so why is the internet so white and western? [online]. *The Guardian*. Available from: https://www.theguardian.

com/commentisfree/2017/oct/05/internet-white-western-google-wikipedia-skewed [Accessed 11 January 2019].

Granville, K., 2018. Facebook and Cambridge Analytica: what you need to know as fallout widens [online]. *New York Times*. Available from: https://www.nytimes.com/2018/03/19/technology/facebook-cambridge-analytica-explained.html [Accessed 11 January 2019].

Gurumurthy, A., 2018. The idea of data justice. Data Justice Conference, May. Cardiff University, UK.

Gurumurthy, A. and Chami, N., 2012. Key findings from the CITIGEN programme [online]. Gender is Citizenship. Available from: http://www.gender-is-citizenship.net/sites/gender-is-citizenship.net.citigen/files/Key_Findings_from_the_CITIGEN_programme_April-2012.pdf [Accessed 11 January 2019].

Jeff, R., 2017. Circulated epideictic: the technical image and digital consensus. *Philosophy and Rhetoric*, 50(3), 272–291.

Kabeer, N., 2005. Gender equality and women's empowerment: a critical analysis of the third millennium development goal 1. *Gender & Development*, 13(1), 13–24.

Kavanaugh, A.L.*et al.*, 2005. Weak ties in networked communities. *The Information Society*, 21(2), 119–131.

Kiger, P.J., 2018. Author Scott Galloway urges breakup of consumer tech giants [online]. Urbanland. Available from: https://urbanland.uli.org/economy-markets-trends/author-scott-galloway-urges-breakup-of-consumer-tech-giants/ [Accessed 11 January 2019].

Latour, B., 2004. Why has critique run out of steam? From matters of fact to matters of concern. *Critical Inquiry*, 30(2), 225–248. Available from: http://www.bruno-latour.fr/sites/default/files/89-CRITICAL-INQUIRY-GB.pdf [Accessed 11 January 2019].

Latour, B., 2005. *Reassembling the social: an introduction to actor-network-theory*. Oxford: Oxford University Press.

Marres, N., 2010. Front-staging non-humans: publicity as a constraint on the political activity of things. In: B. Braun and S. Whatmore, eds. *Political matter: technoscience, democracy and public life*. Minneapolis: University of Minnesota Press, 177–220.

McCambridge, R. and Sengupta, A., 2013. The radical passion economy of Wikipedia: an interview with Anasuya Sengupta [online]. *Nonprofit Quarterly*. Available from: https://nonprofitquarterly.org/2013/09/24/the-radical-passion-economy-of-wikipedia-an-interview-with-anasuya-sengupta/ [Accessed 11 January 2019].

Menon, N., 2015. Is feminism about 'women'? A critical view on intersectionality from India *Economic and Political Weekly*, 50(17), 37–44.

Moawad, N., 2017. Everybody, offline. We need to talk [online]. Available from: https://itforchange.net/e-vaw/wp-content/uploads/2017/12/Opinion-piece-1.pdf [Accessed 11 January 2019].

Mohanty, C.T., 2003. *Feminism without borders: decolonising theory, practicing solidarity*. Durham, NC: Duke University Press.

Morozov, E., 2018. Will tech giants move on from the internet, now we've all been harvested? [online]. *The Guardian*. Available from: https://www.theguardian.com/technology/2018/jan/28/morozov-artificial-intelligence-data-technology-online [Accessed 11 January 2019].

Ojanperä, S., Graham, M., Straumann, R. K., De Sabbata, S. and Zook, M. (2017). Engagement in the knowledge economy: regional patterns of content creation with a focus on sub-Saharan Africa. *Information Technologies & International Development*, 13, 33–51.

Pettit, J., 2018. Solidarity, safety and power: young women organizing in Indonesia [online]. Just Associates. Available from: https://justassociates.org/sites/justassociates.org/files/jass_famm_2018_solidarity_safety_and_power_e-version_19oct.pdf [Accessed 11 January 2019].

Pinto, R.A., 2018. Digital sovereignty or digital colonialism [online]. *Sur: International Journal on Human Rights*, 27. Available from: http://sur.conectas.org/en/digital-sover eignty-or-digital-colonialism [Accessed 11 January 2019].

Raman, U. and Kasturi, S., 2018. The performative periphery: visibilising civic engagement on social media [online]. International symposium: digital politics in millennial India, 15–17 March 2018, Delhi. Munich and Delhi: IITD, 1–65. Available from: http://iiitd.ac.in/ dpmi/final-abstracts.pdf [Accessed 11 January 2019].

Rose, E.J. and Walton, R., 2015. *Factors to actors: implications of posthumanism for social justice work*. Proceedings of the 33rd annual international conference on the design of commu-nication, 16–17 July 2015, Limerick, Ireland. Available from: doi:10.1145/ 2775441.2775464 [Accessed 11 January 2019].

Sardenberg, C.M., 2008. Liberal vs. liberating empowerment: a Latin American feminist perspective on conceptualising women's empowerment. *IDS Bulletin*, 47(1A), 18–27.

Sassen, S., 2014. *Expulsions: brutality and complexity in the global economy*. Cambridge, MA: Belknap Press of Harvard University Press.

Sen, G., 1997. Empowerment as an approach to poverty. Working Paper Series 97.07, background paper for the UNDP Human Development Report. New York: UNDP, 175–194.

Subramanian, S., n.d. *From the streets to the web: feminist activism on social media* (rep.). Banga-lore: Centre for the Study of Culture and Society.

Thampi, B.V. and Kawlra, A., 2012. *Empowering women leaders at the local level: translating descriptive representation to substantive representation through ICTs* [online]. Bengaluru: CITI-GEN Asia Research Programme 2010–2012. Available from: http://www.gender-is-citizenship.net/sites/gender-is-citizenship.net.citigen/files/CITIGENIndia Report_Fina l.pdf [Accessed 11 January 2019].

Vatnøy, E., 2017. *The rhetoric of networked publics: studying social network sites as rhetorical arenas for political talk* [online]. PhD thesis, University of Bergen. Available from: http://bora.uib. no/handle/1956/17262 [Accessed 11 January 2019].

Vemuri, A. (2016). *After Nirbhaya: anti-sexual violence activism and the politics of transnational social media campaigns*. PhD thesis, McGill University, Montreal.

Wellman, B., 2001. Little boxes, glocalisation, and networked individualism. In: M. Tanabe, P.V. Besselaar and T. Ishida, eds. *Revised papers from the second Kyoto workshop on digital cities II: computational and sociological approaches*. London: Springer, 10–25.

PART 3

Analysing power and empowerment: frameworks and approaches

3.1

DID WE FORGET ABOUT POWER?

Reintroducing concepts of power for justice, equality and peace

Alexa Bradley

I met Lisa VeneKlasen and Valerie Miller in 2004 as they were launching Just Associates (JASS), a network of popular educators and activists working in the global South. At the time, I was a senior partner at the Grassroots Policy Project, a movement support organisation partnered with US social change organisations. We were excited to meet because of the intersections in our thinking and practice, most particularly in terms of applied power analysis and strategy development. While working in different contexts, we were drawing on the critical theory of Steven Lukes (1974/2005), Antonio Gramsci (1971), Paulo Freire (1970), Chantal Mouffe (2002) and others to better enable activists to navigate and change power dynamics in their contexts. Engaging with JASS both affirmed and strengthened my work, as it has for countless others involved in human rights, social development and feminist movements.

The jumping-off point for this chapter is an influential report published by JASS in 2006, *Making Change Happen 3: Concepts for Revisioning Power for Justice, Equality and Peace* (Miller at al. 2006, hereafter referred to as MCH3). My hope is to honour the critical insights of that report by refreshing and updating the thinking as it has evolved in the years since its publication. As with all of JASS's work, this chapter builds on theoretical work of various scholars (see reference list) and on both JASS's direct experiences and my own with movements. The 'we' I refer to is the JASS network and the community of activists with whom we work.

Introduction

Did we forget about power? This question sat at the heart of the *Making Change Happen 3* report. Posed at a time when the significant advances for women's and human rights in prior decades had led to an 'over-reliance on policy and technical solutions' and 'superficial approaches to power' by advocacy organisations, the report warned that this 'failure to deal with the complexities of power can lead to missed opportunities and poor strategic choices. And worse, it can be risky and counterproductive' (MCH3, p. 4).

While the global context has changed since the report's publication, the challenges it pointed toward remain as relevant today, if not more so. At that time, it was already clear that the political window in which advances for women and other oppressed groups had gained ground – a period of many liberation movements and the expanded recognition of human rights – was already closing. Yet the sense of confidence and momentum from these earlier years had obscured signs that deeper power dynamics – dynamics that these gains had not eradicated – were behind a growing backlash.

MCH3 argued that in taking so enthusiastically to the technocratic terrain of policy advocacy, activists had unwittingly contributed to the depoliticisation of social justice struggles, and disconnections between advocacy and social movements (see also VeneKlasen, this volume). Consequently, MCH3 argued, '[h]aving a conversation … about how power and change operate in light of real-life politics and organizing experiences [is] absolutely necessary [and] is in itself an organizing and empowerment strategy' (p. 4).

There has never been a shortcut to change, and any change is vulnerable to rollback, particularly if it hasn't shifted who and what are centred in decision-making. Today the increasing influence of private interests within governments jeopardises earlier gains. The capture of state power by non-state actors such as fundamentalist religious groups, transnational corporations and narco-traffickers means not only that laws and regulations favour their private agendas, but also that state resources, including police and military, are dedicated to the promotion and protection of their interests. Laws, policies or protective rights that stand in the way are ignored, attacked or repealed.

Without clarity about these power dynamics, we may miscalculate both the opportunities and obstacles of the moment. And, importantly, we may fail to invest in strategies to amplify the voice and clout of organised constituencies and support their countervailing power.

Why do we forget about power?

With so much at stake, it is worth considering this question as well – why *do* we forget about power? Most simply, thinking about power complicates things. Civics lessons present an idealised version of civic participation – one person/one vote, 'an even playing field' exists in which different interests are negotiated, and so on. If, instead, we face the complexity of inequitable power relationships – from the familial to the global, and their distorting impact on decisions, decision-making and practices – we are pushed to reconsider the adequacy of our strategies for change.

A power analysis reveals what we are up against, and to what degree we are strategically prepared to push back. It clarifies our points of leverage and influence: where political space for our concerns exists and where it does not; who our allies are; what the defining narratives are on our issues; and the inevitable resistance and hostility to our agendas we will face. Navigating and building power in this way takes time, skill and sustained work. It demands coordination between advocacy efforts and grassroots organising, short- and long-term efforts. Perhaps it is not that we forget about power, but that we indulge in the fantasy that it doesn't really matter. But it does. Power matters.

Understanding power

Power, however, is complex and, as MCH3 noted, often a difficult and unsettling topic to address. Many people have had negative experiences with power, and thus perceive it as monolithic and entrenched. 'Such a one-dimensional view can paralyze analysis and action. When people see power as sinister and unchanging, they are unable to recognize their own sources of power' (MCH3, p. 4).

JASS's approach, by contrast, recognises that in reality, 'power is dynamic, relational and multidimensional ... expressions and forms can range from domination and resistance to collaboration and transformation' (MCH3, p. 4). This view opens up possibilities for mobilising alternative forms of power, and for both resisting and re-shaping what appear to be deeply embedded social norms and structures. Power can be created and used for positive change. As Dr Martin Luther King, a key leader in the US civil rights movements of the 1950s and 1960s asserted:

> Power, properly understood, is the ability to achieve purpose. It is the strength required to bring about social, political or economic changes. In this sense power is not only desirable but necessary in order to implement the demands of love and justice. (King 1967, p. 37)

Feminist scholar Srilatha Batliwala (building on the definition developed by Rao et al. in *Gender at Work*) makes understanding power quite practical, explaining that: 'power is the capacity of individuals or groups to determine: who *gets* what, who *does* what, who *decides* what, and who sets the agenda' (Batliwala 2019; see also Rao et al. 2016, Rao and Sandler, this volume).

The personal is political – and intersectional

Batliwala's questions reveal the multiple ways in which power operates, and the resulting impacts and inequities. They validate the feminist assertion that the *personal is political*: 'social power is not acting only in the larger world, but within our households and in our most private relationships' (Batliwala 2019, p. 14).

JASS recognises that without addressing the power dynamics that impact women's private lives – the relationships and roles in families, sexual partnerships and marriage, and in the intimate realm of one's sense of self and body – there will be no real progress for women. 'Political change strategies that focus solely on the public realm will overlook some critical challenges facing women who are leaders, active citizens and public officials when they return to their homes and families' (MCH3, p. 7).

Power and powerlessness also differ because of social identity and hierarchies of race, ethnicity, class, gender, ability, age and sexual orientation. Everyone has multiple, nuanced identities which together shape experiences of relative privilege, vulnerability and oppression. This intersectionality of identity means one can 'experience privilege and subordination simultaneously ... In one setting, a person may be more powerful while in another ... face discrimination' (MCH3, p. 8). JASS incorporates these differences in our analysis and strategy to leverage the collective power and solidarity of diverse communities without leaving some groups vulnerable and isolated.

Power over *from an organising and advocacy perspective*

Generally, if you ask someone what words come to mind when they think of power, they are largely negative – violence, control, abuse, fear. This is a measure of the reality that many people's awareness of power, and certainly women's, reflects experiences at the receiving end of the most commonly recognised form of it – *power over*. Such experiences tend to stifle a desire to think about power, or the ability to imagine it positively. As MCH3 put it, '*power over* ... operates to privilege certain people while marginalizing others. In politics, those who control resources and decision-making have *power over* those without and exclude others from access and participation' (MCH3, p. 5, emphasis added).

Building on the work of Steven Lukes (1974/2005), JASS developed a conceptual framework with 'three interactive dimensions of *power over* that shape the parameters of political action and change, marginalizing some people while privileging others. These range from the more obvious and visible to those hidden and invisible' (MCH3, p. 8, emphasis added). JASS noted that, while defining the three dimensions was helpful for analysing power more effectively, the three in fact 'interact and reinforce one another and need to be viewed holistically as do strategies for challenging their webs of discrimination and subordination' (ibid.). Box 3.1.1 shows how JASS presents these three 'faces' of power.

BOX 3.1.1 THREE FACES OF POWER

Visible power: observable decision-making

This kind of power includes the most visible and public aspects of political power – the formal rules, authorities, institutions and procedures of formal decision-making and enforcing the rules. Examples include elections, laws, regulations, budgets, courts and policing, and government (from local to global). As JASS pointed out, these public spaces are often viewed as an even playing field, but in reality are often 'closed, corrupt or unrepresentative', and not, in fact, neutral (MCH3, p. 9).

Hidden power: setting the political agenda

Hidden power is exercised by powerful people, and organised interests exercise this by using their influence behind the scenes to control who gets to the decision-making table and what concerns shape the public agenda. Hidden power actors include corporate interests, churches, paramilitaries, organised crime and powerful institutions that work 'to exclude and devalue the concerns and representation of other less powerful groups' (MCH3, p. 9). When full and fair public discussion is prevented, decision-making can be skewed to benefit the interests of a few. In response, strategies that focus on strengthening community organisations and movements can build collective power and new leadership to influence and shape the political agenda and increase their legitimacy and voice.

Invisible power: shaping meaning, values and norms

Invisible power is the power of beliefs, ideology, social norms and culture to shape people's worldview, sense of self, values and acceptance of what is normal, right and even real. Invisible power naturalises social inequity. 'Probably the most insidious of the three dimensions of power, invisible power shapes the psychological and ideological boundaries of change. Significant problems and ideas are not only kept from the decision-making table, but also from the minds and consciousness of the people involved, even those directly affected by the problem ... Similarly, key information is kept secret from the public so that issues remain invisible and cannot become part of the decision-making process' (MCH3, p. 10).

(Adapted from Miller et al. 2006)

Power in practice: complexities of visible and hidden

JASS, as a movement support organisation that equips women activists and their organisations, has by necessity iteratively adapted the theoretical framework of the three 'faces' of power – visible, hidden and invisible – to practically serve social change strategy. In particular, we saw that by illuminating the ways in which many decisions were determined by influential interests (hidden power) and were shaped by the invisible but potent realm of beliefs, worldview and political narratives (invisible power) this framework would enable movements to more effectively resist, challenge and transform power inequities.

In adapting the framework as an applied tool for strategy and action, JASS has sought to avoid the paralysis and confusion that can come from overly complex analysis. We have found it helpful, for instance, to clearly differentiate visible and hidden power even as they intertwine to make collusion and undue influence between them easier to identify. To support this clarity, we have tended to describe visible power as an arena of power which is not just 'observable' but is defined by formal and sanctioned decision-making and negotiations. And, by contrast, we have thought of hidden power as that which is exercised by organised interests – at times with the complicity of formal decision-makers (elected, appointed or otherwise) – who seek to control the political agenda, decisions and resources without even the pretence of transparency or accountability.

There have always been powerful interests 'behind the throne', working to influence and control decisions. In our current times, though, they have become increasingly bold and 'visible', explicitly dominating public decision-making and commanding public resources. This make the terms 'hidden' and 'visible' slippery, particularly if you are, for purposes of strategic action, trying to maintain the distinction between those who are supposed to be making decisions and those who are usurping that role. Moreover, as JASS has seen it, just because hidden power interests are now operating in the open, this does not give them the same legitimacy as designated decision-makers. To make these differences clear, we at times refer to visible power as 'formal' power. We also use the sub-category of 'shadow power' within hidden power to refer to efforts by organised *criminal* actors – such as mafias, narco-traffickers – to control public decision-making and resources, and which intensify the levels of corruption, fear and violence within a political context.

The usurpation of power by private interests – especially the capture of the state and other public institutions – is a particular threat that needs to be carefully understood. There are several dimensions of this threat:

- Compromised public institutions cannot be relied on to enforce and uphold rights (human, labour, environmental, women's, indigenous), due process, legal agreements, customary arrangements or the public interest.
- Public services and resources are at risk of privatisation, appropriation or elimination.
- And, perhaps most dangerously, states are corrupted to the extent that they are complicit in attacks on activists and civil society – a dynamic known as the 'closing of civic space'.

These threats pose real danger, both immediate and structural, to activists, movements and the broader citizenry. Communities and movements making demands and seeking change need to carefully assess the interplay of hidden and visible power in their contexts to understand who is actually making decisions, what levers of accountability are functioning and what the risks of advocacy and activism are and from whom. Failure to do so can result in ineffective advocacy at best, and violent repression and criminalisation at worst.

Power in practice: invisible power

For many years, JASS's analysis of invisible power primarily focused on the impact of internalised beliefs and social norms to naturalise conditions of subordination and discrimination, and to stifle people's aspirations and critical questions. This form of invisible power is promulgated through a multitude of social institutions and structures: schools, religion, families, the media, etc. However, beliefs and norms are also manipulated to legitimise specific policies and practices (see Lukes 1974/2005, pp. 7–8). We have gradually drawn more attention to this latter aspect of invisible power in light of the increasingly blatant and, at times sophisticated, use of misinformation and fear to shape the public discourse.

Locating political narratives within an understanding of power, not simply as communications strategy, clarifies their political purpose and potency. Visible and hidden power actors strategically craft and mobilise narratives that draw on existing prejudices and fears, such as anxiety about social difference, to build popular support for a particular agenda and to delegitimise other ideas and opposition. Both these variants of invisible power – internalised and manipulated – operate deep in people's consciousness, anchored in emotion as well as beliefs, and so cannot be challenged simply at a rational level (see Pettit, this volume). JASS uses feminist popular education, a participatory process of critical and experiential reflection and analysis, to foster political consciousness (a multi-faceted awareness of power, privilege and inequality) and to explore alternative ideas in a safe context (see Arce Andrade and Miller, this volume). Whether in the case of political narratives or other more diffuse forms of invisible power, it is strategically useful to analyse whose interests these forms of invisible power serve, and how they impact every part of our lives.

Transformative power

Power, of course, is not static – it is always being contested; and *power over* is not the only form of power. JASS encourages community-based organisations to build and mobilise their own power. Cognisant that without alternative models activists could unconsciously replicate dominating forms of power, JASS offers a *transformative power* framework (called 'vital power' in MCH3, p. 6) to cultivate patterns of power rooted in equity, inclusion and liberation. The report explained that 'activists cannot expect that the experience of being excluded prepares people to become democratic leaders. New forms of leadership and decision-making must be explicitly defined, taught, and rewarded in order to promote democratic forms of power' (ibid.). The term *transformative power* indicates the goal of fundamental change in power dynamics at all levels – from the most intimate to the most public (see Box 3.1.2).

BOX 3.1.2 TRANSFORMATIVE POWER

Power within

Power within has to do with *a person's sense of self-worth and self-knowledge.* Grounded in a belief in inherent human dignity, *power within* is the capacity to value oneself, think independently, challenge assumptions and seek fulfilment. Effective grassroots organising efforts help people affirm personal worth, tap into their dreams and hopes, and discover their *power to* and *power with*.

Power to

Power to refers to *the unique potential of every person to speak, take action, shape her life and world.* Leadership development for social justice provides new skills, knowledge and awareness, and opens up the possibilities of joint action, or *power with* others. Nurturing people's *power to* is a critical antidote to resignation and political withdrawal.

Power with

Power with refers to the collective strength that comes with **finding common ground and community with others.** *Power with* – expressed in collaboration, alliances, and solidarity – multiplies individual talents, knowledge and resources for a larger impact.

Power for

In recent years, JASS has added *power for* as a dimension of transformative power. It refers to the combined vision, values and demands that orient our work. It inspires strategies and alternatives that hold the seeds of the world we seek to create. *Power for* provides a logic to transformative power – motivating the sustained movement-building efforts that generate *power to, with* and *within* as building blocks for change.

(Definitions of power within, power with *and* power to *are adapted from Miller et al. 2006, p. 6; the definition of* power for *is the author's own.)*

Underlying JASS's conception of *transformative power* is an understanding of the layers of oppression that keep people subordinated, isolated and feeling powerless, and of the necessity to re/construct identities and strategies from a different logic that can 'unleash creative human capacity to act and change the world' (MCH3, p. 6).

At a time of rising right-wing populism, it is important to note that not only pro-gressive social movements build transformative power. Current mass movements rooted in fundamentalism and 'white nationalism' are providing a sense of collective identity and political power to groups that feel menaced by change, real or perceived, in their status in the social order. While these reactionary formations don't look like traditional *power over*, they often reinforce conservative actors, institutions and belief systems in society – dynamics which progressive activists must take into account in order to offer alternative directions for change.

Power and strategy

Strategy in a movement context is by necessity concerned with efforts to both resist and challenge *power over* and to build *transformative power*. In fact, it is often the case that doing either one well contributes to the other.

Influencing and impacting visible power

Efforts focused on visible power often work to 'change the "who, how, and what" of policy-making – the decision-makers, the transparency and inclusiveness of the process, and the policies – so that decision-making is more democratic and accountable, and people's needs and rights are addressed' (MCH3, p. 9). Strategies include advocacy, policy development, accountability efforts, legal action, reform-ing institutions, securing and enforcing rights, and impacting elections.

Challenging and countering hidden/shadow power

Strategies to shift the power dynamics of hidden power have two principal dimen-sions: 1) work to expose who's really calling the shots and reveal their interests (MCH3, p. 9); and 2) work to strengthen the political capacity and legitimacy of less powerful groups. The former often includes boycotts, 'name and shame' campaigns, law suits, protests and other 'outside' strategies to undermine the clout and impunity of hidden actors and to pressure others to distance themselves. The latter focuses on building countervailing power through 'leadership development, organizing, coali-tion-building, research, media and public education efforts' (MCH3, p. 9).

Disrupting and changing invisible power

'[S]trategies to counter invisible power target social and political culture [and make] alternative values and worldviews alive and visible' (MCH3, p. 10). Strategic interventions include fostering individual and collective critical consciousness, questioning dominant ideologies and norms, healing internalised stigma and fear, and cultivating vibrant visions of self and society – a form of *power for*. 'These strategies can help transform the way people perceive themselves and those around them, and how they envision future possibilities and alternatives' (ibid.).

Challenging negative political narratives includes both revealing the interests behind them and offering contrasting narratives and values able to shift public sentiment and debate.

The power matrix

Table 3.1.1 presents a contemporised view of different dimensions of power and how they interact to shape the problem, and offers potential responses and strategies for challenging *power over* and building our own transformative and countervailing power.

Power analysis for community organising and movements

A close look at power makes clear that 'it is nearly impossible to make policy headway on issues … without challenging the multiple dimensions of power at work' (MCH3, p. 12). This awareness is on the one hand discouraging – advocacy alone will not solve the challenges we face; but on the other:

> this closing off of opportunities in the visible realm of power presents big possibilities for re-energizing education and organizing strategies that nurture new leaders and voices. By challenging dominant ideologies and worldviews, people not only deepen their understanding of power dynamics and them-selves [but also open themselves to] alternative worldviews and agendas that incorporate rights, justice, equality and democracy. (MCH3, p. 12)

In what may seem a prescient comment today, MCH3 underscored the need for this work, warning that:

> Creating new spaces for the articulation of alternatives is an increasingly urgent task, because submerging the debate about neoliberal and fundamentalist worldviews presents troubling implications for democracy as well as rights. Without channels for surfacing and resolving conflicts through collective mobilization and engagement in democratic politics, there is a danger that anger and frustration will curdle into extremism. (MCH3, p. 12)

Nuanced power analysis not only enables people to better understand what is hap-pening in a given context; it also enables them to see that current power realities are not pre-ordained, and to imagine other possibilities and strategic interventions. Spe-cifically, '[f]or most marginalized groups, the only way to create meaningful pressure is by building broad-based organized alliances and movements capable of mobilizing informed, active people combined with strategic public media attention to create "noise"' (MCH3, p. 13). A critical dimension of movement strategy is assessing the context, opportunities and avenues in which such 'noise' will best advance the goals and strength of the movement.

TABLE 3.1.1 The power matrix

MECHANISMS How power over operates to exclude and privilege	EXAMPLES Power over	RESPONSES AND STRATEGIES	
		Challenge and resist power over	*Build and create our own transformative power*
Visible: making and enforcing rules Presidents, legislatures, courts, ministries, police, military, United Nations, World Bank, chambers of commerce Instruments: policies, laws, constitutions, budgets, regulations, conventions, agreements, enforcing mechanisms, etc.	Biased laws/policies Decision-making structures that favour the elite and powerful and exclude others Unrepresentative governance bodies Lack of transparency and accountability Laws not upheld/gap between law and practice	Demand accountability to existing laws and agreements using advocacy, law suits, direct action, petitions, etc. Challenge inequitable policies and practices Expose corruption and ties to hidden Impact elections	Impact decisions and governance: laws, policy, judicial and spending Mobilise community power for accountability Leverage relationships with allies in key positions Engage in legal, political and judicial advocacy Reform institutions Shape policies and practices
Hidden/shadow: setting the agenda Political control over what and who is part of decision-making Exclusion and delegitimisation of others through 'unwritten rules', intimidation, misinformation and co-optation (e.g. industry suppression of climate science)	Activist leaders discredited as troublemakers or outsiders and their issues as elitist, impractical, anti-tradition, etc. (e.g. LGBT rights/labour rights are 'special' interests) Media does not consider these groups' issues newsworthy	Research and expose hidden power actors and their influence and interests Expose and discredit shadow actors Develop strategies to protect ourselves from threats and backlash	Build our own movement infrastructure Build collective power of communities Strengthen movement leadership and organisation Build strategic alliances Participatory research to legitimise our issues Use alternative media and communications

| MECHANISMS | EXAMPLES | RESPONSES AND STRATEGIES | |
How power over operates to exclude and privilege		Challenge and resist power over	Build and create our own transformative power
Power over	*Power over*		
Invisible: shaping meaning, values and what's 'normal' Socialisation: cultural norms, values, practices and customs shape people's understanding of their needs, rights and roles, and normalise inequities and the status quo	*Socialization/oppression* Belief systems (e.g. patriarchy) cause internalisation of inferiority, powerlessness, shame, anger, resignation, etc.	Challenge and disrupt repressive social norms and traditions	*Create consciousness and our own narrative* Foster critical consciousness, self-esteem and solidarity
Control of information and political narrative to 'manufacture consent' and silence dissent	Dominant ideologies and narratives in popular culture, education and media reinforce bias and inequality, and stifle other ways of thinking (e.g. women blame themselves for abuse)	Question taboos and use of shame/guilt to control	Amplify non-dominant voices, ideas, views and beliefs
Dominant ideologies validate social realities	Crucial information is misrepresented or withheld	Name and expose underlying interests and values driving political narratives	Influence and inform public discourse, attitudes and behaviour
		Draw attention to contradictions and impacts of invisible power	Creatively produce media and forms of cultural intervention
		Understand fear as a tool of control and its impact on our bodies	Cultivate alternative ideas and practices

Adapted by the author from 'The Power Matrix' in Miller et al. (2006, p. 11, from the original in VeneKlasen and Miller 2002). Columns 1 and 2 are adapted from MCH3 and columns 3 and 4 are the author's own.

Spaces for political engagement: invited, claimed and created

There is rich scholarship on what conditions and kinds of civic space are conducive or open to real citizen involvement (Brock et al. 2001, Cornwall and Coelho 2006, Gaventa 2006). 'Space' means institutional and community spaces of engagement and deliberation, both in person and virtually. Discerning the 'strategic relevance' of potential spaces for political engagement – those to which citizens are invited, those which are closed to us and to which we might lay claim, and those autonomous ones we create ourselves – is essential for activists and civil society (MCH3, p. 5). Invited political spaces are generally highly controlled and orchestrated. Relying on them can be of limited value in the best of circumstances, given all the other ways in which power is being exercised to impact decision-making; but if and when those invited spaces are 'closed', we could find ourselves without other strategies for impact.

> While invited spaces can offer possibilities for influence and networking, they rarely produce long-term results on vital justice issues. The more pressing danger, however, is that they can serve to legitimize the status quo and divert civil society energies and resources. (MCH3, p. 5)

Activists have creative ways to make political space, including taking over or *claiming* existing spaces (hearings, forums, conferences, board meetings, etc.) not intended for our use, and *creating* more and less-public events ourselves, including virtual spaces – people's forums, delegations, dialogues, installations, community consultations and more. Claiming a space created by others can provide an opportunity to intervene in the power dynamics controlling that space, and to lay claim to its visibility and legitimacy. But it also involves navigating the political and practical limitations of that space (Cornwall and Gaventa 2001).

Created spaces can 'provide groups a chance to develop agendas, knowledge and solidarity without interference or control by corporate or government power-holders' (MCH3, p. 10). As self-authorised processes of deliberation and decision-making, they create a platform from which otherwise marginalised people are able to intervene in the public discourse and presentation of 'reality'.

Of course, all political spaces are always at risk of shut-down, co-optation or atrophy. Civil society groups, movements and activists must constantly reinvigorate or re-imagine all political spaces to ensure their strategic value (Just Associates 2005, Miller et al. 2006, VeneKlasen and Miller 2002, Brock et al. 2001).

Global to local/local to global

Power is multi-dimensional in other ways too. Powerful actors and forces operate across borders and boundaries, from local to global. For instance:

> key powerful actors are increasingly geographically distant from the local injustices they produce, as is the case with factories or oil companies whose

shareholders and corporate decision makers are far from the environmental destruction or labor violations they are responsible for. (MCH3, p. 15)

This complicates strategy as it can further obscure who is behind decisions and who can be held to account. Organising efforts confront the reality that 'corporate globalization has reshuffled power such that it is almost impossible to fight local issues without taking into account and targeting global power dynamics and actors' (MCH3, p. 15).

Global corporate accountability campaigns have had some important successes over the years – for example forcing Big Pharma to reduce prices for HIV treatment drugs in the global South – but 'the corporate sector is adept at making minor adjustments to deflect public criticism, and slipping back into business as usual when activists aren't looking' (MCH3, p. 15). Recognising such strategic power imbalances can lead to a realistic appraisal of the dynamics of power that impact our lives and concerns. We can avoid wasting time with ineffective strategies and explore creative ways to use the power we have.

Interestingly, the challenges of global–local organising are giving rise to new, multi-pronged strategies. For instance, in the face of alarming climate news and dauntingly powerful fossil fuel industries, movements are combining on-the-ground local efforts – blockades, direct action – with global divestment efforts, social media pressure and the development of economic alternatives. Local struggles become global rallying points: examples include the indigenous-led pipeline blockade at Standing Rock in the US (Worland 2016), and the divestment campaign to stop a dam after Honduran environmental defender Berta Cáceres was murdered for protesting against it (Ford and Jones 2018). Such aligned local–global collaboration can leverage resources, maximise political pressure and spark and inspire related organising struggles.

Confronting risk, organising for safety

Unfortunately, for those standing up to powerful interests, intensifying levels of threat and violence are a reality; and, at the same time, communities organising resistance are discovering the limits of human rights mechanisms and protection. The resulting risk has led to innovative strategies for collective and community-based safety. For instance, the Mesoamerican Women Human Rights Defenders Initiative and FAMM Indonesia are networks which connect and support activists so they are less isolated, can share strategies for safety and collectively speak out on issues of concern.[1] For women and others facing exclusion and violence within movement organisations and homes in addition to public threats, these networks provide safe spaces, mutual support and a

1 For further details on the Mesoamerican Women Human Rights Defenders Initiative see Lopez with Bradley (2017) and https://justassociates.org/en/ally/mesoamerica n-women-human-rights-defenders-initiative-im-defensoras. For details on FAMM Indonesia see Pettit (2018) and https://justassociates.org/en/resources/solidarity-safety-a nd-power-young-women-organizing-indonesia.

platform from which to challenge those realities (a similar point is made by Flores, this volume). Collective approaches reflect a recognition that, day to day, what makes activists and organisations stronger – connectedness, organising, alliances, unity, knowledge of context and power dynamics, joint action – also makes them safer and more resilient in the face of backlash and repression.

JASS's movement-building praxis, forged from years of equipping and accompanying movement activists and organisations, continues to evolve in response to changing contexts. Yet many of the movement-building fundamentals remain the same as when MCH3 was published:

- the need to understand power in its many forms
- to cultivate the capacity to 'think and act beyond the confines of existing rules' (*power within and to*)
- to 'bring people together across differences for a larger purpose' (*power with*)
- to negotiate disagreement and conflict
- to embrace a shared vision of equity and liberation while making specific demands (*power for*)
- to cultivate a '[inter]generational and collective leadership to ensure our continuity'
- and, most of all, to continually to seek opportunities to practice and grow transformative power through creative and strategic action (MCH3, p. 14).

Emerging strategies reflect hard-won knowledge that organised, unified communities which also integrate preparation for backlash are not only more powerful but also less able to be divided, individually targeted and undermined by defamation. The connections being made between power, solidarity and safety are rich and a critical complement to building transformative power.

Conclusion

If there is one central point of MCH3, it is that creating change requires power – which means understanding it, navigating it, challenging it and transforming it. Those in power are rarely responsive to outside demands without the pressure of an organised political force. As Frederick Douglass, the nineteenth-century African American abolitionist, writer and political leader, knew well, 'power concedes nothing without a demand. It never did and never will' (Stauffer and Gates 2016, p. 288). JASS centralises feminist movement-building – the sustained work of building the organised and strategic capacity of grassroots women and their allies – to help create the 'demand' that Douglass speaks of.

As MCH3 put it, '[t]here is probably no more compelling form of power than the force of large numbers of different people united in a collective cause for justice' (p. 14). Perhaps the gift of our contradictory times – with rising authoritarianism and repression on one hand and uprisings and counter-mobilisations on the other – is the clarity of the value of 'agile [forms of] collective power', the 'power of numbers and movements' (ibid.).

References

Batliwala, S., 2019. *All about power: understanding social power and power structures*. New Delhi: Creating Resources for Empowerment in Action.

Brock, K., Cornwall, A. and Gaventa, J., 2001. Power, knowledge and political spaces in the framing of poverty policy. IDS Working Paper, 143. Brighton: Institute of Development Studies.

Cornwall, A. and Coelho, V.S., 2006. *Spaces for change? The politics of participation in new democratic arenas*. London: Zed Books.

Cornwall, A. and Gaventa, J., 2001. From users and choosers to makers and shapers: repositioning participation in social policy. IDS Working Paper, 127. Brighton: Institute of Development Studies.

FordL. and Jones, S., 2018. Bank faces lawsuit over Honduras dam project as spirit of Berta Cáceres lives on [online]. *The Guardian*, 18 May. Available from: https://www.theguardia n.com/global-development/2018/may/18/bank-faces-lawsuit-over-honduras-dam-pro ject-spirit-of-berta-caceres-fmo-agua-zarca [Accessed 4 April 2019].

Freire, P., 1970. *Pedagogy of the oppressed*. New York: Herder & Herder.

Gaventa, J., 2006. Finding the spaces for change: a power analysis. *IDS Bulletin*, 37(6), 23–33.

Gramsci, A., 1971. *Selections from the prison notebooks of Antonio Gramsci*. New York: International Publishers.

Just Associates, 2005. *Strategic opportunity or black hole? Assessing policy spaces to advance women's rights*. Washington DC: Just Associates.

King, M.L.Jr., 1967. *Where do we go from here? Chaos or community*. Boston: Beacon.

Lopez, M. with Bradley, A., 2017. *Making change happen 6: rethinking protection, power and movements. Lessons from women human rights defenders in Mesoamerica*. Washington DC: Just Associates.

Lukes, S., 1974/2005. *Power: a radical view*. London: Macmillan.

Miller, V., VeneKlasen, L., Reilly, M. and Clark, C., 2006. *Making change happen 3: power. Concepts for revisioning power for justice, equality and peace*. Washington DC: Just Associates.

Mouffe, C., 2002. *Politics and passions: the stakes of democracy*. London: Centre for the Study of Democracy.

Pettit, J., 2018. *Safety, solidarity and power: young women organizing in Indonesia*. Washington DC: Just Associates.

Rao, A., Sandler, J., Kelleher, D. and Miller, C., 2016. *Gender at work: theory and practice for 21st century organizations*. London: Routledge.

Stauffer, J. and Gates, H.L., 2016. *The portable Frederick Douglass*. London: Penguin.

VeneKlasen, L. and Miller, V., 2002. *A new weave of people, power and politics: the action guide for advocacy and citizen participation*. Rugby: Practical Action.

Worland, J., 2016. What to know about the Dakota access pipeline protests [online]. *Time Magazine*. Available at: http://time.com/4548566/dakota-access-pipeline-standin g-rock-sioux/ [Accessed 4 April 2019].

3.2

APPLYING POWER ANALYSIS: USING THE 'POWERCUBE' TO EXPLORE FORMS, LEVELS AND SPACES

John Gaventa

Introduction

In a complex, globalised and rapidly changing world, power dynamics are multi-dimensional, constantly evolving and full of complexity. The 'powercube' (Gaventa 2006) is an approach to power analysis which can be used to examine the multiple forms, levels and spaces of power, and their interactions. Building on earlier work on power – and elaborated and popularised in collaboration with other colleagues through the website powercube.net and numerous other resources – the powercube has been widely used around the world for analysis of power, education and aware-ness-building, context analysis, programme and strategy development, and monitoring and evaluation. This chapter briefly outlines the evolution of the powercube, and provides examples of the issue areas in which it has been used, and for what purposes. Drawing on these, we then offer eight lessons in how to apply the powercube fra-mework for analysing and transforming power relations.

Background

Many years ago, as a fledging researcher and volunteer fresh out of university, I was working in a mining valley deep in the heart of the Appalachian Mountain chain in rural America. While the people were poor, the land was rich – full of coal, timber, water and natural beauty. Yet the vast majority of this was absentee owned by a secretive corporate empire based in London; and in the valley the social and economic effects of this unequal, extractive economy were seen everywhere: land and water destroyed through unsustainable mining practices; dilapidated housing, poor schools and local services due to a low tax base; a deep sense of dis-empowerment, yet also a strong and resilient local community bound together by culture and history. The situation here was but a microcosm of the profound inequalities and its effects that we now see globally. And yet, at least as an outsider, I saw little visible protest. Why, I asked, in a situation of glaring inequality, did we not see more open resistance and challenge to the status quo? (Gaventa 1980).

To answer this question, I turned to the work of my then professor at Oxford University, Steven Lukes, who was about to publish his classic book, *Power: A Radical View* (1974/2005). In this book, Lukes argues that power can be seen in three dimensions, from the more visible to its hidden and invisible *forms*.[1] Over the years, as I continued to work in this field, I began to realise that these forms of power are a continuum, but reflect only one dimension of power (Gaventa 2006), and that a more complex approach was needed.

Influenced by the work of other colleagues in the Participation Team at the Institute of Development Studies (IDS) – e.g. Brock et al. (2004), Cornwall (2002) – we began to realise that power manifests itself differently in different *spaces*, which ranged from the *closed* to *invited* to *claimed*, and that power was relative: those who were perceived by themselves or others as powerless in one space might be seen as more powerful in other spaces. Increasingly concerned also about how in a globalised world power becomes disconnected from territory, we were clear that it was also critical to move beyond the realm of 'community power' to examine the dynamics of power and citizen action across levels, from the *local* to the *national* to the more *global* (Gaventa 2007).

In a short paper for a workshop at IDS in 2002, and later for the *IDS Bulletin* (Gaventa 2006), I brought these ideas together in what I called the 'powercube' (see Box 3.2.1). Building on the dynamic metaphor of Rubik's Cube, the powercube approach suggests that we must examine these three aspects of power (forms, spaces, levels) not only separately but also in their interactions. Moreover, each dimension of the cube also reflects a spectrum of possibilities that also interact with one another, opening and closing the entry points for influence and change. Power strategies which only focus on one element, or one dimension, often simply reproduce or strengthen power in another. Really transformative change happens when social actors (movements, civil society organisations, donors) work across all aspects of the cube, necessitating the emergence of coalitions and networks of actors, which themselves are affected by power dynamics.

BOX 3.2.1 THE POWERCUBE

Forms relate to how power manifests itself:

- *Visible*: focuses on who participates and predominates in observable decision-making
- *Hidden*: keeps certain issues, interests and voices out of the decision-making process or off the public agenda

---

[1] To my knowledge, the terms *visible, hidden* and *invisible* to refer to Lukes's three dimensions of power were first developed by Lisa VeneKlasen and Valerie Miller (2002) of Just Associates (JASS).

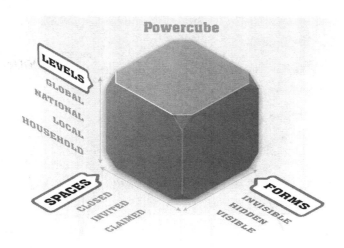

- *Invisible*: internalised beliefs and norms, or lack of awareness – which means that certain voices do not speak and certain issues and inequities go unquestioned

Spaces of power refer to potential arenas for participation and action:

- *Closed*: decisions are made behind closed doors without broad consultation or participation
- *Invited*: people are invited to participate in public arenas but within set boundaries
- *Claimed*: less powerful people or groups create their own spaces where they can shape their own agenda

Levels refer to the multiple layers or levels of power in a global world:

- *Global*: formal and informal sites of decision-making beyond the nation state
- *National*: governments, parliaments, political parties, coalitions or other forms of authority, usually linked to nation-states
- *Local*: sub-national governments, councils and associations at the local level
- *Household*: the micro-level, which may be outside of the public sphere but which helps shape what occurs within it(*Author's elaboration, powercube.net*)

While it was never our intent to turn the powercube into a widespread tool for analysis and action, it was quickly picked up by others. In one of the first substantial applications, Irene Guijt led a group of colleagues to use it to evaluate strategies of civil society participation as supported by four Dutch non-governmental organisations

(NGOs) in five countries (Guijt 2005, Guijt 2008). Oxfam and other NGOs, community-based organisations, IDS students and alumni from around the world, and government aid agencies began to apply it internally in their work, often supported through action learning journeys, trainings or accompaniment by Jethro Pettit from IDS and colleagues (Pettit 2013).[2] With growing take-up and refinement of the approach, in 2008 we brought together a number of users of the powercube for a workshop to share lessons and experiences. On the basis of this collective experience, in 2009 the web resource powercube.net was launched. Since that time, the approach has continued to spread, with hundreds of thousands of visits to the website, and hundreds of articles, manuals and background briefs drawing upon and developing the approach further.

This chapter briefly shares some of these applications and uses, and concludes with some lessons drawn from this experience. Given space considerations, this is necessarily an overview, and readers are encouraged to go to the references cited to understand further how the powercube was applied as well as the insights that were developed as a result.

Using the cube for power analysis in multiple fields and domains

One of the most important uses of the powercube is for the analysis of power dynamics across a range of fields and domains by a broad array of development actors, including international and local NGOs, social movements, think tanks, universities and donors.[3] These include analysing power in relationship to participation, policy and governance issues (the areas from which the first applications emerged). But the powercube has proven itself to be highly versatile and relevant to other fields and issues as well, including digital inclusion, economic justice, environmental issues, trade (including fair trade), health, housing, humanitarian relief, human rights, hunger and nutrition, legal empowerment, mental health, peacebuilding, and water and other natural resources. Some selected examples of these, drawn from an extensive search of many more examples, may be found in Table 3.2.1.

2   International NGOs that hosted action learning, workshops and trainings in power analysis and the powercube during this period include the Swedish Cooperative Centre (Sweden, Latin America), Christian Aid (UK, Kenya, Colombia), PSO (Netherlands), Trócaire (Ireland, Cambodia), Oxfam GB (UK, Latin America), Oxfam International, Oxfam Novib (Netherlands) and Hivos (Netherlands, Latin America). Government aid agencies that have hosted workshops and trainings include the Swiss Agency for Development Cooperation (SDC) and the Swedish International Development Cooperation Agency (Sida). Training and accompaniment was provided by the author, the editors of this volume, Irene Guijt, Jo Rowlands and others, including staff of these organisations.

3   Google Scholar shows over 500 citations of the powercube, and we have found over 60 publicly available documents where the framework is used in a substantive way.

TABLE 3.2.1 Analytical applications of the powercube in various fields (selected)

Field/issue	Selected references	Summary of approach
Digital inclusion	Roberts and Hernandez (2017)	Employ the powercube to examine which forms, spaces and levels of power affect the use of citizen participation technologies in the Philippines.
Economic inequality	Gaventa and Martorano (2016)	Drawing on evidence from the 2016 World Social Science Report on inequality and social justice, the authors use the powercube to analyse how inequality shapes forms, spaces and levels of participation, and to suggest strategies for change.
Environment	Rodríguez de Francisco and Boelens (2014)	Analyses the dynamics and entwining of visible, hidden and invisible power mechanisms in shaping payment for environmental services in the Chamacah Watershed in Ecuador. The study argues that disregarding the political dimensions of these services management is likely to end up favouring the interests of the most powerful.
Fair trade	Brugger (2017)	Uses the powercube to analyse decision-making arenas and power relationships between producers (i.e. plantation workers or small farmers), traders (i.e. plantation owners), retailers and consumers in Fairtrade tea production from East Nepal and Darjeeling. Looking across local and global levels and across spaces in the bargaining process, the analysis shows how power relations limit both the power of workers and consumers in the chain.
Health	Kaim (2013)	Looking at participation, knowledge and power in health systems, the author suggests that in people-centred health systems, visible, hidden or invisible power do not always limit citizen engagement, but may be mobilised as strategies to challenge or transform existing power relations.
Housing	Muir and McMahon (2015)	Focusing on Northern Ireland, the authors use the powercube to assess who is excluded in housing policy, the barriers to improvement and how improvements might be made.
Humanitarian	Larkin and Clark (2017)	Work on how refugees in Kenya 'assert their agency' points to the importance of power analysis in situations of conflict or emergencies to illuminate threads of power that are not otherwise obvious.
Human rights	Andreassen and Crawford (2015)	Focuses on how local and national struggles for rights have been constrained by power relations, and how civic action has been able to challenge and change power structures, drawing on case studies in six countries and using the lens of the forms and spaces of power.

Field/issue	Selected references	Summary of approach
Hunger and nutrition	Blay-Palmer (2016)	Draws on the powercube to analyse power imbalance, food insecurity and children's rights in Canada, and shows how this analysis can help inform strategies to shift power imbalances, including building power at multiple levels.
	Harris (2017)	Uses the powercube to map the levels, forms and spaces of power that shape nutrition policy in Zambia, helping to identify entry points for change.
Legal empowerment	Feruglio (2017)	Examines how invisible, visible and hidden power shape access to services in legal empowerment initiatives in Kenya and South Africa, arguing that policy-level impacts are the result of long-term processes that rely on multi-pronged and multi-level actions (e.g. mass mobilisations, international mechanisms, national courts and parliamentary processes).
Mental health	Brosnan (2012)	Argues that power dynamics are primary obstacles to equitable involvement of mental health users. Analysis of the spaces and levels of power, as well as the hidden and invisible aspects, can help service users strategise around their potential to influence decision-making in mental health services.
Participation and governance	Rabé and Kamanzi (2012)	In Tanzania the powercube was used to analyse the quality of participation in decision-making at the village level. The forms of power are found in all of the spaces of participation, across levels.
	Lay Lee (2012)	In China, applications of the powercube show that the Party-state is the dominant visible power at local and national level, but the international level presents local NGOs with the opportunity to engage with global NGOs to strengthen their voice.
Peacebuilding	Idler et al. (2015)	Applies the powercube to explore how spaces, forms and levels of power interact in local peace initiatives, particularly in consultation forums in Guatemala. While these forums promoted the participation and empowerment of a variety of social sectors, they also reproduced structures of inequality and were prey to invisible power, which made them less effective in enabling marginalised social groups.
Policy processes	Sida (2013)	Examining attempts for more inclusive policy dialogues in Mozambique, work by donors and development agencies examines how power manifests itself in invited spaces for policy dialogue, arguing that these forums became spaces for manipulation and co-optation rather than for strengthening the voice of civil society.

Field/issue	Selected references	Summary of approach
Water	Whaley and Weatherhead (2015)	Examines power dynamics that exist among farmers, and between them and key stakeholders involved in water management in the UK. The work points to the barriers that preclude framers from participating in water governance processes, including *power within*, the power that government water managers still exercise 'over' the farmers; and the relationship between lowland farming and environmental interests where the *power to* act has been historically opposed.

Emerging insights

Taken together, these applications of the powercube offer a number of useful insights into a range of issues and areas for power analysis. While it is beyond the scope of this chapter to consider these in depth, a few of the important contributions are considered below.

Community power analysis

The genesis of much of the debate on the study of power that led to the work by Steven Lukes, as well as my earlier study, *Power and Powerlessness in an Appalachian Valley* (1980) arose from studies of power at the community level, particularly in North America – including the famous work by Robert Dahl, *Who Governs? Democracy and Power in an American City* (1961). Perhaps because many of us involved in developing the powercube worked in international development, the approach has been used in a number of places to help us understand community-level power in other countries as well. Of these, one of the most in-depth is the study by Rabé and Kamanzi which sought to uncover the 'character of power' in 15 villages in Tanzania using the powercube model. As outlined in Table 3.2.1, they found multiple crossovers and interlinkages between the dimensions: 'visible, hidden and invisible forms of power traverse all three spaces of participation, across multiple levels of decision making' (2012, p. 73). While they found the powercube to be useful for the Tanzania context, they also found it was not particularly helpful on the questions of livelihoods and economic empowerment, 'as a prerequisite for social and political empowerment (or at least, as a simultaneous development alongside social and political empowerment)'. They call for new categories of power involving livelihoods and resources, as well as 'shadow power', e.g. 'the omnipresence of bribery and corruption at the local level' (ibid.).

Markets, trade and value chains

The Tanzania study points to the importance of linking power analysis not only to the political domain, but also to the economic domain. Gaventa and

Martorano (2016) similarly argue for the need to link economic and political empowerment if we are to confront inequality. Several more recent studies have begun to apply the powercube to the market arena. The work by Brugger (2017) sheds light on the 'black box' that exists between consumers and producers of Fairtrade Orthodox Himalayan Tea. The certification process is a buyer-driven and top-down process which recreates colonial dependencies in production and trade of agricultural products. The bargaining process over welfare for workers and small farmers takes away the power from the workers and small farmers to demand adequate welfare on local levels and in created spaces through such mobilisations as labour unions or political actions. Similar work on power in value chain governance in the Horticultural Ethical Business Initiative (HEBI) used the lenses of visible, hidden and invisible power to show how the excessive power of the retailers dominated value chain governance but also interacted with local context and place, in ways that led to the undermining of the HEBI initiative (Nelson et al. 2016). In both the tea and horticulture cases, power analysis linking local, national and global levels showed how power at one level can influence the manifestation of power at another level by either restricting or enabling opportunities for meaningful engagement.

Human and social services

While one strand of work takes us towards economic domain, a series of other applications have been more focused on power in the delivery of social services. The work on health, housing and mental health cited in Table 3.2.1 used the powercube frame to develop approaches for service users to participate in defining their own problems, overcome aspects of invisible, internalised power, and engage in dialogues with service providers. However, another author (Schutz, 2019) argues that within social services, 'empowerment' has largely been reduced to individual empowerment of users and clients, ignoring more collective and more confrontational approaches to challenging more systemic roots of power. Schutz builds on the ideas of spaces and forms of power, adding also the continua of 'types' of power (*power to, with, over*) and 'amounts' of power (from zero–sum to non-zero–sum). He then looks at five strategies of empowerment, ranging from the less to the more conflictual – including individual empowerment, collaborative empowerment, counterscript (e.g. symbolic protests), solidarity (e.g. community organising) and civil resistance.

Human rights

One of the most extensive analytical applications of the powercube has been that by Andreassen and Crawford in their book *Human Rights, Power and Civic Action* (2013; see also summary in Andreassen and Crawford 2015). As Schutz argues in relation to the idea of empowerment in human services, these authors argue that while much of the literature on human rights-based approaches emphasises the need for empowerment of rights-deprived groups, there has been a neglect of the power structures that obstruct securing such rights. Looking at rights struggles in six countries, they use the visible, hidden and invisible continuum in the powercube to develop a more comprehensive power analysis of the obstacles that these struggles faced. Using this analysis, they argue for three more collective strategies for achieving rights, ranging from collaboration with public authorities as duty-bearers, confrontation with power-holders such as the state and alliance-building with other non-governmental actors. Which strategy or combination of strategies will work is affected by how power works in a given context. Drawing on the concepts of spaces discussed in the powercube, the authors analyse how civil society actors might participate with decision-makers in 'invited spaces' and seek to make 'closed spaces' more transparent. Yet they also warn of the risk of co-optation: 'to avoid engaging with powerful elite actors on highly unequal terms where officially invited, for instance, it would seem essential for civil society organizations to initially strengthen their own countervailing power in more autonomous spaces' (Andreassen and Crawford 2015, p. 688).

These few examples give insights into just a few ways in which the powercube has been used as a tool for analysis across many different issues and domains, in many different countries and contexts. While they point to the importance of understanding the workings of power in particular contexts, they also offer some common elements that seem to cut across these, including:

- the importance of invisible power in shaping or precluding citizen voice, participation and action
- the interactions of power across levels, from the local to the global, to create and close opportunities for engagement
- the risk that 'invited' spaces for participation become sites for co-optation if they are not also strengthened by popular forms of citizen action in claimed spaces, such as social movements.

Moreover, as several of the studies and follow-up interviews point out, the 'power of the powercube' is found when it is used to examine the dynamic interrelations across two or all three of its dimensions – forms, spaces and levels – in turn helping to break down binary, linear or simplistic understandings of how and where power manifests itself.

Applications of the powercube for learning and action[4]

Such conclusions not only offer analytical insights into how power works, across issues and contexts, but they also have enormous implications for action. It is perhaps because of these that we have seen the take-up of the powercube as a tool used (alongside others) by practitioners such as community activists and the staff of

---

4   This section draws upon and further updates the earlier very useful review by Pantazidou (2012).

NGOs and development agencies to build awareness, do context analysis, develop new programmes and strategies, and evaluate the impact of their work.

Education and awareness-building

The powercube has been widely used as a tool to help people build awareness of power and how it affects their work, strategies and actions. A number of civil society organisations, trade unions and development agencies have hosted learning processes on power analysis for their staff and partners. These have included workshops and trainings ranging from a few hours to a few days in duration, to longer action learning journeys conducted over a period of several months – supported by facilitators and by resources and case studies related to the participants' actual work, issues and contexts.

In one example, 15 staff and partners from Oxfam Novib (Netherlands) took part in a nine-month Learning Trajectory, working in small teams to understand how power was operating in five key programmes around the world. Intensive workshops were held every few months, alternating with practical application and inquiry by the participants in their day-to-day programme work, with occasional check-ins and distance coaching from the facilitators. The issues explored by the participants ranged from indigenous rights to extractive industries, to HIV/AIDS prevention to partnership dynamics, to campaigns for sustainable palm oil.

In a similar action learning process, the powercube was used with grassroots organisations in marginalised communities in the UK to explore power related to issues of racial justice, migrant rights, gender-based violence, female genital mutilation, unemployed youth and homelessness, among others (Hunjan and Pettit 2011). Participants were community leaders from the affected groups, and used the powercube and related frameworks to deepen their understanding of power dynamics and to explore implications for strategy and action. Staff from the charitable foundations supporting these leaders, and their groups also took part in the learning process to improve their grant-making and partnerships.

The framework has been used for teaching power in more formal classroom settings as well (see McGee, Pettit and Wegner, this volume), to build awareness of the power relationships involved in research partnerships between communities and university researchers (Ferreira et al. 2015), and to analyse power relationships within higher education (Boni and Walker 2016).

Context analysis

The dynamics of power vary enormously across context, and in a rapidly changing world, being able to assess power dynamics is critical for any type of action or intervention designed to change power relations. Many groups have used the powercube for this purpose, adding it to other approaches for context mapping. For instance, Pettit and Mejía Acosta (2014) argue for complementing more traditional forms of political economy analysis with power analysis using methods like the powercube. Doing so, they argue, allows the analysis to go beyond the visible and more institutional analysis of actors and their networks to look at more invisible forms of power, internalised norms, and at how power operates in more informal and hidden spaces (see also Rowlands, this volume). Reviewing a number of examples of application of the powercube, Pantazidou provides examples of its use by NGOs, donors and social action groups to do context analysis for three purposes:

> to analyse the local, national or international context in order to design a programme or to develop or refine action strategies; to explore the effects and potential of current organisational practices; and to understand the power dynamics that shaped a past event, policy change or decision making process. (Pantazidou 2012, p. 9)

Programme planning and organisational learning

Building on such context analysis, a number of NGOs, donors and other organisations have also used the powercube to design and implement programme interventions for development or social change. For instance, Oxfam GB developed a guide on 'power and fragility' to support governance programming in fragile contexts (Fooks 2012). In the UK Christian Aid (2016) has similarly developed a 'practice paper' to help to 'reposition themselves, to create or enter new spaces ... to develop new ways of working' and to 'review the power in our own personal and professional relationships'. Donor agencies such as the Swiss Agency for Development and Cooperation (SDC) and the Swedish International Development Cooperation Agency (Sida) have also developed the tool for internal planning. For instance, work for SDC on 'operationalising empowerment' examines how the powercube can 'help identify entry points for change and to encourage self-reflection on the power which donors exercise' (Luttrell et al. 2007, pp. 1–2). Pantazidou points out that the powercube can help identify or sharpen theories of change, highlight the need to develop alliances with others and develop new tactics or approaches in order to deal with the multiple forms of power and their inter-relationship (2012, pp. 14–18).

Advocacy strategies and campaigns

While the powercube can be used for mapping contexts and contributing to programme planning, it can similarly be used to contribute to movement building and advocacy campaigns for change. As Guijt pointed out in her study of power and participation, 'Defining and recognizing the importance of different manifestations of power can ensure more consciously adopted, strategic action – and the identification of alternatives to current strategies – that can effectively transform power inequalities' (2008, p. 169). For instance, as a result of the Learning Trajectory described above, Oxfam Novib very systematically applied the tool to look for ways to build a campaign on the palm oil industry to improve the situation for smallholders and labourers in Colombia (Seeboldt and Salinas Abdala 2010). Action Aid International's Strategy 2028, 'Action for Global Justice', scales this idea up to develop a theory of change across the whole federation, affecting programming in 47 countries: 'Social justice, gender equality and poverty eradication are achieved through purposeful individual and collective action to shift unequal and unjust power, whether it is hidden, visible or invisible, from the household level to local, national and international levels' (Action Aid 2017). The Power Matrix developed by Just Associates is particularly helpful to think about what types of strategies need to be developed to address different forms of power in the context of movement building (Miller et al. 2006, p. 12; see also Bradley, this volume).

Protecting human rights

Other activists have elaborated on the powercube to develop strategies for dealing with violence and protecting human rights. Pearce (2007) used the concepts of the cube with activists in Colombia to map and assess the range of strategies that civil societies use to challenge power, but found that in this context, the cube did not explicitly address the role of violence. She developed a parallel 'violence cube' which like power, has its visible and invisible dimensions (Pearce 2009). More recently, work by Just Associates has further developed approaches of power analysis to identify strategies for human rights defenders, arguing that power can be a positive force as activists and communities organise to protect themselves against repercussions in hostile settings (Lopez with Bradley 2017, see also VeneKlasen, this volume). Amnesty International has used the approach widely, including in an action research programme on transitions to democracy in Egypt, where it was applied to map power relations and to strategize on actions for change.[5]

Monitoring, evaluation and learning

In addition to helping to map and plan new programmes and strategies for action, the powercube serves as a tool for evaluating and reflecting on the impact of these programmes. As referenced earlier, Guijt (2005) led a team of researchers to evaluate the impact of Dutch government-funded NGO programmes on shifting power and civil society participation in five countries. Macleod (2011) explored the powercube as a tool for evaluation in workshops with partners in an aid agency's women's rights programme in Nicaragua, El Salvador and Guatemala to examine shifts of power within women's movements. IDS applied the framework to evaluate Christian Aid's 'Power to the People' programme, using it to map the relationship of communities with

5 Interview with Maro Pantazidou, 22 December 2017.

authorities and to assess the nature of government responsiveness (McGee and Scott-Villiers 2011). As Pantazidou found, 'using the Powercube as a basis for evaluation can be very helpful for looking beyond the outputs and outcomes of projects towards a recognition and assessment of the various levels of power shifts entailed in processes of change' (2012, p. 20).

In support of all these applications, a wide array of resources have been developed that build upon, add to and popularise core concepts of the powercube, while also linking them to other resources and tools. For instance, the UK community work above led to the very useful publication *Power: A Practical Guide for Facilitating Social Change* (Hunjan and Pettit 2011). Just Associates has been at the forefront of developing resource materials on power analysis for activists and social movements, including their important book *A New Weave of People, Power and Politics* (VeneKlasen and Miller 2002), which pre-dated and contributed to the powercube, and more recent resources found in their online *Making Change Happen* series (e.g. Miller et al. 2006). Oxfam developed a short and very useable guide for its staff and partners, *A Quick Guide to Power Analysis* (2014). Danish NGO DanChurchAid's Learning Lab has produced an animated online guide for practitioners in power analysis (ActAlliance 2017); and Sida published a power analysis guide for its staff and partners which includes an introduction to the powercube (Pettit 2013). Versions of the powercube have been translated into a number of languages, including Spanish, French and Arabic.

Reflections on how to apply the powercube[6]

The multiple applications of the powercube have given us numerous insights about the nature and dynamics of power, as well as how the powercube can be used to understand and illuminate them. Along the way there have been many helpful adaptations, as well as critiques, which have also deepened our learning about its applications. Eight key lessons have emerged: four related to how the cube is applied for power analysis and action, and four concerning how it is used in processes of learning and reflection.

Lessons for power analysis

Thinking dynamically: going beyond the checkbox

One of the problems with the 'Rubik's Cube' visualisation is that it can appear as relatively static, with fixed categories and boxes. There is a risk that people will simply try to 'fill in the boxes' rather than analysing the relationships between

---

6   This section builds on lessons also from earlier work, including Gaventa (2005) and Pantazidou (2012). These have been supplemented by interviews with a number of users and an online survey conducted in 2017, led by Fiammetta Wegner.

them. In fact, each dimension should be seen as a spectrum, interacting with the other dimensions in a highly dynamic way. For instance, the possible spaces for action (closed, invited, claimed) open and close over time. Similarly, the levels of power (and which are most important) are far more complex than the 'local, national or global', and can range from the household to the village, county, state, national, regional, global and others, depending on the local context. Spaces and levels interact with forms of power, and shift over time. As Pantazidou writes, 'power constellations change', highlighting 'the need for the power frameworks to encourage a dynamic and historical assessment of the conditions out of which any current context was born and not to see it as at "still picture"' (2012, p. 10). In turn, as found by researchers using the cube in Guatemala, there was the need for social change organisations to have the '"staying power" to move across spaces of engagement over time, to retain links with groups working with other spaces, and to have the different capacities for engagement demanded by different spaces in differing moments' (Gaventa 2005, p. 20).

Contextualising the categories

While power needs to be seen as dynamic, how it is experienced and mani-fested is also very contextual. The terminology used − such as 'visible, hidden and invisible' − can sometimes be difficult to understand, and may be read quite differently based on differences in language, history and culture. What appears a space for action in one context, in another may be bounded by invisible forms of power, or historical experiences such as violence or reprisals, which limit its possibilities for change. Particularly challenging in some cases has been the idea of 'hidden' power, presented in the cube as forms of keeping certain issues and actors off the political agenda. But in Latin America, where there is a strong experience with military and paramilitary forces (often asso-ciated with drug cartels), discussions on hidden power can quickly elide into considerations of 'shadow' or 'dark power', referred to as *poder oculto*, or 'co-optation of the state by violent and criminal interests' (Pantazidou, 2012, p. 12, Pearce and Vela 2005; see also VeneKlasen and Bradley in this volume). In Tanzania, Rabé and Kamanzi (2012) also report that the forms of power in the cube didn't take into account the extent of corruption, which they suggested be called 'shadow power', similar to Latin American colleagues. But in Egypt, the 'secret' police were found to be not hidden or secret at all, but very visible in their presence − to the extent that NGO activists found themselves 'nor-malising' this power (Tadros 2010 quoted by Pantazidou 2012, p. 13) One way of contextualising the concepts of the cube is by keeping them very open, asking participants to define the levels, spaces or forms that most affect their lives, without imposing the categories given in the cube. Taking this approach in Guatemala, Colombia and elsewhere, participants identified far more levels of power and spaces and strategies for engagement than implied by the 'boxes' in the cube (Gaventa 2005, drawing from Pearce and Vela 2005).

Highlighting gender

Aspects of the powercube approach resonate with and have drawn from feminist thinking on gender and power, especially the idea of invisible power, which focuses on norms and internalised forms of oppression, and which links closely to ideas of strengthening *power within* widely used in feminist analysis (Rowlands 1997). Using the powercube can highlight issues of violence against women often hidden from public spaces (Pearce and Vela 2005). The Swiss Peace Foundation has used the cube to focus on women's participation in peacebuilding, supplementing other forms of gender analysis, especially in conflict settings (Brank et al. n.d.). Others have used it to analyse women's participation in local governance, also combining gender and power analysis (Hossain and Akhter 2011).

However, some have found that the powercube framework is not easily applied to gender analysis as earlier versions did not explicitly introduce 'private' or 'intimate' spaces or 'household' levels, which have also been shown in the extensive work on gender and power to be critical realms. As a result, some later versions of the cube have extended the levels dimension to the 'household level' in order to make more explicit the link between power in domestic, private spaces and public spaces (see Box 3.2.1). To avoid the risk of understanding gender as confined to its 'box', others have argued for the need to bring gender analysis explicitly to every dimension of the cube. Edström (2015, p. 74) expands the powercube to the idea of 'power dice', in which one of the dice is based on the dimensions of the powercube, and another focuses on more material, cultural and ideological dimensions.

Looking at the interactions

What is most powerful about the cube is not to look at any one dimension, but to think about how each interacts with the others. This is important on at least two levels. First, one has to think about what happens inside any one of the 'boxes' as it is in turn affected by what is going on in the other dimensions. For instance, while 'invited spaces' may seem like opportunities for participation, if the quality of what goes on inside the space is inhibited by forms of invisible and hidden power, then the participation that occurs may simply mean that relatively powerless groups 'echo' what the relatively powerful want to hear, rather than using the space for more meaningful engagement. Similarly, Cornwall (2004, p. 78) reminds us that spaces are not firmly separable: 'what happens in one impinges on what happens in others, as relations of power within and across them are constantly reconfigured.'

Second, though, one must think about strategies for change that link across the dimensions, especially if the aim is to develop a more transformative agenda. In what some called the 'boomerang effect' (Keck and Sikkink 1999), challenging power at one level may open up spaces for action elsewhere. For instance, the demands for making a 'closed space' more transparent at the global level (e.g. World Bank) may provide information or pressure that can be taken up or claimed by actors at a local level. Ultimately, we have argued, it is when strategies for understanding and shifting power connect across levels, spaces and forms that fundamental transformation happens. The powercube can be used to map and visualise these connections: to think about gaps in the ecology of strategies that are being used, and about how to build alliances that link social change actors across all the levels, spaces and forms. In this process, understanding the role of 'intermediaries' – those individuals, organisations or channels that link across the aspects of the cube – is particularly important.

Lessons for learning and reflection

Dealing with complexity

In training others to use the powercube, a number of users have found that it can be complicated for people to understand and to apply, and can be perceived as abstract from everyday experience. On the one hand, as observed earlier, the complexity of the cube is one of its strengths: by looking at interactions of forms, levels and spaces of power we move away from simplistic and binary understandings of power to a focus on the multiple ways and places in which it manifests itself. But, on the other hand, as a social change tool it needs to be accessible and useable by those who want to apply it to their everyday experience. A number of techniques have been found to help strengthen its application, including the following:

- Link to personal experience – rather than starting with analysis of power 'out there', start with asking people about their personal experiences. When have they felt powerful or powerless? What kinds of spaces do they enter? Where are decisions made that affect their lives?
- Break it down into parts – particularly when being used with groups to analyse their own experience, start with an understanding of one dimension at a time and then move to the others, asking how each builds on the previous. Where you start – through the lens of forms, spaces or levels – depends on what seems most appropriate to the context and the users. Some users of the powercube have observed that understanding power across levels can be most challenging, especially when starting at the local level, as national and global levels may be perceived to be out of the realm of everyday experience.
- Use visualisation – for many the 'cube' is not a useful visual representation. Many have found the use of cartoons, drawings or animations useful to illustrate the core ideas (ActAlliance 2017, Macleod 2011, powercube.net 2009).

Combining with other tools

The powercube is by no means meant to be the only tool for power analysis; nor should it be. Other tools for power analysis are also useful. For instance, the powercube does not explicitly focus on the actors who hold or wield power, though actors can be mapped against the various dimensions. It can be used with other approaches, which can help focus more explicitly on actors – including network analysis, stakeholder influence mapping and tools such as Net-map (Pantazidou 2012, p. 9). Nor does the cube focus explicitly on power that grows from identities of race, gender, ethnicity, age and sexual orientation, where approaches based on intersectionality can be useful (Edström et al. 2016). The work by Just Associates – including the *The New Weave* (VeneKlasen and Miller 2002) and later publications in their *Making Change Happen* series (e.g. Miller et al. 2006, Lopez with Bradley 2017) – brings a strong feminist understanding to power analysis, including using approaches such as the 'power flower', which focuses more on how one's various identities affect the possibilities of agency. In another project involving Action Aid's programming on livelihoods and women's rights, the powercube framework was combined with the Gender at Work Framework (which uses a quadrant to map individual vs systemic forms of power) to assess the shifts of power in favour of women (Delgado et al. 2016; see Rao and Sandler, this volume). Hunjan and Pettit's *Practical Guide for Facilitating Social Change* (2011) also offers a variety of tools that may be combined with the powercube.

Being reflexive: putting oneself and one's organisation in the picture

Oftentimes NGOs, donors, social movements and charismatic individuals play a role of critical mediator in processes of change; but in so doing they are themselves part of the power picture. By putting themselves within it they can reflect on their own roles, values and strategies for change. For instance, though doing an exercise known as 'power twister' (ForumSyd 2009) in which actors use their bodies to show at which levels and spaces they are spending their time and resources, some donors and NGOs have come to realise how disconnected their work in closed and invited spaces, at national and global levels, is from the spaces experienced by the grassroots communities they hope to support. The powercube has been useful in multiple ways to encourage such self-reflection, by both organisations and individuals. In an online survey of powercube users in early 2018, a number of respondents commented that the powercube helped them become more critical, encouraged them to go beyond binary thinking, to be reflexive about their own power, and to reflect and react in new ways. By reflecting on their own forms of power – such as their internalised norms of gender, race or class – users can also be more aware of their roles as actors for change.

Towards transformative power

The powercube is often introduced and used with another framework of forms of power – including *power within, power with, power to* and *power for*, as contrasted with *power over* (see Rowlands 1997, and Bradley in this volume). Much power analysis has traditionally focused on *power over* – the power of one actor (individual, group, institution) over another, which was the focus of the earlier theoretical work by Steven Lukes (1974/2005), whose work formed an important part of the powercube's intellectual roots. Others emphasise that power can be seen in more positive and productive terms. In their study of human rights struggles, for instance, Andreassen and Crawford conclude: 'Our studies have emphasized that power is essentially dichotomous, both positive and negative, and not a zero-sum game but dynamic, relational, and potentially expansive (collaborative power or alliance power)' (2013, p. 250). In my uses of the powercube, I see these types of power as highly interrelated. The *power within*, recognising one's own agency and capacities, is closely linked to over-coming 'invisible' power. The *power with* has to do with the need to build alliances to work across all the spaces and levels of the cube, as it is difficult for any single actor to be able to do so alone. Both *power within* and *power with* are important for achieving the *power to* act, especially if our model of empower-ment is one that emphasises collective forms of action.[7] *Power within, power with* and *power to*, taken together, are necessary to challenge *power over* in a trans-formative way. Just Associates (Bradley, this volume) call this 'transformative power', and have added to the lexicon the term *power for*: the combined vision, values and agenda of change that motivate and orient the work we do. By encouraging the imagining and creation of other possible futures, *power for* encourages, gives meaning to and practically demands the sustained movement building efforts that generate *power to, with* and *within* – building blocks toward that changed future.

Ultimately, power analysis is not an end in itself, but a tool to leverage change. Yet, as we know, tools can be used for many purposes, both progressive and regressive. The powercube and other tools can be valuable starting points in which we can ground our work for change. But, equally important, we must complement the powercube analysis with this final question: what is the world that we wish to see? What is our vision of the norms, values and institutions that we hope to achieve through challenging existing power relations? With this compass, we are more likely to be able not only to analyse power, but also to use such analysis to contribute to a more just and sustainable world.

References

ActAlliance, 2017. *Introducing the Powercube* [online]. Available at: https://vimeo.com/253176500 [Accessed 20 August 2018].

Action Aid, 2017. *Action for global justice: strategy 2028* [online]. Available at: http://www.actionaid.org/sites/files/actionaid/strategy_2028_lr.pdf [Accessed 20 August 2018].

Andreassen, B.A. and Crawford, G., 2013. *Human rights, power and civic action: comparative analyses of struggles for rights in developing societies*. Abingdon: Routledge.

Andreassen, B.A. and Crawford, G., 2015. Human rights and development: putting power and politics at the center. *Human Rights Quarterly*, 37(3), 662–690.

---

7   Schultz (2019) argues that the *power to* has often been reduced to individual forms of empowerment, which can easily be co-opted unless they are linked to more collective forms of action.

Blay-Palmer, A., 2016. Power imbalances, food insecurity, and children's rights in Canada. *Frontiers in Public Health*, 4, 117. Available at: https://doi.org/10.3389/fpubh.2016.00117 [Accessed 19 August 2018].

Boni, A. and Walker, M., 2016. *Universities and global human development: theoretical and empirical insights for social change*. Abingdon: Routledge.

Brank, B., Keller, U. and Fischer, R., n.d. Gender and peacebuilding. AMS factsheet series on gender and peacebuilding [online]. Swiss Peace Foundation. Available at: http://koff.swisspeace.ch/fileadmin/user_upload/koff/Publications/AMS_Fact_Sheet_GePB_web site052014.pdf [Accessed 21 August 2018].

Brock, K., McGee, R. and Gaventa, J., 2004. *Unpacking policy processes: actors, knowledge and spaces*. Kampala: Fountain Press.

Brosnan, L., 2012. Power and participation: an examination of the dynamics of mental health service-user involvement in Ireland. *Studies in Social Justice*, 6(1), 45–66. Available at: https://doi.org/10.26522/ssj.v6i1.1068 [Accessed 19 August 2018].

Brugger, A., 2017. *Power relations in the global production net-work for Orthodox Himalayan Tea analyzing Fairtrade tea production in East Nepal and Darjeeling through the Power-as-Translation Framework and the Power Cube*. MA thesis, University of Zurich.

Christian Aid, 2016. Power analysis: programme practice [online]. Available at: https://www.alnap.org/system/files/content/resource/files/main/power-analysis-programme-practice-paper-jan-2016.pdf [Accessed 20 August 2018].

Cornwall, A., 2002. Making spaces, changing places: situating participation in development. IDS Working Paper, 170. Brighton: Institute of Development Studies.

Cornwall, A., 2004. Spaces for transformation? Reflections on issues of power and difference in participation in development. In: S. Hickey and G. Mohan, eds. *Participation: from tyranny to transformation? Exploring new approaches to participation in development*. London: ZED Books, 75–91.

Dahl, R., 1961. *Who governs? Democracy and power in an American city*. New Haven: Yale University Press.

Delgado, M., Guijarro, D. and OteroE., 2016. *Description and analysis of the methodology applied to the evaluation of ActionAid work on women's rights* [online]. Available at: http://multiplyingimpact.care2share.wikispaces.net/file/view/Methodology+report_final.pdf [Accessed 22 August 2018].

Edström, J., 2015. Undressing patriarchy in the male order development encounter. In: E. Esplen, ed. *Engaging men in building gender equality*. Newcastle upon Tyne: Cambridge Scholars.

Edström, J., Singh, S.K. and Shahrokh, T., 2016. Intersectionality: a key for men to break out of the patriarchal prison? *IDS Bulletin*, 47(5), 57–74.

Ferreira, R., Ebersöhn, L. and Mbongwe, B.B., 2015. Power-sharing partnerships: teachers' experiences of participatory methodology. *Progress in Community Health Partnerships: Research, Education, and Action*, 9(1), 7–16.

Feruglio, F., 2017. *Do more empowered citizens make more accountable states? Power and legitimacy in legal empowerment initiatives*. Making All Voices Count Research Report, Brighton: Institute of Development Studies.

Fooks, L., 2012. Power and fragility: governance programming in fragile contexts: a programme resource [online]. Oxford: Oxfam GB. Available at: https://policy-practice.oxfam.org.uk/publications/power-and-fragility-governance-programming-in-fragile-contexts-a-programme-reso-253944 [Accessed 20 August 2018].

ForumSyd, 2009. Power and democracy [online]. Available at: https://www.powercube.net/wp-content/uploads/2009/11/powertwister_forumsyd.pdf [Accessed 22 August 2018].

Gaventa, J., 1980. *Power and powerlessness in an Appalachian valley.* Oxford: Clarendon.

Gaventa, J., 2005. *Reflections on the uses of the 'Power Cube' approach for analyzing the spaces, places and dynamics of civil society participation and engagement.* CFP Evaluation Series 2003–2006, no. 4. Netherlands: Mfp Breed Netwerk.

Gaventa, J., 2006. Finding the spaces for change: a power analysis. *IDS Bulletin,* 37(6), 23–33.

Gaventa, J., 2007. Levels, spaces and forms of power: analysing opportunities for change. In: F. Berenskoetter and M.J. Williams, eds. *Power in world politics.* London: Routledge, 214–234.

Gaventa, J. and Martorano, B., 2016. Inequality, power and participation: revisiting the links. *IDS Bulletin,* 47(5), 11–30.

Guijt, I., 2005. Assessing civil society participation as supported in-country by Cordaid, Hivos, Novib and Plan Netherlands: synthesis report. CFP Evaluation Series 2003–2006, 4.Netherlands: Mfp Breed Netwerk and Learning by Design.

Guijt, I., 2008. Civil society participation as the focus of northern NGO support: the case of Dutch co-financing agencies. In: A. Bebbington, S. Hickey, and D. Mitlin, eds. *Can NGOs make a difference? The challenge of development alternatives.* London andNew York: Zed Books, 153–175.

Harris, J. (2017) *National manifestation of an international idea: multi-sectoral approaches to stunting reduction and the transfer of nutrition policy to Zambia.* PhD thesis, SOAS, University of London.

Hossain, N. and Akhter, S., 2011. *Gender, power and politics in Bangladesh: a study for the Upazila support project* [online]. Dhaka: UNDP Bangladesh. Available at: http://www.undp.org/content/dam/bangladesh/docs/Publications/Gender%20Power%20and%20Politics%20study.pdf [Accessed 21 August 2018].

Hunjan, R. and Pettit, J., 2011. *Power: a practical guide for facilitating social change.* Dunfermline: Carnegie UK Trust.

Idler, A., Mouly, C. and Miranda, L., 2015. Power unpacked: domination, empowerment and participation in local Guatemalan peace forums. *Journal of Peace, Conflict & Development,* 21, 1–40.

Joint Evaluation, 2013. *Support to civil society engagement in policy dialogue* [online]. Bangladesh Country Report. Available at: https://www.sida.se/contentassets/fc5901a e284f4e85bf72bb46a3544297/support-to-civil-society-engagement-in-policy-dia logue—bangladesh-country-report_3447.pdf [Accessed 19 August 2018].

Kaim, B., 2013. *Who are we to care? Exploring the relationship between participation, knowledge and power in health systems.* Zimbabwe: Training and Research Support Centre (TARSC) and Community of Practitioners on Accountability and Social Action in Health (COPASAH).

Keck, M.E. and Sikkink, K., 1999. *Activists beyond borders, advocacy networks in international politics.* Ithaca: Cornell University Press.

Larkin, L. and Clark, S., 2017. *Refugees flexing social power as agents of stability: creating modes of economic livelihoods in Kenya's camps.* Champaign, IL: US Construction Engineering Research Laboratory.

Lay Lee, T., 2012. Rethinking power and rights-promoting NGOs in China. *Journal of Asian Public Policy,* 5(3), 343–351.

Lopez, M. with Bradley, A., 2017. *Making change happen 6: rethinking protection, power and movements. Lessons from women human rights defenders in Mesoamerica.* Washington DC: Just Associates.

Lukes, S., 1974/2005. *Power: a radical view.* 2nd ed. New York: Palgrave Macmillan.

Luttrell, C., Quiroz, W.S. and Bird, K., 2007. Operationalising empowerment: a framework for an understanding of empowerment within SDC. ODI Working Paper 308. London: Oversees Development Institute.

Macleod, M., 2011. Exploring the Power Cube as a tool for use in evaluation: identifying shifts in power within women's movements in Central America [online]. Available at: http://mornamacleod.net/wp-content/uploads/2015/04/Exploring-the-Power-Cube-as-a-Tool-for-Use-in-Evaluation-Final.pdf [Accessed 22 August 2018].

McGee, R. and Scott-Villiers, P., 2011. Christian Aid 'power to the people' mid-term review report, unpublished.

Miller, V., VeneKlasenL., Reilly, M. and Clark, C., 2006. *Making change happen 3: power. Concepts for revisioning power for justice, equality and peace.* Washington DC: Just Associates.

Muir, J. and McMahon, M., 2015. Involving easy to ignore groups in housing policy and strategy in Northern Ireland. Housing Rights [online]. Available at: https://www.housingrights.org.uk/news/involving-easy-ignore-groups-housing-policy-and-strategy-ni [Accessed 19 August 2018].

Nelson, V., Tallontire, A., Opondo, M. and Martin, A., 2016. Pathways of transformation of transgression? Power relations, ethical space and labour rights in Kenyan agri-food value chains. In: M. Goodman and C. Sage, eds. *Food transgressions: making sense of contemporary food politics.* Abingdon: Routledge, 15–38.

Oxfam, 2014. Quick guide to power analysis [online]. Oxford: Oxfam GB. Available at: https://policy-practice.oxfam.org.uk/publications/quick-guide-to-power-analysis-313950 [Accessed 20 August 2018].

Pantazidou, M., 2012. What next for power analysis? A review of recent experience with the powercube and related frameworks. IDS Working Paper, 400. Brighton: Institute of Development Studies.

Pearce, J., 2007. Violence, power and participation: building citizenship in contexts of chronic violence. IDS Working Paper, 274. Brighton: Institute of Development Studies.

Pearce, J., 2009. Bringing violence into the Power Cube [online]. Available at: http://www.powercube.net/wp-content/uploads/2009/11/violence_powercube.pdf [Accessed 20 August 2018].

Pearce, J. and Vela, G., 2005. *Assessing civil society participation as supported in country by CORDAID, HIVOS, NOVIB, and Plan Netherlands.* Colombia Country Report, report on the Programme Evaluation. Netherlands: Mfp Breed Netwerk.

Pettit, J., 2013. *Power analysis: a practical guide.* Stockholm: Swedish International Development Cooperation Agency.

Pettit, J. and A. Mejía Acosta, 2014. Power above and below the waterline: bridging political economy and power analysis. *IDS Bulletin*, 45(5), 9–22.

Powercube.net, 2009. Handout on power cartoons [online]. Available at: https://www.powercube.net/wp-content/uploads/2009/11/power_cartoons.pdf [Accessed 22 August 2018].

Rabé, P. and Kamanzi, A., 2012. Power analysis: a study of participation at the local level in Tanzania. ASC Working Paper, 105. Leiden: African Studies Centre.

Roberts, T. and Hernandez, K., 2017. The techno-centric gaze: incorporating citizen participation technologies into participatory governance processes in the Philippines. Making All Voices Count Research Report. Brighton: Institute of Development Studies.

Rodríguez de Francisco, J. and Boelens, R., 2014. Payment for environmental services and power in the Chamachán Watershed, Ecuador. *Human Organization*, 73(4), 351–362.

Rowlands, J., 1997. *Questioning empowerment: working with women in Honduras.* Oxford: Oxfam.

Schutz, A., 2019. *Empowerment: a primer.* London: Routledge.

Seeboldt, S. and Salinas Abdala, Y., 2010. *Responsibility and sustainability of the palm oil industry: are the principles and criteria of the RSPO feasible in Colombia?*Bogotá and The Hague: Indepaz and Oxfam Novib.

Tadros, M., 2010. What you see is NOT what you get: fluid, opaque, amoebic power. Available at: https://www.powercube.net/wp-content/uploads/2009/11/Fluid_opaque_amoebic_power.pdf [Accessed 20 March 2012].

VeneKlasen, L. and Miller, V., 2002. *A new weave of power, people and politics: the action guide for advocacy and citizen participation*. Rugby: Practical Action.

Whaley, L. and Weatherhead, K., 2015. Power-sharing in the English lowlands? The political economy of farmer participation and cooperation in water governance. *Water Alternatives*, 8, 820–843.

3.3

CRITICAL REFLECTIONS ON SHIFTING THE TOXIC ALCHEMY OF INSTITUTIONAL POWER

Aruna Rao and Joanne Sandler

Introduction

In 2015, at the sixth annual Women in the World Summit in New York, the then US presidential candidate, Hillary Clinton, declared that 'there's never been a better time to be a woman'. Now, a few years later – when cases of sexual harassment, abuse and exploitation in organisations as different as CBS, Fox News and Google in the US, the United Nations (UN), and Oxfam and Save the Children globally have rocketed to centre stage – that proposition is being severely tested. After the *New York Times* published its report in 2017 detailing decades of incidents of sexual exploitation allegedly carried out by media mogul Harvey Weinstein (Abrams and Rashbaum 2017), legions of women around the world have told their 'MeToo' stories on social media. A year later, in June 2018, the same paper published another article (Moore 2018), this time focusing on the UN, on how *not* to investigate sexual harassment cases. It pointed out the contradictions between the UN's public stance of 'zero tolerance' against sexual abuse and its internal system for examining sexual misconduct by its own employees, which is designed to protect the organisation rather than to get at the truth, support victims and punish perpetrators.

- How does this happen despite decades of work in every industry on gender and diversity training, clear feminist analyses of 'hegemonic masculinity' (Connell 1987) and its manifestations in organisational culture?
- How does this happen despite the scores of policies, laws and regulations that have been introduced at national and organisational levels since 2000?
- How does this happen with the legions of gender advisers, gender specialists and gender focal points who/that work in large government and development organisations?

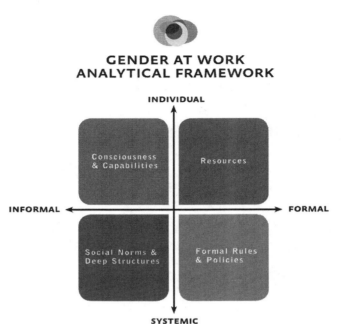

FIGURE 3.3.1 Gender at Work analytical framework
Source: Adapted from Rao and Kelleher (2002, p. 2)

- What enables the silencing of the collective chorus of feminist activists within those organisations to name, challenge and change sexism and gender discrimination?

We believe the answers lie in how power dynamics work to maintain what we call the 'toxic alchemy' of institutional power. This has four key dimensions. First, *patriarchal norms of discrimination* live in the foundations of our institutions, both formal and informal – in the rules of the game. Each time we manage to chip away at aspects of norms and deep structures that are amenable to change, others surface with renewed resilience.

Second, these *rules are maintained by a culture of silence*, allowing harmful and discriminatory norms and practices to live just below the radar. This culture silences different people in different ways: young women; those on insecure contracts; those who are ethnic or racial minorities who are the most vulnerable and have a lot to lose by speaking out. Staff with expertise in gender equality censor themselves as gender-equality work is always vulnerable to being cut back. They silence themselves as part of a culture of leadership that deals with infractions of official policy with a wink and a nod. It is common practice for alleged perpetrators to be moved to another part of the organisation or simply promoted to a position that takes them out of direct line authority over the victims.

Third, cases of gender discrimination or sexual harassment and abuse are *treated as isolated individual events* – a case of a few 'bad apples' in an otherwise nourishing if 'patriarchal cooking pot' (Longwe 1997, p. 148). Despite policies and procedures, old habits of doubting women, failing to protect their confidentiality, blaming them for refusing to 'take one for the team', and punishing them for speaking out are alive and well.

And, fourth, there is a *complete absence of systemic accountability and transparency* and few consequences for transgression. Instead, the onus is on the aggrieved individual to speak out and then be blamed for wearing skirts that are too short. Power works in hegemonic and insidious ways to maintain the toxic alchemy of institutional power.

In this chapter, we will show how the Gender at Work Framework (Figure 3.3.1) encourages attention to systemic features of what needs to change for women's rights and gender equality. We will then take a deep dive into the lower-left quadrant of the Framework on social norms and deep structures to look at how these enable discrimination and underpin the toxic alchemy of institutional power, and to examine ways of transforming these norms and structures (Rao et al. 2016).

The Gender at Work Framework views institutional change as being multi-factorial and holistic; it links organisational change, changes in institutional norms ('rules of the game') and gender equality. This is based on an analysis of the role of social institutions or rules – both formal and informal – in maintaining and repro-ducing women's unequal position held in place by gender power dynamics in society and in organisations. The Framework is concerned with both individual and systemic dimensions of change. It takes into account the individual psychology and capacity of women and men, their access to resources and the social structures in which they live.

In the Framework, the top two quadrants are *individual*. On the right are chan-ges in noticeable individual conditions – e.g. increased resources, women in lea-dership positions, training and capacity-building opportunities, voice, etc. On the left are individual consciousness and capabilities – knowledge, skills, political con-sciousness and commitment to change toward equality.

The bottom two clusters are *systemic*. The cluster on the right refers to formal rules as laid down in constitutions, laws and policies. The cluster on the left is the set of social informal norms and deep structures – including those that maintain inequality in everyday practices. These vary by context.

Sustainable changes for women's rights and gender equality need to take place in all four domains, and especially in the lower-left quadrant. The Framework can be used to look at what changes we want to see in organisations or in communities, to map change strategies and outcomes, and to monitor and evaluate progress.

Typically, change for gender equality and women's rights, including addressing violence against women, has relied on solutions on the formal side of the Frame-work. In India, for example, in the wake of the 2012 Delhi gang rape, the Parlia-ment passed the Sexual Harassment of Women at Workplace (Prevention, Prohibition and Redressal) Act 2013, requiring all organisations (public and private) to set up an internal complaints committee with an external member, train the members in the substance of the law, and provide a safe and confidential process to address sexual harassment cases. These are changes on the right-hand (formal) side of the Framework; they are visible and measurable.

According to the Indian Ministry of Women and Child Development there was a 51 per cent rise in sexual harassment cases at workplaces in 2014–15, and in the 2016–17 academic year a 50 per cent increase in reported cases of sexual harassment from various higher education institutions. Compliance with the law was poor, even though non-compliance can result in fines on employers followed by cancellation of their licence to operate. According to a survey conducted by the Indian Bar Association in 2017, 70 per cent of women said they did not report sexual harassment by superiors because they feared the repercussions. Anagha Sarpotdar, a researcher who works on sexual harassment in the workplace and who is an external member appointed to monitor such trials by Mumbai city, said: 'often, women go to committees believing them to be independent and find that they are actually puppets in the hands of their superiors' (Chachra 2017). Again and again we see that while formal changes are necessary, they are insufficient. Not addressing discriminatory social norms and the power imbalances that keep them intact often leads to failure.

This toxic alchemy of power also ensures that those in power protect each other. In the sexual harassment cases that have recently come to the fore in international development organisations, there is a perception that men and women in charge often protect their own and preserve a culture of silence. The examples also show that these transgressions are treated as isolated, individual events rather than being symptomatic of a larger culture where power is routinely abused. This makes it easier to deal with, and allows the dominant culture to continue unchanged.

The Gender at Work Framework helps makes the toxic alchemy of power more visible, and it is adaptable to many settings and situations. For example, Gender at Work Associates have used it in a gender action learning process to work with a change team in the South African Commercial Catering and Allied Workers Union (SACCAWU) to build women's leadership.[1] The process helped union members identify how power worked in the union to maintain deep structures and social norms that enable discrimination – the lower-left quadrant of the Framework. In the union, deeply rooted traditions of male dominance meant that women, particularly black African women, had little voice and influence in the union, bore the brunt of economic retrenchment and job insecurity, and had no childcare and maternity benefits. Sexual harassment was used as a weapon to undermine women's power, and the threat of violence operated at a very deep level. Women often colluded in their own oppression by not challenging the norms of patriarchy.

The Gender Coordinator at SACCAWU tried to get women members to vote for women in leadership positions, but this didn't happen until an alternative model

1 For more on Gender Action Learning, see http://genderatwork.org/gender-action-learning.

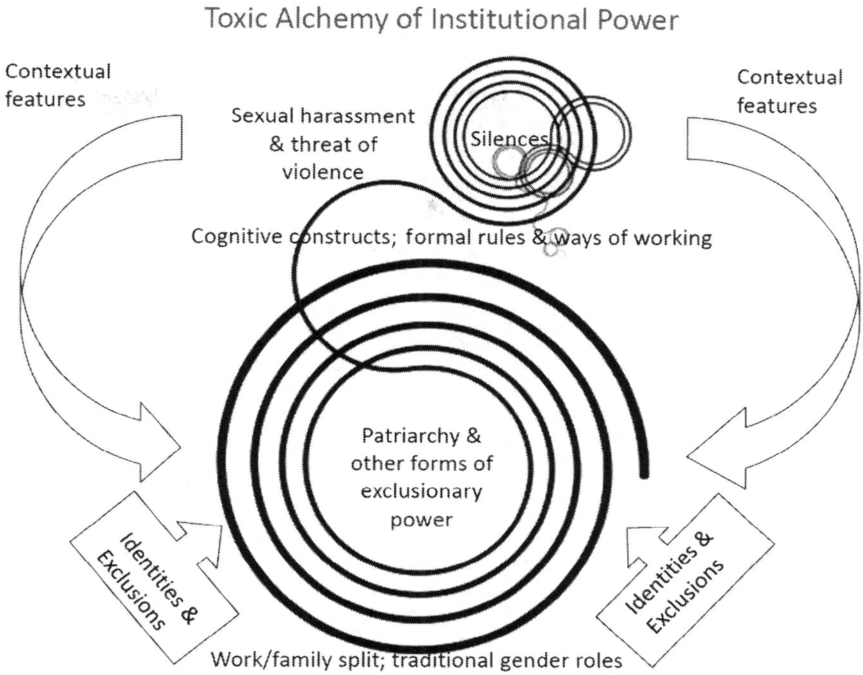

Toxic Alchemy of Institutional Power

FIGURE 3.3.2 Toxic alchemy of institutional power
Source: Rao et al. (2016, p. 147)

of leadership through a different structure – Mall Committees – was created and women began to question the culture of silence around gender discrimination in the union. Women also learned that cultural change required shifting the gender division of labour – not only in the workplace but also in the home and within the family – because traditional family norms burdened women with household responsibilities, thus restricting them from taking on leadership roles. In other words, organisational change required personal change and social change. Women needed to talk about issues that affected them: to not be silent but instead to share their experiences, particularly around sexual violence, with other women; and they had to deal with resistance from men who feared losing status if women advanced in union leadership.

Breaking silence and increasing accountability are key strategies for challenging deep structures of inequality, represented in the lower-left quadrant of the Framework. Organising is key to this. The organising by and in support of housekeeping staff in hotels in the US after the case of alleged sexual abuse by Dominique Strauss-Kahn, the former French Finance Minister and former head of the International Monetary Fund, is an example. While there is little data on the incidence of sexual harassment and abuse that hotel housekeepers face, the publicity garnered by the arrest of Kahn in 2011 for attacking a housekeeper at the Sofitel in New

York encouraged housekeepers around the country to report and sparked awareness and organising, including by unionised housekeepers. While still developing, concrete responses are emerging. In New York City, Seattle and other US cities, hotels are now required to provide housekeepers with panic buttons or electronic whistles, the concrete tools that would represent action in the top-right quadrant of the Framework. Unions and women's rights groups in the US are supporting organising to make this a standard across hotel chains, building on the laws and policies represented in the lower-right quadrant. Attitude change will hopefully follow. As one Seattle housekeeper pointed out: 'Now guests know that we are carrying a panic button … they'll probably think twice if they try to do anything bad' (quoted in Eidelson 2017).

The toxic alchemy of institutional power

Multiple factors and dynamics influence the form and character that discriminatory social norms and deep structures take in organisations. Figure 3.3.2 depicts the *toxic alchemy of institutional power* as it interacts with deep-seated societal norms that perpetuate exclusions which are condoned though silences and enforced by the threat of violence. This figure represents our take on making 'visible' key features of the bottom-left quadrant of the Gender at Work Framework. Circles and spirals are used to suggest movement – forward, backward and around – as well as layers of abuse and threat.

Patriarchy manifests in many different forms as depicted in Figure 3.3.2, for example in the *cognitive constructs* that influence how gender equality issues are

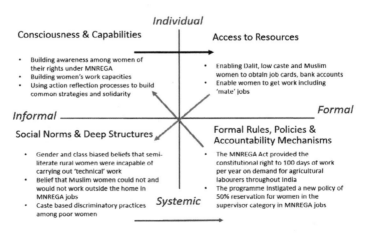

FIGURE 3.3.3 Mapping strategies to change institutional power: Dalit women's accountability project

Source: Aruna Rao's elaboration

framed and in the *rules and ways of working* within organisations, including which identities are privileged and which are silenced. Perhaps the most pervasive cognitive construct in the toxic alchemy of institutional power relates to the notion of public/private divides that deeply undervalue care work (unpaid work). Women disproportionately carry the responsibility for care work, especially the care of children and the elderly (Elson 2005). In organisations this is manifest in myriad ways: for example, women union members of SACCAWU were unable to attend union meetings at night because of lack of childcare and safe transport, thereby forfeiting power and influence.

Gender at Work's engagement with the Mahatma Gandhi National Rural Employment Guarantee Act (MGNREGA) in India offered many illustrations of the ways in which the toxic alchemy of power subverts and interrupts visionary efforts to advance equality from an intersectional perspective. MGNREGA came into force in India through an act of Parliament in 2005. It was the culmination of a long struggle by trade unions, workers' movements, and women's organisations and civil society groups supported by left parties. It guaranteed 100 days of work annually as a legal right, provided for unemployment benefits and made special provisions for women – including a 33 per cent reservation of jobs as well as equal wages for men and women.

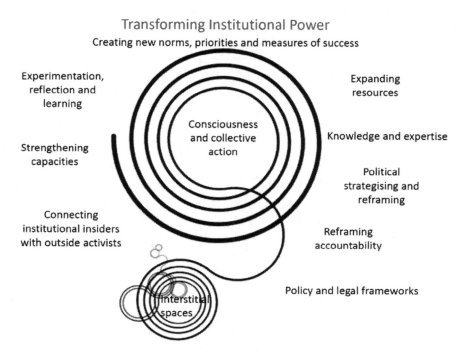

FIGURE 3.3.4 Transforming the toxic alchemy of institutional power
Source: Rao et al. (2016, p. 159)

While the legislation was visionary, its benefits were spread unevenly because of the gap that existed between what the legislation guaranteed and its implementation on the ground. Dalit women – who are on the lowest rung of the caste hierarchy – were denied their right to jobs and income because of the biases and actions of the people who implemented the programme: from programme officials who believed them to be incapable of taking on supervisory tasks, to members of the local governance councils who systematically kept them from accessing MGNREGA jobs. Because of their caste status, Dalit women would only get the most menial jobs, including within MGNREGA. Because they are women, they are condemned to having to endure the double burden of working within and outside the home. Moreover, the programme also bypassed poor Muslim women, who were believed not to be interested in or not permitted to do manual labour outside the home.

Gender at Work, in partnership with four local non-governmental organisations (NGOs), realised that for Dalit women to have equal access to MGNREGA resources, they would need to challenge and break deep-rooted discriminatory practices and stereotypes about women and work reflected in the programme's implementation. For example, in one pilot, Vanangana (one of the local NGOs) initiated an all-women's worksite engaged in building a large pond where Dalit women actively participated in all stages of planning and implementing the work. This model proved that women were capable of managing and taking decisions on 'technical' matters of a large worksite, including as 'mates' or supervisors. At the same time, it enabled greater interaction between women and local officials in the *panchayats* (village councils) and block and district administration with whom they had not interacted before.

At the end of Gender at Work's three-year engagement with the MGNREGA programme, vast numbers of Dalit and Muslim women were aware of their rights under MGNREGA and were trained in supervisory jobs: there was a 30 per cent increase in workdays for Dalit women; they gained job cards, bank accounts and income; and gained recognition in the eyes of their families and community. The programme strategies and outcomes are mapped onto the Gender at Work Framework (shown by arrows in Figure 3.3.3).

The action learning process, however, did something far more important: it enabled these women to connect to each other across class, caste and religious lines to form a sense of shared interests and solidarity, and to gain confidence in their abilities to act and advocate for themselves. This example starts to unpack the range of strategies that can be deployed to disrupt the toxic alchemy of power.

Strategies for transforming institutional power

We have used the toxic alchemy of institutional power as a metaphor for deep structures and how power works to help us understand and explore the bottom-left quadrant of the Analytical Framework. Figure 3.3.4 depicts strategies drawn from our experience that change agents have used to transform toxic institutional power. These strategies are multilayered and dynamic, and work across the other three quadrants by mobilising individual consciousness and agency, policy change and political strategising – using resources and opportunities, analysis and reflection, and calling on collective voices to demand, push for and make 'another world possible'. The strategies cascade together to appear again and again in stories of feminists and women's rights advocates engaged in social justice initiatives. Below is a quick overview of these:

- *Political strategising and reframing* are often starting points. The years of work that were invested in strategising and reframing violence against women from being a private issue to a public policy issue, followed by intensive *conscious-ness-raising and collective action*, have been translated into scores of *new norms, priorities and measures of success* as well as growing (though still inadequate) *resources* for support systems such as shelters, one-stop centres, hotlines and other spaces.
- The call in the UN's Sustainable Development Goals (SDGs) to recognise, reduce and redistribute unpaid care work emerged after decades of generation of *knowledge and expertise* by feminist economists to make a case for women's domestic work to be counted as having economic value.[2]
- The recent focus of many governments and the UN Security Council on women, peace and security – including recognition of the rape of women as a tactic of war and a national security issue – emerged (in part) because *feminists occupied interstitial spaces* within mainstream organisations to co-create more strategic pathways of action and work to *connect these institutional insiders with outside activists who effectively stepped up demand*. Together, insiders and outsiders continue to push *to generate institutional accountability with real consequences for transgression*, although the toxic alchemy of power often conspires to thwart these efforts.

In some ways, one of the most challenging strategies to deploy for transforming toxic alchemy is making space for *experimentation, reflection and learning*. Feminist organisations are starting to recognise this and make provision for it. Gender Action Learning processes use a variety of embodied and reflexive practices, including tai chi, to provoke this kind of reflection. Recently, Gender at Work Associates con-sulted Remmoho, a South African group that was interrogating problematic gender dynamics within activist collectives, as part of an ongoing effort to combine political strategising with reflection and learning. As Omotayo Jolaosho wrote:

> Together with a number of key facilitators, Remmoho members worked to create sessions where participants could freely discuss their daily lives, encom-passing and extending beyond their activism, including their familial relation-ships, sexuality, and living conditions … Sexuality was an important theme in discussions because it directly affected women's mobility in the world … Nomvula, a founding member of Remmoho, noted the transformation that

2   See https://www.un.org/sustainabledevelopment/.

came with discussing sexuality: *The biggest concept that gave us a breakthrough was being the owners of our own bodies because we realised that as women we don't own our bodies … I think sexuality is key when you're doing gender work because until someone knows how all these gender roles are actually constructed and what it means to me as an individual and as a woman in society you can't really get a breakthrough* (Jomalosho 2018, emphasis in original).

Chipping away at the toxic alchemy of institutional power is very challenging, not least because it is invisible, and has become so normalised and pervasive that it is taken for granted. Making progress in peeling back the layers can look like a small act – such as voting in more women leaders in a union – or can be a massive sea change in perceptions, such as the one provoked by the #MeToo movement.

In almost every example of progress toward equity and equality, however, as layers are peeled back, new manifestations of the toxic alchemy emerge. For example, around the world, information and communication technologies (ICTs) open up new job possibilities for young women, enable flexible work schedules and, through virtual work platforms, seem to reduce traditional hierarchical structures. IT companies such as Google have instituted diversity programmes to promote an inclusive environment to foster a culture in which those with alternative views, including different political views, feel safe sharing their opinions. However, in July 2017 a Google engineer published an internal memo – the 'Google Memo', which since went viral – in which he slams the diversity programme, saying that 'it is extreme to ascribe all disparities to oppression, and it is authoritarian to try to correct disparities through reverse discrimination' (quoted in Wakabayashi 2017). Instead, he argues that male/female disparities can be partly explained by biological difference; for example, women generally have a stronger interest in people rather than things, and tend to be more social, artistic and prone to neuroticism. This argument harkened back to an age-old belief that women are suited to specific kinds of tasks because they are biologically built that way and men are more competitive, and showed how hard it is to dislodge such inherently biased views despite education and generational change.

The devaluing of what is seen as 'care work' in organisations is a manifestation of gender bias transposed to the workspace that persists today. In CIMMYT, an agriculture research centre which is part of a 15-member network of the Consultative Group for International Agricultural Research (Merrill-Sands et al. 1999, p. 95), 'those who contributed in terms of strengthening collaborations, problem-solving, facilitating effective work processes, developing new methodologies, or managing tended to believe that their work was invisible'. Not only did this have consequences for individuals in the organisation, but it also militated against the kind of collaborative work that became increasingly necessary for developing farmer-oriented, sustainable solutions in a resource-poor and highly competitive market.

Moreover, the recent focus on sexual harassment is instructive: while individuals have been forced to step down from powerful positions in some instances, organisation-wide power inequities have rarely come under scrutiny in spite of the fact that it is widely acknowledged that sexual harassment thrives in environments where abuse of power is rampant. Organisations have often responded by mandating half-day training programmes for senior managers or engaging lawyers and human resources staff in formulating new policies and investigative procedures: in other words, taking action that remains (for the most part) on the formal side of the Gender at Work Framework. These actions send a strong signal that the response is, primarily, about maintaining the status quo when it comes to organisational power. These are responses that are often more focused on minimising organisational liability than they are on changing the norms and practices that enable sexual harassment in the first place.

For change experiments to create new norms and standards to sustain, organisations need to systematise accountability for what Malayah Harper, general secretary of the World YWCA, calls 'systemic backlash' (quoted in Wolfe 2018). First, this means enforcing rules about transparency of information on the extent of the problem and how it is being addressed in the organisation. Most of the information held by offices of internal oversight, which are often tasked with investigating transgressions, remains inaccessible and secret. Second, it means changing the rules about immunity when transgressions are serious and break the law. And, most importantly, it means confidential reporting mechanisms and third-party investigation and adjudication. According to one of the women who says she was harassed by Luiz Loures, the deputy executive director of UNAIDS: 'This is not just one individual, it's more than that … 'It's about how you establish a system that creates perks for the chosen ones, which is a group of senior men' (quoted in Ratcliffe 2018). Independent investigation mechanisms and processes can help crack the immunity of privileged senior men.

On the other hand, when organisations pull together multi-sectorial change teams – engaging women and men from all levels of the organisation who have been victims of sexual harassment in formulating policies and procedures, alongside top-level managers – this might signal a change in business as usual. When organisations listen and learn, bring in outside experts and engage in an emergent process of experimentation to understand what will disrupt abuse of power, this can signal that they are serious about interrogating the toxic alchemy and ushering in cultures of equality.

But are organisations now willing to invest in the long hard work of changing toxic institutional power? Without strong internal champions, dedicated resources and a strong push from outside constituencies, good intentions and initial enthusiasm often fizzle out. For example, BRAC – the largest NGO in the world, based in Bangladesh – had an innovative gender action learning programme covering all staff. It began in 1994 with top leadership support, and was led by a gender team with 50 programme facilitators to increase women's voice and leadership, build a culture of equality between women and men staff, and strengthen programmatic outcomes for women's welfare (Stuart et al. 2017). Within a short time span it achieved phenomenal success in changing discriminatory attitudes and behaviours – creating a safe space to question abusive power, challenge patriarchal values that underpin programmes and build new ways of working and relating. The programme was stopped after seven years, though some of its core features have survived in different initiatives. Now these focus exclusively on community groups. With changes in programme leadership and staff turnover, and a questioning of the value of this kind of investment in the current 'value for money' climate measured in dollars and cents, there is little chance for this work to be revived. As a result, an opportunity to genuinely 'mainstream' gender equality in BRAC's programmes by learning from this experience is slipping away.

Conclusion

Our experience has taught us that changes in social norms and deep structures are seldom caused by single interventions. As long as the rush is to 'get the policy right', gender equality policies will rarely take on deep structures directly. Policies and programmes are expected to deliver results in the short term, whereas changing social norms and deep structures – while critical to policy and programme success – take longer to deliver results. Instead, change is associated with a nexus of causalities, including forces in the larger society, social mobilisation, feminist leadership, policy change and resource increases. As well, changes in the deep structure do not happen all at once. Change is likely to be a slow process in which different aspects become more visible over time, are challenged and new ways of working are formulated.

The Gender at Work Framework helps us focus on these interconnected changes and norms and deep structures, and encourages us to unpack and understand what they look like in the particular context in which we work, untangle what is specific and what is universal, and look at how these dynamics interact with other domains of change in the Framework. If institutional power has been an important site for per-petuating gender inequalities and discrimination, it can also be transformed to become an important microcosm for demonstrating pathways for achieving cultures of equal-ity. As our examples illustrate, while discriminatory social norms and deep structures are resilient, they can be challenged – and new, more gender-equitable norms can emerge. Our most important learning is that when working on complex social change problems where solutions are unclear and pathways are tangled, strategising must include mapping deep structures and a clear intention to change them – or at least factor them in. Doing so is a means of ensuring that gains in other quadrants of the Gender at Work Framework can deliver their intended benefits to all.

References

Abrams, R. and Rashbaum, W.K., 2017. Harvey Weinstein paid off sexual harassment accusers for decades [online]. *New York Times*, 8 Oct. Available from: https://www.nytim es.com/2017/10/05/us/harvey-weinstein-harassment-allegations.html [Accessed 20 December 2018].

Chachra, M., 2017. Despite law, 70% working women do not report workplace sexual harassment; employers show poor compliance. *IndiaSpend*, 4 March. Available from: http://www.indiaspend.com/cover-story/despite-law-70-working-women-do-not-rep ort-workplace-sexual-harassment-employers-show-poor-compliance-94743 [Accessed 20 December 2018].

Connell, R.W., 1987. *Gender and power: society, the person and sexual politics*. London: Polity Press.

Eidelson, J., 2017. Hotels add 'panic buttons' to protect housekeepers from guests. *Bloomberg*, 13 December. Available from: https://www.bloomberg.com/news/articles/2017-12-13/hotels-add-panic-buttons-to-protect-housekeepers-from-guests [Accessed 20 December 2018].

Elson, D., 2005. Unpaid work, the Millennium Development Goals, and capital accumulation. Presentation at the Conference on unpaid work and the economy: gender, poverty, and the Millennium Development Goals, 1–3 October. New York, Levy Economics Institute.

Jomalosho, O., 2018. How movements like #metoo can address marginalization among activists. Gender at Work, 16 March. Available from: http://genderatwork.org/news/bringing-our-bodies-back-in [Accessed 20 December 2018].

Longwe, S.H., 1997. The evaporation of gender policies in the patriarchal cooking pot. *Development in Practice*, 7(2), 148–156.

Merrill-Sands, D., Fletcher, J. and Acosta, A., 1999. Engendering organizational change: a case study of strengthening gender equity and organizational effectiveness in an international agricultural research institute. In: A. Rao., R. Stuart, and D. Kelleher, eds. *Gender at work: organizational change for equality*. Hartford, CT: Kumarian Press.

Moore, J., 2018. U.N. cases read like 'manual in how not to investigate' sexual assault. *New York Times*. Available from: https://www.nytimes.com/2018/06/29/world/united-nations-sexual-assault.html?fbclid=IwAR2q_S0fcG6U7ptePS2SUUdK27D0XLHyyb FIYwFKxE70jrkyWVVWDkJ1O6c [Accessed 20 Dec 2018].

Rao, A.*et al.*, 2016. *Gender at work: theory and practice for 21st century organizations*. Abingdon: Routledge.

Rao, A. and Kelleher, D., 2002. What is Gender at Work's approach to gender equality and institutional change. Republic of the Philippines, National Machinery for Gender Equality and Women's Empowerment. Available from: https://library.pcw.gov.ph/sites/default/files/Gender%20at%20work%20Gender-Equality-and-Institutional-Change.pdf [Accessed 3 June 2019].

Ratcliffe, R., 2018. 'A boys' club': UN agency accused over sexual harassment claims. *The Guardian*. Available from: https://www.theguardian.com/global-development/2018/feb/24/un-former-employee-call-for-inquiry-sexism-bullying-harassment [Accessed 20 December 2018].

Stuart, R.*et al.*, 2017. *Advancing gender equality in Bangladesh*. Abingdon: Routledge.

Wakabayashi, D., 2017. Contentious memo strikes nerve inside Google and out. *New York Times*. Available from: https://www.nytimes.com/2017/08/08/technology/google-engineer-fired-gender-memo.html [Accessed 20 December 2018].

Wolfe, L., 2018. U.N. sexual assault investigations die in darkness. Foreign Policy. Available from: https://foreignpolicy.com/2018/03/08/how-u-n-sexual-assault-investigations-die-in-darkness/ [Accessed 20 December 2018].

3.4

FINDING THE RIGHT POWER TOOL(S) FOR THE JOB: RENDERING THE INVISIBLE VISIBLE

Jo Rowlands[1]

Introduction

There has been much thinking about understanding power and power relations and dynamics over the past few decades. You might imagine by now it would have become a strong focus of attention for anyone thinking about making change. You might also think that the activist would have access to many tools and much experience to assist in taking a wider and deeper view of how power is manifested in their area of action; that this would be actively used to inform effective approaches and contributions to change. In practice, while some people and organisations are deliberately exploring power in their practice (see chapters by VeneKlasen, Bradley, and Arce Andrade and Miller in this volume as prime examples) and using it to explore very innovative approaches to change and to work with methodologies that are themselves empowering, they remain outliers. Other organisations are clearly innovating, deliberately or accidentally, but not necessarily as a result of power analysis and specific intention. For many, power remains an implicit and opaque element of their work – something they somehow 'sense' or 'intuit' rather than approach deliberately. As someone interested in exploring, understanding and shifting power in favour of the well-being of people who generally lose out in current dominant power relations (Rowlands 1995), I have great curiosity about how to bring nuanced understanding of power into the everyday thinking and practice of activists and change agents. In my role as Governance Adviser for Oxfam over many years, I have had multiple opportunities to try different things to support both staff and partners in a wide range of contexts to deepen their analysis. Elsewhere, I have reflected on some of the

1   This chapter draws on conversations with and comments from Oxfam staff in Viet Nam, Mexico, the Democratic Republic of the Congo (DRC), Nepal, Myanmar, Peru and a number of individuals in cross-boundary roles. Particular thanks to Rosie McGee and Jethro Pettit for comments on earlier drafts.

experience of using power analysis to inform programmes of action and attempts to develop capacities to do so within Oxfam (Rowlands 2016). In this chapter, I will explore further some of the issues raised there, and continue to explore the challenge of embedding these approaches systematically into the work of a large organisation. Through my work with Oxfam over the years, I have seen that people need three interconnected elements to support effective power analysis. One element is to have frameworks, or approaches, which help to disentangle the complex web of dynamics that make up power so that power can be better understood. A second is to have a way of exploring how change happens so that power can be navigated. The third element is to have a set of tools to support the building of power where power is not a zero-sum thing, which is essential if power relations are to change in practice. In my work supporting teams to do, among other things, power analysis, I am often asked for a tool that will make all of this easy, and I hope this chapter will help those people understand why they do not get exactly what they ask for.

Why power analysis?

People analyse and navigate power all the time, both in their daily lives and in their communities and organisations. Commonly, if activists carry out power analysis, it is done 'instinctively' and based on what we already know or think we know about the world, the issues, the actors and the structures within which we operate.[2] This is inevitably a partial picture. How we personally experience power is affected by our own positionality, our life experience, our values and our accumulated knowledge. This is one of the strongest arguments I know for working with diverse teams, so that we aggregate that knowledge and experience and bring a wider range of values and assumptions and experiences to bear on our efforts. That may be enough for some to identify increasingly effective approaches. However not everyone's 'instinctive' approach is grounded on sufficient experience or accurate knowledge and understanding about existing power and change dynamics. If people want to be effective change agents in situations of unfair power relations, and avoid investing effort in areas that are unlikely to be productive, gaps in understanding need to be identified and, if possible, filled. My working assumption is that addressing power deliberately and intentionally to inform understanding of context and processes of strategy and design will open up fresh entry points and enable creative combinations of approaches, methods and alliances for change. It will also help us challenge the limits of our own knowledge and identify areas where it is insufficient. This is particularly essential if the purpose of so doing is to transform power relations in some way, and where power is unequally distributed.

---

2   I use 'we' to refer to activists and change agents working for progressive change in power relations in favour of those normally disadvantaged by existing dominant power dynamics – of whom I consider myself one. This is not intended to imply any uniformity of perspective among what is a very diverse group.

The realities within which most if not all activists and changemakers work are constrained. We have limited resources – people, time, money and capacities – and so many of the changes we seek are surrounded and shaped by complexity. One motive for doing a good power analysis then is to identify ways of aligning those resources to best effect. This is as useful to a large organisation as it is to a small one. In a large one there is a sizeable challenge in supporting people to develop the skills and incentivising investment in their application. In Oxfam, different parts of the organisation use different frameworks to guide their work, so we need to equip people to apply power analysis through whatever approaches and tools they need to use in practice – whether they are part of a campaigning focus, a humanitarian response or longer-term development programming.[3] Then there is the issue of how individuals think, learn and operate: some people are comfortable with absorbing theoretical ideas and then trying to apply them; others prefer much more detailed guidance, and to work from checklists. One size does not fit all.

I am particularly interested in how people learn to do broader, deeper power analysis, and how it becomes embedded in their thinking so that it actively shifts into part of what I earlier referred to as an 'instinctive' approach to power analysis. How does it become a habit, something automatic, constantly reiterated, rather than something that needs to be added on – an extra task which will always look like more work, more effort, for which more time and resources are needed? Can it help generate understanding of puzzling questions such as why people support things that don't appear to be in their interests, or go along with situations that do not appear to benefit them?[4]

Ways of analysing power

Frameworks/approaches

As mentioned earlier, one element of power analysis needs to be thinking about what power is, the forms it takes and how it behaves. There are frameworks or approaches available to support power analysis, such as the powercube (Gaventa 2006 and Gaventa this volume), which provide a conceptual frame for deliberately unpacking and explicitly exploring the aspects of power embedded in the issues, actors, structures and processes surrounding the issue. There is also the framework I explored in my earlier work that supports thinking about the kinds of power – *power with, power within, power to* – that can be built and strengthened (Rowlands 1997). These frameworks or approaches support users to stretch and question their understandings of power and its dynamics explicitly. They can help identify gaps in knowledge, and explore how different aspects of power might be articulating with each other (across levels, for example, or in the ways the different expressions of

---

3   My exposure has been more to the long term and campaigning work, and this is reflected in the experience I draw on in this chapter.
4   What Pettit (2016) refers to as 'civic habitus'.

power interact). The powercube provides a way of differentiating and mentally organising different elements to support a systematic approach to analysing reality. Many framings of power are useful; but the goal I have in mind in using them is to work with people to internalise and embed the ways of thinking required to develop what we might call 'power literacy',[5] which can then be applied through whichever frameworks or approaches are chosen.

Our positionality can affect how and what we perceive as reality. For many in the formal development sector, for example, the habit of thinking that what we do is about 'development', and therefore not about politics, can restrict the ability to perceive the full range of power relations. This includes the power embedded in our own roles, organisations and resources, and our individual personal power. It often keeps us overly focused on the economic elements of power, curtailing our thinking to within the frame of 'project' approaches.[6] This has contributed to perhaps an over-reliance on the framework of political economy analysis, with its particular emphasis on actors and their interests, to the detriment of the use of other approaches to understanding power that is socialised and internalised. It has thereby limited the kinds of 'solutions' sought in many major problem areas. That doesn't mean the political economy framework has no use or relevance to power analysis; but it should be used with an awareness of its limitations, and as a minimum overlaid with gender analysis (Haines and O'Neill 2018). It is a very different approach from solidarity, for example, which would introduce very different elements of invisible power.

How does change happen?

One useful constant refrain that can add value to power analysis, whichever approach or tools are being used, is: How does change happen, on this topic, in this context, at this moment in time? Combining work on theories of change and action with power analysis can ensure that power analysis is used purposefully, and can help us avoid getting lost in detail or side-tracked into fascinating but not immediately relevant analysis. A good power framework doesn't necessarily help unpack how change might happen; but when combined with thinking through how change happens (or, significantly, is prevented from happening) – whether as part of the development of a formal 'theory of change' or 'theory of action', or not – it can lead to many insights and possibilities for the activist. Thinking about how change happens can be a good vehicle for introducing a power-aware perspective, and very much lends itself to power-aware application of the 'indirect power tools' (see below) that help one understand how change happens around here and can be expected to happen in a particular initiative. This in turn informs the kinds of coalitions or

5   Thanks to Duncan Green for suggesting this term.
6   There is, of course, also the issue of how power is embedded in the concept and 'mindset' of development itself, shaping thinking about what kind of activity it requires – but that is a story outside the scope of this short chapter.

constellations of allies that will be needed, the kinds of actors, institutions or processes to target with action and so on.

What tools and methods?

Another element is the many and various tools that are not necessarily designed to explore power directly, but which unpack the way power dynamics operate in the world, as embedded in particular actors and structures or institutions such as government, enterprise, community group, etc. or in particular processes, and in the interests pursued by them. When we use such 'indirect power tools', such as stakeholder mapping, force field analysis, or problem trees, we implicitly draw and map power – but it is very easy to overlook some forms of power. Commonly, for example, the invisible power of the norms and beliefs that hold a particular set of actors in relation to each other in a particular way, and that are deeply linked to history and culture, are overlooked. These generally applicable tools can be made much more potent if we find ways of using the 'lens' of a power framework to overlay them with explicit attention to the forms and expressions of power. They can also be supplemented with work on narratives. In this way, tools that were designed for a general (often management-focused) purpose and application can become aids to identifying power issues and support power-aware strategising. Tools can make us feel safe and confident; but it is clear that we have to bring our wider understanding of power – our frameworks and approaches as well as our wider knowledge and experience, which together form the way we see and understand reality – to inform their use.

Power is also embedded and embodied in individuals in various ways: privilege, knowledge and experience; wealth and control over resources; manner (arrogance, humility); personality or celebrity. Identity plays a big part in power. As activists and changemakers, how do we see ourselves in the power mix? This affects how we perceive what is possible. Being able to step back, be self-reflexive and observe is a useful skill to cultivate. It will affect the way we are able to make use of the range of tools to support analysis and to apply effectively a power lens to their use.

Use of one or more frameworks to think about power, in conjunction with thinking about how change happens and then bringing practical 'indirect power tools' to bear to unpack how power is present and operating – can open up a wide range of possibilities and options for contributing to change. Then comes the critical part: making political judgements and choices, and putting those choices into action. Doing a thorough job of the power analysis can be immobilising if it does not include the essential process of strategic choice-making that takes it towards action. It should make it possible to go forward with confidence – and with a good awareness of how plans may need to adapt as action tests the accuracy of the analysis and any assumptions that were made, or opens up new areas of deeper understanding to inform what comes next.

Examples from practice: Oxfam's experience

Overview

In Oxfam, we do not tell people how to do power analysis, or how to use it to inform the work we do. We do, however, require our teams to work with a set of values, as mentioned above, and objectives that require attention to power to implement. Oxfam's core mission is about reducing poverty and suffering. So, for example, gender equality and women's rights will be central components, along with any intersectional issues needed in the particular context. Inequality and injustice are centre stage. If you work on these you have to address power. Our teams are free to use the tools they choose, that are judged useful for the purpose they are pursuing – whether that be a campaign or support to local partners in addressing some governance issue.

Many teams use political economy analysis (PEA) (Pettit and Mejía Acosta 2014). This is quite an undertaking, can be expensive and can easily sit on a shelf once done, especially if findings are sensitive. We have experimented with using PEA in a way that makes sure to focus on invisible power as well as the formal and shadow elements of political economy, and which uses the bottom-up experience and knowledge of our staff and partners rather than external 'experts' (Oxfam GB and Oxford Policy Management 2013). Done this way, the findings may be less 'rigorous' in the sense usually used in conventional, and especially quantitative, research (with the limitations that implies), but with more locally based and informal knowledge that brings a different kind of rigour through drawing on local and subaltern knowledge and the granularity of lived experience. It is still a time-consuming and laborious exercise. One challenge with PEA is that, as mentioned earlier, the terminology tends to confirm people's thinking into conventional framings around politics and economics. PEA is generally based on a neo-classical world view and behaviourist assumptions about human behaviour and motivations – in other words, it springs from a particular form of invisible power that is deeply embedded in development approaches, and which may not be exposed by working from within that frame. It assumes a primary focus on maximising utility, incentives and rewards, and looks at opportunity costs and forms of cooperation based on self-interest. This PEA approach to analysis also generally fails to render describable much of the invisible power that holds any given political economy in place through people's expectations, assumptions and attitudes. In particular, it tends to fix in place an understanding of economics that excludes non-monetised elements such as care work and environmental common goods, which can particularly skew benefits and control away from women and more marginalised groups. PEA approaches to power analysis are therefore easily skewed towards particular perspectives and values that can very subtly limit the user's ability to see a full picture or go beyond the dominant frame of analysis. So it takes a determined effort to use PEA in ways that do not limit thinking to the familiar dominant narratives.

Most Oxfam programmes, if not all, will use stakeholder mapping as a core approach to power analysis. As I have described elsewhere (Rowlands 2016), the degree to which deep and broad power analysis is achieved with the use of these tools varies considerably; but there has been a noticeable and steady, if not even, increase in quality achieved over time. Where people used to approach stakeholder mapping as an exercise in listing individuals and organisations with an interest in the issue under exploration and categorising and assessing the nature of their interest and influence, more often now it is approached as a way to unpack power dynamics, to explore interrelationships and identify pressure points, gaps, opportunities and new potential alliances. Some of our teams have deliberately sought out the invisible power in how stakeholders are mapped in order to identify new approaches to the change processes they are supporting (see the Peru example in Box 3.4.1).

BOX 3.4.1 ON STAKEHOLDER ANALYSIS

Stakeholder analysis is a common method which can be used in a range of ways:

- *Basic*: a list of stakeholders, perhaps with interests and attitudes to the issue; power on the specific issue, e.g. as blockers, champions or undecided.
- *Sometimes*: Now what? – how they interrelate, what would be needed to make change happen; how to reach and create an influencing coalition to tip the balance.
- *Rarely*: looking at individuals within organisations and institutions. Can we engage (or isolate) – need a lot more knowledge of the internal workings of institutions and often can't go there – black box effect. Knowing the people takes TIME; enough nuance to 'dance with the system' (Meadows 2008). Do not underestimate the power of personal connections (church, family, etc.).

Some of the problems with stakeholder analysis include:

- a tendency to focus mostly on visible power – you have to dig hard for hidden power (e.g. church, private sector, military, illicit) and it can be risky;
- it can be hard to reflect invisible power in a stakeholder map – it's easier through stories and narrative;
- a tendency not to look beyond national borders, even if most power is elsewhere in the system.

In specific areas of work, most notably the work on gender justice, our teams use an approach to gender analysis that makes some of the historically less visible power explicit (see Rao and Sandler, this volume). Up to now, on the whole if a team is working with one of these tools for making gendered power explicit, they are likely to use that as the primary approach to power analysis for the work in question. There is great potential in combining frameworks – using this one alongside the powercube, for example – since they flag up very different things. This would support people in checking that their habitual ways of thinking (presuming that these are reflected in the initial choice of primary framework/approach) are challenged, since each gives a very distinctive framing of an issue. My expectation would be that this would be helpful in working to join up and create synergy across some of the different areas of work/activism, particularly between campaigning approaches and the ground-level work that underpins the organisation's legitimacy in campaigning. In practice, many people are uncomfortable with mixing frameworks, and a process facilitator very comfortable with the complexity involved can be helpful.

Putting it into practice

At this point I want to share some small examples from Oxfam's experience in its country programmes.

Tanzania: Chakua Hatua (Take Action)

This programme to encourage 'active citizenship' in two regions of Tanzania was designed to address the issue that many people in the country are deterred from taking action as citizens. There are many reasons for this which can't be unpacked here; but the programme was designed to build levels of confidence, knowledge and skills among a group of local people to enable them to play what was called an 'animator role': this would have them work with their local community to identify, understand and act on issues identified by local people as being of priority concern. Oxfam did not want to identify or prescribe what those issues might be. It wanted to provide support for locally prioritised activism, without directing it in any way. People already active in some way, but not as conventional leaders, were invited to participate in the programme. In an early programme visit I joined the Oxfam team meeting these people and hearing how they were thinking about local issues. Early in the trip, we found ourselves waiting for half an hour to make a necessary courtesy call to a local dignitary. I used the opportunity to introduce the team to the basic ideas of visible, hidden and invisible power, and to the ideas of *power to, power with, power within* and *power over*: a 30-minute, top-level theoretical introduction to some new ideas. The official turned up, we met and went on our way. A week later, we had a meeting to do a detailed debrief of the visits. With no prompting from me, all the analysis of the various conversations that had been held came out through the lens for those ways of thinking about power, combined with a gendered perspective. The team was excited to use this thinking to shape the training and accompaniment that would be provided over the following few years, and to guide programme staff in keeping the initiative focused on supporting the building of power for some pretty marginalised communities. The programme had significant successes in supporting communities to act on a wide range of issues of their own choosing and initiative, including financial compensation for land taken, the removal of corrupt officials and restitution of funds diverted for local people.[7]

Myanmar

Oxfam's programme of work in Myanmar has, among other areas, had a strong focus on issues of power and governance. Post Cyclone Nargis, this was in support of the opening up of a newly democratised country after decades of military rule. Things were very fluid after the 2010 election; the legal framework was evolving rapidly and there was great scope for supporting ordinary people to be part of the extraordinary shift in how power was organised. Oxfam set up a step-by-step social accountability programme, supporting civil society groups to begin to build constructive relationships with local government, as the latter was working out how to play its role. After initial caution on both sides, this began to be built. More recently, however, it has become clear that the opening up, at least in its democratic angle, was slowing – and in some dimensions beginning to reverse. In the parts of the country affected by violent conflict, the context is becoming increasingly difficult and is not meeting people's expectations of the new government.

The Oxfam team has had to change from trying to keep up with power relations that were moving rapidly in a positive direction, to understanding and navigating a rapidly shifting (politically and socially) context, particularly for civic actors. It has proved very helpful to use a careful focus on hidden and invisible power in thinking about how to work within such a sensitive aid context. Understanding hidden power is challenging, given that it involves the internal dynamics of the military, which maintains significant power despite partial democratisation. This not only takes time, it also takes great sensitivity and political literacy; it has to be about specifics. And you cannot always be sure that what you think you know is accurate. The environment is filled with unreliable information and rumour. The team has to pay attention to detail and nuance, both of which are constantly fluctuating. Invisible power is a major factor: not only in terms of understanding the cultural environments (there are many) within which we work and the roles of identity in relation to power, but also to factor in the effects of decades if not centuries of physical and psychological violence and trauma, fear and disinformation. The widespread absence of trust is a strong feature. Invisible power also leaves people vulnerable to manipulation and constrained expectations and

7   https://oxfamblogs.org/fp2p/building-accountability-in-tanzania-applying-an-evolu tionaryventure-capitalist-theory-of-change/; https://oxfamblogs.org/fp2p/what-use-a re-models-of-change-an-experiment-in-tanzania/; https://oxfamblogs.org/fp2p/shoul d-you-keep-innovating-as-a-programmeme-matures-dilemmas-from-a-ground-brea king-accountability-programmeme-in-tanzania/; https://oxfamblogs.org/fp2p/what-dif ference-does-accountability-make-six-real-life-examples-from-tanzania-and-a-grea t-job-opportunity/.

ambition. We have used conflict-sensitive PEA[8] – done both by our staff and partners and by 'experts' – and have found conflict analysis to be another frame through which to understand power and power dynamics. We have also used the powercube and gender analysis. No single approach has given us everything we need. In addition, as an external organisation working with government permission, we have to constantly navigate our own position and power, how it is perceived by others and how it might play into or fall foul of the power dynamics of the shifting space.

Peru

The Oxfam team in Peru have worked hard to get to grips with a context characterised by the capture of formal political power by specific entrenched economic interests. Substantial but un-redistributed growth has further concentrated decision-making power in the hands of elites. Political parties do not offer real mechanisms for representation, and the familiar civil society strategies have failed to open up decision-making to address serious inequality and meet the needs of poor and marginalised people. Many spaces for activism are blocked, with the digital space emerging as one avenue for discussion, debate and dissent. Traditional media houses are owned by the same elite with vested interests in perpetuating narratives of neo-liberal growth and investment. Following a dismantling of the left during the dictatorship of Alberto Fujimori, social movements have traditionally focused on confrontational mechanisms like strikes and road blocks – protests that have failed to deliver change, failed to capture the imagination of young people or engage the middle classes – and their leadership is not being renewed. A fresh analysis of power dynamics and power mapping led the team to seek out new approaches that centre on invisible power (power of elites), focusing on shifting the terms of debate and supporting voices to come through that do not easily get heard. Through a series of 'inequality labs', a form of participatory action research, they have built intergenerational and intersectional bridges between civic actors, formal non-governmental organisations (NGOs), informal youth movements, academics, investigative journalists and progressive influencers that intentionally level the power dynamics between old and new movements. This has enabled the construction of a shared, coherent narrative. Part of the strategy has been creating an online neutral space where narratives that challenge the dominant story in Peru can safely emerge and be amplified, pushing these out into the wider public domain, and where new connections and alliances can be made in a way that supports young people to challenge. The team sees power analysis and understanding politics as essential and continuous processes.

These three very different snapshots of Oxfam's experience of power analysis show the wide variety of approaches that can be taken. They illustrate that power analysis is not about using magic tools, but about embedding a way of thinking and seeing things to help uncover how power of different kinds flows through the actors, institutions

---

8   http://www.conflictsensitivity.org/how-to-guide/.

and processes of society to inform action. None of them claim to be complete or authoritative; all of them illustrate the need for power analysis to be ongoing rather than a one-off exercise; all of them led the teams to understand the issues they were addressing at a significantly deeper level than previously. This has been a deeper exploration where the team included a diversity of experience and perspective, including partners and other trusted people with local knowledge.

Lessons from Oxfam's experience

Two simple tools for digging deeper

As explored earlier, tools are best when used within the wider frame of a framework/approach and an understanding of how change happens. With that proviso, here are some that may be less familiar to the general reader, which we have found useful in Oxfam.

The five whys[9]

This one is useful for all sorts of things; but used with a power analysis perspective, it can be very helpful in digging deeper, and helping people go into a more nuanced and complex understanding. It is very simple: you keep asking why? Five iterations usually deliver useful thinking. We have used this quite a lot with our teams in Latin America, and they find it simple and unintimidating. Why is there violence against women, for example, or why is person x able to have so much influence? And why is that; and why is that; and why is that; and why is that? It helps go beyond simple description, to understanding the policy blocks, the implementation issues and the invisible power of the underlying ideas and beliefs and norms. Unlike a problem tree, it doesn't allow people to get stuck trying to work out if something is a symptom or a cause; it just keeps digging.

Power analysis focusing on the 'subject'

A lot of power analysis looks at an issue or a system to understand the kinds of power flowing through it and the actors and institutions involved. That approach can make it too easy to lose sight of the purpose of the analysis. We have found it useful to turn this upside down by exploring the power relations that surround a particular person we are trying to support, such as an indigenous woman in her daily life.

What power surrounds her? How does it prevent her getting out of poverty?
What language is used?
Which norms and attitudes affect her on a daily basis, negatively or positively?
Which actors and institutions does she engage with or not engage with?
How does she make her voice heard?

9   My colleague Thomas Dunmore Rodrigues affectionately calls this the 'toddler tool'.

What visible and formal power most impinges on her life?
Which hidden or shadow power affects her most?
With whom can she build *power with*? and so on.

Getting help

One lesson that stands out across many experiences of doing power analysis is that, whatever frameworks and tools you might choose to use, most people benefit significantly from having someone accompanying the process and providing facilitation support where needed. Often we are doing power analysis of something where we have a personal involvement; and someone a bit outside the context can be a great help in stepping back and taking a wider perspective than usual, perhaps looking at a wider view of a system. In particular, accompaniment and facilitation have value when the issues are emotive, or where divergent opinions, passionately held, are brought together to strengthen the thinking. It is also very useful when different ways of thinking about power are being combined, or where the people are not familiar or perhaps comfortable with the more abstract and theoretical elements. An added benefit can be that someone accompanying a process over time, through various iterations, can be very helpful in managing the discontinuities of changes in people's involvement, staff turnover and so on, helping build on previous work rather than repeatedly covering the same ground.

Accompaniment and facilitation are different issues from that of who might lead a process of power analysis. In Oxfam's Viet Nam programme, for example, a decision was made to support a partner to lead a key power analysis process. This was seen as the right thing to do, in terms of the power relationship between Oxfam and the partner organisation, and was useful in achieving a shared analysis that was based on important local readings of power relations and in validating the partnership; but at the same time, the process was constrained by how concepts and tools were understood and used, and through the ways that people in that context were used to thinking and working, given the political environment around them. In that particular instance, shared leadership might have supported some more challenging power analysis, without losing the crucial element of informed interpretation for a sensitive context.

One particular challenge in the process of power analysis is how to identify what you don't know. A lot will always be unknown; some things can only be guessed at. How do you work out what is essential to unpack and what can wait? What level of power analysis is 'good enough'? In particular, it will not be enough to conclude 'it's hidden power' or 'political capture' or 'there's a lack of political will': to be useful, specific detail is needed. If power is well hidden, what can be done to uncover enough to make good choices of where to invest effort and what to avoid?

Conclusion

I have told the story of my perception of the organisational journey Oxfam has been on in relation to power analysis (Rowlands 2016), the obstacles faced, the challenge of preparing people effectively to do power analysis, and how to bring continuity in a continuously changing combination of people and areas of focus. It is inevitably a partial picture. One conclusion I have reached more recently is that the set of values that underpins our power analysis matters; and that if individuals have internalised those values – in Oxfam's case, accountability, empowerment and inclusiveness – the application of power analysis will have clear motivation behind it and be easier to address through whichever tools or approaches are chosen. Power analysis, in itself, may be a neutral thing; but its use in practice has purpose behind it and is therefore necessarily normative.

In working with power analysis, we are undertaking a triple process of: disentangling and understanding power; exploring how to navigate power within an understanding of how change happens; and building and mobilising power, seeking where possible to reduce or remove obstacles to shifting power relations in favour of people are disadvantaged and excluded. For that you need to look at potentials for building power, and at the obstacles to building power. I am increasingly convinced that this requires a strong emphasis on invisible power in terms of ambition to shift norms and culture – people's expectations. This matters for building hope, exploring the potential for collaboration and looking beyond the traditional familiar ways things are done for approaches that will break the cycles, challenge assumptions and explore what possibly could be, and not just what you think could be – none of which is easy. But a strong focus on invisible power is also significant for understanding what holds visible and hidden forms of power in place. There is a sense in which I think power analysis, done well, is as much about stretching the imagination as it is about describing and explaining things.

Power is fluid and constantly shifting, so the process of analysis is essentially never complete or finished. This gives us a tension to navigate between pragmatism and effectiveness: how to judge when a power analysis is good enough? On the one hand we probably never have the full picture in all its complexity and multi-dimensionality; but there are risks inherent in not doing enough, especially where there is a strong role played by hidden power such as in the Myanmar and Peru examples above. The solution to this tension is probably a combination of seeing it as a constant, ongoing process rather than as a one-off or periodic exercise, and of designing action to be adaptable – especially in more fragile contexts – with reflection and learning moments built into our plans from the start.

Power is a personal thing, not an objective 'out there' force; and putting ourselves into the analysis is important, wherever in the scheme of things that puts us: realism matters, as do honesty and humility. Because of this, any use of frameworks and tools cannot be separated from intent, values and purpose, as I have already said – or from who is using them.

Power operates at many levels in interconnected ways. The frameworks and approaches to think about each level may stay constant; but the tools we use and the methods will need to fit the needs of the people and cultures at the different levels. So adaptation, flexibility and good judgement are also required in the choice and use of tools and methods, and in the language and examples used in communicating about power. Everyone lives surrounded by power, and will have knowledge and experience to contribute about how it works – so long as they are not expected to use technical language they are unfamiliar with.

It is both energising and daunting to keep remembering that striving to understand and work with power is no abstract exercise: the conclusions we draw and the choices and actions we take as a result can be risky, for us or others, can lay us open to attack and at the same time can contribute to real and positive change in real people's lives. Power analysis, beyond any academic curiosity, is not an end in itself, but is always connected with understanding how change happens in relation to specific changes and, I very much hope, to supporting those changes to increasingly materialise.

References

Gaventa, J., 2006. Finding the spaces for change: a power analysis. *IDS Bulletin*, 37(6), 23–33.

Haines, R. and O'Neill, T., 2018. Putting gender in political economy analysis: why it matters and how to do it. Gender & Development Network Briefings. May 2018. London: Gender and Development Network. Available from: http://gadnetwork.org/ga dn-news/2018/5/9/putting-gender-in-political-economy-analysis-why-it-matters-a nd-how-to-do-it [Accessed 30 Oct 2018].

Meadows, D., 2008. *Thinking in systems: a primer*. Chelsea: Green Publishing.

Oxfam GB and Oxford Policy Management, 2013. *How politics and economics intersect: a simple guide to conducting political economy and context analysis* [online]. Oxford: Oxfam GB. Available from: http://policy-practice.oxfam.org.uk/publications/how-politics-and-economics-inter sect-a-simple-guide-to-conducting-political-eco-312056 [Accessed 30 Oct 2018].

Pettit, J. and Mejía Acosta, A., 2014. Power above and below the waterline: bridging political economy and power analysis. *IDS Bulletin*, 45(5), 9–22.

Pettit, J., 2016. Why citizens don't engage: power, poverty and civic habitus. *IDS Bulletin*, 47(5), 89–102.

Rowlands, J., 1995. Empowerment examined. *Development in Practice*, 5(2), 101–107.

Rowlands, J., 1997. *Questioning empowerment*. Oxford: Oxfam.

Rowlands, J., 2016. Power in practice: bringing understandings and analysis of power into development action in Oxfam. *IDS Bulletin*, 47(5), 119–130.

PART 4

Understanding agency: social action for shifting power

4.1

POWER AND AGENCY IN VIOLENT SETTINGS

Marjoke Oosterom[1]

Introduction

This chapter discusses how power analysis can be used to gain an understanding of how experiences of violent conflict affect people's agency and positions in power relationships, and can help identify potential avenues for people regaining a sense of agency. Violent conflict has diverse and lasting impact on the people who have experienced it. This is not just the result of violence itself: dynamics of violence affect society and the public sphere at large, when powerful actors exercise control over public discourses (Oosterom 2016), and when social norms and institutions change (Justino et al. 2013). Conflict and violence thus become social conditions in which people live their lives (Lubkemann 2008). Often, conflict-affected settings are highly dynamic, with shifting configurations of power and high levels of uncertainty (Vigh 2006). Yet in the midst of these dynamics, people continue with everyday life struggles alongside their efforts to stay safe. The agency people have extends to trying to create order in the dynamic environment that is a conflict setting, and trying to influence configurations of power and maximising opportunities to their advantage (Utas 2005, Vigh 2006).

I address a number of questions. How can power analysis help to understand the impact of violence, on local power relations and especially on people's voice and agency? How can it help identify ways to overcome fear and move from individual to more collective forms of agency? When would people consider their agency to be empowering? The chapter offers some examples of people who managed to help protect others or reduce the impact of a violent environment. Rarely, however, were such instances likely to scale up to overcome the deeper causes of

1 I am very grateful to all participants of the different studies cited here, who were willing to share their stories, and my co-researchers who cared deeply about them. I thank Rosie McGee and Jethro Pettit for valuable feedback on earlier drafts of this chapter.

violence. Using evidence from different contexts, I want to convey two points. First of all, while people living in violent settings are agents who try shape their lives to the best of their ability, they may not think of their agency as empowering or as influencing a wider process of change. In these contexts it is extremely challenging to go beyond coping agency and have 'citizen agency' that challenges or negotiates more powerful actors. Secondly, I want to show that invisible power in violent contexts is not limited to social norms and beliefs, but extends to the embodied knowledge of past experiences of violence.

The chapter is based on various qualitative studies I carried out between 2010 and 2016 in Uganda, South Sudan and Zimbabwe, together with researchers based in academia and civil society.[2] All studies focused on the effects of violence on people's agency in one way or another, but were situated in very different contexts in terms of the dynamics of violence and conflict. The study in northern Uganda looked at the effects of conflict and displacement on citizenship and citizen engagement in the aftermath of the armed conflict between the Government of Uganda and the Lord's Resistance Army (LRA), an insurgent group which evolved from the late 1980s to 2006 (Oosterom 2016). The study in South Sudan was conducted in Imatong State in 2013, thus prior to the third civil war, when insecurity was mainly caused by numerous inter- and intra-community conflicts, as well as militia groups. Conducted with researchers from women's human rights organisations, this study explicitly addressed gendered experiences and responses to insecurity (Oosterom 2017). The study in Zimbabwe focused on the agency of youth in response to political violence in a repressive regime context (Oosterom and Pswarayi 2014). The chapter thus speaks mainly to the context of Sub-Saharan Africa, and the methods were designed with particularities of the contexts in mind. Violence dynamics and the effects on people will be different in other contexts, and this is important to consider when applying the learning from these studies to other settings.

I start this chapter with a review of the literature that links everyday experiences of violence and violent conflict to agency and power. I will then discuss a number of methodological issues that need to be considered when doing research on power relations in violent settings. In subsequent sections I will explain the methodologies used to generate in-depth understandings of power and agency in relation to violence, and how power analysis frameworks help reveal how people cope with, and in some instances mitigate, violence and its effects. This leads to a final section in which I reflect on different forms of agency, and when it leads to empowerment.

2   The project entitled 'The effects of conflict on citizen engagement in northern Uganda' was carried out between 2009 and 2013. The studies in South Sudan and Zimbabwe were part of the programme 'Power, Violence, Citizenship and Agency', which ran from 2013 to 2015. All three studies were supported by ICCO and Hivos, international non-governmental organisations based in the Netherlands.

Experiences of insecurity and violence in everyday life

It was long assumed that violent conflict results in chaos: a vacuum of authority and a disintegration of social institutions and other forms of social life (Vigh 2006). Although social institutions *are* constantly being disintegrated during prolonged periods of crisis, they are also being transformed and rebuilt, as are different configurations of power (Justino et al. 2013, Lubkemann 2008, Vigh 2006). The concept of the 'everyday' draws attention to the ways in which people seek to influence, reorganise and appropriate the structures that influence their lives, and seek to reorganise power (Certeau 1988). Further, Vigh (2006) argues that if crisis becomes *chronic* it becomes the anticipated reality for most people. They will 'normalise' certain forms of violence as something that is part and parcel of their environment; and when uncertainty becomes the norm it becomes the context, or background, against which everyday life continues to be produced (see also Lubkemann 2008). Rather than mere acts of violence that people witness, experience, or commit, violence becomes a social condition (ibid.).

Considering the everyday also brings into focus the diverse forms of violence and insecurity that matter from a bottom-up, people's perspective, and how this affects their lives. This has also been conceptualised as 'vernacular security' (Lind and Luckham 2017, Luckham 2017). Using this lens again takes us beyond direct acts of violence to include an understanding of symbolic violence and how narratives of violence are communicated and transmitted (Luckham 2017, McGee 2017). Experiences of violence can have long-lasting legacies, and produce a culture of fear in which fear penetrates social memory (Green 1995) and may create a 'culture of silence' (Hume 2009). As a consequence, people are reluctant to openly talk about certain issues with their peers, let alone raise them with more powerful actors. It is also possible that people are comfortable engaging more powerful actors on certain issues, while they actively self-censor themselves when it comes to issues they consider more risky (Oosterom 2016). When acknowledging that agency is not just the product of rational action but also effected through embodied, psychological processes, then the role of fear in (post)conflict settings needs to be recognised. Someone's decision not to engage openly may not be 'apathy', but her deliberate strategic choice to remain passive (Pettit 2016a, Pettit 2016b).

More often than not, conflict-affected settings are highly dynamic, with configurations of power shifting frequently, and abruptly. People living in violent settings cannot take anything for granted. They need to assess the ongoing changes and shifts in their context, and this underpins their everyday social practice. To depict this behaviour Vigh introduced the concept of 'social navigation', which he defines as the process whereby 'agents seek to draw and actualize their life trajectories ... in a shifting and volatile social environment' (2006, p. 4). Importantly, it captures both people's current assessment of their social environment *and* the anticipated future: when taking decisions they assess how configurations of power might develop, and how they might maximise the returns of their efforts. In the midst of uncertainty, people are constantly trying to maximise opportunities and reduce risk in order to protect their livelihoods and safety (Vigh 2006, Vigh 2009). One way of doing this is to come up with different coping mechanisms – such as, for instance, adjusting livelihood activities, using hide-outs to spend the night or temporarily leaving 'hot' areas. This is different, however, from agency that actively take issues into the public sphere, which is considered a defining characteristic of 'citizen agency' (Lister 2003). Agency is then about engaging more powerful actors in order establish (a level of) security at a broader scale or address the causes of conflict.

This distinction between coping agency and political agency that involves engaging with more powerful actors has been alluded to in the literature. Moser and Horn (2012), for instance distinguish coping agency from resolving agency; and MacGinty (2014) refers to coping mechanisms and practices that are more 'ambitious' and challenge the fixity of conflicts. It has been asserted that people can actively negotiate with powerful armed actors while also confronting and resisting them (Barter 2012, McGee 2014, McGee 2017). They may also have to comply with the rules and orders set by such actors (Baines and Paddon 2012, Barter 2012), even if in some cases this may be 'performative compliance' (Simone 2005). In other cases they may need to actively support violent actors in order to stay safe, offering them food, shelter and intelligence (Justino et al. 2013). Similar tactics and strategies have been documented for authoritarian regime settings, where people navigate, and sometimes defy and resist, the state and state-sponsored entities (Ansoms and Cioffo 2016, Oosterom and Pswarayi 2014, Thomson 2011). Beyond this focus on actors it is important to find out how different forms of violence have shaped social norms as well as perceptions of the public sphere, and which issues are considered sensitive (Oosterom 2016). In many places it may be too risky to confront powerful actors, and people may need to resort to compliance or tacit resistance.

All of this goes to show that people living in violent settings respond to and negotiate power, and are not just 'receivers' or victims of violence and state repression. If empowerment is a process of change that is meant to lead to gaining or consolidating power of relatively powerless or marginalised people, then this distinction between coping agency and political agency is key. Being able to cope and carry on with addressing everyday life issues without much interference from more powerful actors may feel satisfactory in a way, but not necessarily empowering.

Researching experiences of violence

In each of the country studies, a range of methods was used to map forms of violence, the actors involved in perpetrating and mitigating violence, the effects of violence on agency and people's responses. The research then explored experiences of empowerment and disempowerment, and to what extent people felt their agency was actually empowering. Methods had been adapted from existing participatory methods used to map manifestations and causes of violence (McIlwaine and Moser 2003), which have also been applied to African urban settings (Moser and Horn 2012). Yet our methods differed from those methods through our emphasis on conceptualisations of power in all research instruments, guided by frameworks developed by Gaventa (2006), VeneKlasen and Miller (2002) and

Miller et al. (2006) in particular (see also chapters by VeneKlasen, Bradley, and Arce Andrade and Miller in this volume). These frameworks are particularly suitable for analysing how legacies of violence constituted or changed social norms through the concept of 'invisible power' and to exploring people's agency through the concept of *power within, power with* and *power to* (VeneKlasen and Miller 2002). Further, when asking about agency the studies made use of literature on subversion and on tacit and passive resistance, recognising that people affected by conflict and violence are not just victims, but actively shape their lives and negotiate and even resist violent actors (Barter 2012).

The choice of methods needed to respond to sensitivities in each country. Thus, while PhotoVoice was appropriate in South Sudan, the team considered this methodology risky when working with youth participants in Zimbabwe, where state security actors are more likely to be suspicious of groups of people using cameras in public spaces.[3] Here, we asked youth to draw short cartoon stories, and we also used storytelling and theatre in private venues where we could create a 'safe space' for self-expression, reflection and discussion. As part of creating safe spaces for exploring sensitive topics, rapport building at the start required the utmost attention. When working with youth this required a mix of activities that were fun and made people laugh, alongside establishing ground rules for listening and confidentiality in focus group discussions.

Context strongly influences the language that can be used in research methods: whereas it was possible to discuss notions of empowerment and disempowerment in urban Zimbabwe, owing to the relatively better average levels of education, methods in rural Uganda and South Sudan needed to deploy a more accessible and descriptive language when mapping the range of responses to insecurity before going into a more in-depth discussion about whether participants felt their actions had 'brought them something', 'led to some improvement', 'made them feel better or stronger' in an attempt to gauge their sense of empowerment. Such discursive challenges are often overlooked when methodologies are being developed, although this is crucial when working with less-educated participants, when addressing complex concepts like power and sensitive issues like violence, and when working in larger teams and through interpreters.

Recognising that social identity strongly influences experiences and responses to violence, we tried to include and engage participants from different backgrounds. Research instruments would explicitly address social difference through questions and probing, asking participants to reflect on their own and others' identities, and how this impacted experiences of violence. This was crucial for understanding gendered experiences of violence. Studies that focused on youth needed to address

---

3   PhotoVoice is a participatory research methodology in which research participants are invited to take pictures in response to one or more questions. It enables participants to show perspectives or aspects of life that may not be captured in interviews. Through subsequent discussions or interviews about the pictures the method produces rich visual and narrative data. See Prins (2010).

how social hierarchies based on local, socially constructed notions of 'youth' or 'adult' status influenced both experiences of and responses to violence.

In each of the studies we used a combination of visual and narrative methods, including theatre, aimed at generating people's perceptions and experiences of violence and violent conflict, as well as generating theoretical insights into how different violence dynamics shape agency. The following sections look across the studies, and will highlight how conceptualisations of power generated new understandings of how violence is experienced, and of what influences people's responses.

Mapping configurations of actors and relationships

Often, participants have no trouble identifying forms of visible power when mapping the actors that enact different forms of violence, or who mobilise violence through others. In the studies discussed here, this was done through visual mappings such as Venn diagrams, whereby participants were asked to name all actors that perpetrate violence, whom they consider a threat or are afraid of. We subsequently ranked these actors by asking who was more threatening than who, and why; and we also conducted causal flow diagrams to discuss the causes and effects of different forms of violence.

Usually participants are very able to distinguish how actors exercise hidden forms of power. With some further probing on the actors and relationships between them, it is possible to map the ways powerful actors maintain 'behind the scenes' networks in order to sustain their control over resources (trade networks, land, assets), and how more powerful actors use others to mobilise violence on their behalf. For instance, in South Sudan these exercises showed connections between parliamentarians, arms traders and cattle raiders, which helped explain the role of hidden forms of power behind certain violent clashes, which at first appeared to be the result of inter-community rivalries.

Importantly, and informed by the notions of the 'everyday' and 'vernacular security', researchers encouraged participants to name all kinds of violence and the relevant actors, and instances of when they felt scared or under threat. In South Sudan, this promoted female participants to talk about gender violence and domestic violence, which they experienced far more often than violence inflicted during cattle raids (Oosterom 2017). The male participants, on the other hand, prioritised cattle raids and inter-community conflicts over land that might escalate into violence – all forms of 'public violence' in which it is their role to protect their villages.

Similar mappings were also carried out to identify actors that contribute to peace or are able to mitigate violence. This, alongside the 'peeling the onion' exercise discussed further below, helps identify people's own mechanisms for reducing violence. Mappings are likely to bring out 'conventional' leaders like religious leaders, but can also identify informal leadership figures and local activists. Following the mapping, an in-depth discussion concentrates on the diverse ways in which the local actors handle violence and insecurity, encouraging participants to recount anecdotes and real examples from the past. In South Sudan, this helped identify certain elderly women in the community who could offer refuge to younger women who were beaten by their husbands, and who were the only women allowed to approach the customary authorities (Oosterom 2017). Non-governmental organisations that were working on gender-based violence in Imatong State were completely unaware of the role of such women, and were trying to pursue formal mechanisms like gender desks at police stations. Often these stations are very far away; but in any case this course of action would require women to challenge their husbands in a public office, which they were reluctant to do. Here the analysis thus helped identify avenues for addressing domestic violence that were closer to home and custom.

Invisible power, past and present

In our studies, invisible power was usually not addressed at first instance, but only after we had obtained a detailed understanding of the local context and the configuration of actors and the relationships between them, as well as of the different forms of violence people experienced. This is also in recognition of invisible power as one of the more difficult forms of power to understand (Scott-Villiers and Oosterom 2016). The role of invisible power has often been discussed in relation to social norms and beliefs (Gaventa 2006, VeneKlasen and Miller 2002). When researching violence it also helps to understand the ways in which violence becomes psychologically embodied, and how this impacts people's agency in the present. The methodologies for assessing the role of invisible power varied across the studies, but were mainly discursive: we added questions to focus group discussions after mappings had been completed; or in individual interviews we asked how past experiences continued to affect how someone engaged certain actors, probing for potential risks and fears.

In the case of domestic violence among the Latuko in Imatong State, South Sudan, the analysis of invisible power centred on norms governing the relationship between husbands and wives. These discussions showed that women and men find a certain level of beating is acceptable (Oosterom 2017). Women were reluctant to share incidents in public because a marital dispute was considered a very private issue, and presenting it in public damages the good reputation of a home. Only when a woman was seriously injured or, in the words of one of our participants, 'when blood comes out', would other men intervene by arranging a meeting between the couple and other adult men. In most cases they would reprimand the wife for not respecting her husband, but among themselves they would tell the husband not to beat his wife so severely. Here, the analysis of invisible power in relation to violence showed two things. First of all, it showed the social norms that women are not meant to discuss marital affairs in public. Secondly, it showed how experiences of violence become embodied: women accept a certain degree of physical violence as normal, and will not question it. In combination, these manifestations of invisible power contributed to the reproduction of certain forms of domestic violence.

In northern Uganda as well as in Zimbabwe the analysis of invisible power revealed how past experiences of violence undermined certain forms of agency in the present through invisible power. In northern Uganda, the Acholi people had often found themselves caught between the rebels and the army during the conflict (Baines and Paddon 2012, Oosterom 2016). Anyone who critiqued the state could easily be accused of supporting the rebels, and be subjected to state violence. These experiences added to historic perceptions that the incumbent regime, largely made up of southern and south-western tribes, was against the Acholi ethnic group (Oosterom 2016). Specifically, in the aftermath of the war it deterred people from publicly questioning and critiquing the state, afraid this might have repercussions (ibid.). These sentiments only came out in individual interviews in which past experiences of state violence were linked to current perceptions of the state, although they seemed more strongly felt by older participants who had had direct experience of military violence. Past experiences had become embodied knowledge of what the state was capable of when critiqued or challenged, and many people resorted to a nearly subconscious self-censorship – an example of invisible power limiting citizen agency.

In Zimbabwe, the experience of constant state surveillance contributed to a sense of insecurity. Having learnt and witnessed how the Mugabe regime dealt with dissidents and vocal members of the opposition parties, youth had good reasons not to speak out against actors linked to the ruling party. Further, memories of the excessive political violence during the 2008 elections had a big influence on those youth who – at the time - were old enough to understand what was going on, and who had been actively targeted by partisan actors in their campaigns. For many, it had been a crucial moment for deciding never to become active members of a political party (Oosterom and Pswarayi 2014). Some expressed awareness of the risks of developing strong ties to politicians and buying into party patronage, saying this could potentially increase the risk of being mobilised into violent militias come the next elections (Oosterom 2019).

Social norms and habits are transmitted through socialisation processes, and therefore invisible power and its effects can be reproduced across generations (VeneKlasen and Miller 2002). As these studies on violence have shown, past experiences of violence can also have a socialising effect on people through invisible power: over time people have learnt what to say and do, and what not to in order to minimise risk. Their experiences have thus developed into embodied, nearly subconscious knowledge. Such embodied violence and trauma can have a limiting effect on people's agency. However, the effects of violence are not uniform. There are cases of people who have spent much of their life in violent conditions but who developed into vocal activists, challenging state violence and taking immense risks in fighting for justice (JASS 2012).

Discussing empowerment and disempowerment

In Zimbabwe, researchers used a combination of visual methods, theatre and storytelling to generate an understanding of empowerment and disempowerment among youth, using them to facilitate a discussion about how they could help each other reduce the risk of experiencing further political violence. Working in groups of five to six youths, with men and women separate, research-facilitators asked youth to draw two instances from their lives: one when they experienced empowerment, and one when they felt disempowered. They were given large, spacious flipcharts and asked to also draw the circumstances of their stories. After drawing, we asked them to present their drawings and tell their stories with as much detail as possible. We then facilitated a discussion to talk through the actors involved, as well as *power within, power with* and *power to* – adjusting questions to the stories we heard. For the majority of the participants the repressive, violent context figured strongly in drawings and narratives of disempowerment. Drawings by male youth chased by state security agents reflected how youth are targeted by the ruling party, particularly in the run-up to elections, and forced to attend political meetings and commit political violence. Stories about empowerment brought up the first time an individual went to vote, or when they had taken a leadership role such as in youth groups. The structured discussions about power and agency revealed that family and peers were especially important for helping youth to stay safe and find ways to avoid the political, usually partisan actors that target youth.

To discuss agency in response to violence and insecurity in greater depth we adapted the 'peeling the onion' exercise (Hunjan and Pettit 2011) to discuss individual agency and *power within*, and collective agency or *power with* at the level of family and friends, the community, and beyond – the layers of the onion representing the different levels, starting from the individual at the centre. Using the concept of *power over* we asked probing questions about who is helping and hindering individual and collective responses to violence, and how violence is overcome. These exercises brought out important differences between young men and women, with young women often choosing to hide at home to avoid risky public spaces, while young men spoke of temporary migration to places they considered to be safer, often through family networks. In this context it is hard to confront and challenge security agents, members working for the Central Intelligence Organisation (secret police) and ruling party officials that can exercise power over youth; hence exit and avoidance strategies prevail as forms of agency. An important instance of collective *power with* came out when working with members of a group of young dancers and artists, who actively used their group to model new ways of civic engagement and purposefully refused to perform at political rallies in order to prevent being 'captured' and tied into party patronage (Oosterom and Pswarayi 2014). Though subtle, the group members rejected the acts of political parties without articulating their critique openly. In this context, few will dare to stand up and 'speak truth to power', or exercise agency in a confrontational way.

Visual mappings of actors who help mitigate violence are likely to bring out the actors that publicly take on violent actors, individually or collectively, but are less likely to generate information about people's more subtle tactics of defying and tacitly resisting violent actors. Doing this requires a dedicated discussion or individual interviews guided by notions of passive resistance and defiance (Barter 2012), with a focus on the range of ways through which one avoids getting into trouble, or how one relates to, interacts with and deals with powerful actors. In Zimbabwe for instance this led to participants talking about *zino irima* – a term that refers to people just exchanging greetings with people who they know are part of the state security apparatus, but avoiding any further engagement with such people (Oosterom and Pswarayi 2014). Youth also reported that stealing fruit and crops from the land that belongs to the village heads, who usually are regime collaborators, was a way to defy and resist them (ibid.). Visual and narrative methodologies that used a power framework thus helped identify individual and collective tactics used by youth in their response to political violence, sometimes reducing the risk of being affected by it.

Agency and empowerment

The instances of agency I have described in this chapter are quite remarkable, given the rather disempowering circumstances people face in violent settings. The question of whether these actions are also empowering needs to be approached carefully. From the perspective of the individual one can use questions such as those suggested by VeneKlasen and Miller's (2002) conceptual framework as to whether participants felt their actions strengthened their *power within* or contributed to *power with* and *power to*. Left aside here is the issue of those who have decided to join violent groups or take part in violence, while recognising that the sensation of carrying a gun and membership of violent groups can feel very empowering (Utas 2005). Whether people felt their agency contributed to any broader process change or gaining power is an entirely different matter, and many may not even think of their actions in this way.

The groups of young artists in Zimbabwe felt empowered because they had so far managed to stay out of political parties. They felt they had overcome something that not everyone can: stay out of party patronage, which is a form of *power over* that may increase access to opportunities but puts youth in vulnerable positions (Oosterom and Pswarayi 2014). They had set an example for other youth in their neighbourhood and their actions may have prevented other youth from joining violent party structures, but this could not be assessed at the time. Even if it did, the impact of the art group was highly localised. The female leadership figures in South Sudan recognised their agency as *power to* but not empowerment (Oosterom 2017). They were aware they were helping women who were experiencing domestic violence by intervening in marital disputes and talking to male leaders, but also felt their limitations and the magnitude of the problem when saying 'everyday at least five women are beaten here [in the village]' (Oosterom 2014, p. 39). These women maintained a level of influence and, most likely, were helping to prevent domestic violence from getting out of control. Yet, they alone could not stop high levels of alcohol consumption and address the absence of state protection – major contributing factors to domestic violence. In northern Uganda, the Acholi people did feel empowered when they had the opportunity to directly address political leaders when they had come for a village meeting, enabled by *power with*. In these situations they could even be critical of gaps in service delivery.

On the other hand, speaking individually to a civil servant or political leader in an office was often disempowering because, due to their authority, they felt they had to be humble and deferential (Oosterom 2016).

All of these examples are instances of 'citizen agency' as participants actively took issues into the public domain (Lister 2003). A sense of empowerment was prompted by people's awareness of *power over* by other actors and the instances in which they were actively negotiating this *power over*, even if it did not lead to peace or a transformation of the overall relationships of power. Participants usually recognised that they were not necessarily gaining power, or making progress towards a more peaceful society. We often heard answers like 'Yes this felt empowering, but ...'. The realisation of how difficult it was to change larger systems of violence, in which states often play a role, had a tempering effect on feelings of empowerment.

Conclusion

In this chapter I have used examples from settings that are affected by different forms of violence and violent conflict to show how violence impacts agency. The range of methods used in each study was firmly based on concepts of power in order to establish the diverse ways in which violence shapes agency, and also people's responses. The chapter has pointed at a new understanding of invisible power in these contexts: not just as social and cultural norms, but also as embodied experiences of violence. Both forms of invisible power are socially reproduced, and both can affect agency through creating nearly subconscious boundaries around what a person thinks can be questioned, challenged and changed.

The distinction between 'coping agency' and 'citizen agency' and more political acts of negotiating and resisting the power of other actors helped us to think about what empowerment really means in these settings (Barter 2012, Lister 2003). While effects of violence are usually experienced locally by real people, its causes are multidimensional and at multiple levels. This makes it so difficult to resolve. I would agree with others who caution against romanticising all forms of agency in violent settings (Bordonaro and Payne 2012, Seymour 2012). At the same time, examples of people who are quietly or actively resisting violence are impressive and can be taken as a starting point for thinking about how others can be supported and encouraged to do the same.

References

Ansoms, A. and Cioffo, G.D., 2016. The exemplary citizen on the exemplary hill: the production of political subjects in contemporary rural Rwanda. *Development and Change*, 47 (6), 1247–1268.

Baines, E. and Paddon, E., 2012. 'This is how we survived': Civilian agency and humanitarian protection. *Security Dialogue*, 43(3), 231–247.

Barter, S.J., 2012. Unarmed forces: civilian strategies in violent conflicts. *Peace & Change*, 37 (4), 544–569.

Bordonaro, L.I. and Payne, R., 2012. Ambiguous agency: critical perspectives on social interventions with children and youth in Africa. *Children's Geographies*, 10(4), 365–372.

Certeau, M.D., 1988. *The practice of everyday life*. Berkeley: University of California Press.

Gaventa, J., 2006. Finding the spaces for change: a power analysis. *IDS Bulletin*, 37(6), 22–33.

Green, L., 1995. Living in a state of fear. In: C. Nordstrom and A.C.G.M. Robben, eds. *Fieldwork under fire: comparative studies of violence and culture*. Berkeley: University of California Press.

Hume, M., 2009. Researching the gendered silences of violence in El Salvador. *IDS Bulletin*, 40(3), 78–85.

Hunjan, R. and Pettit, J., 2011. *Power: a practical guide for facilitating social change*. Dunfermline: Carnegie UK Trust.

JASS, 2012. *From survivors to defenders: women confronting violence in Mexico, Honduras, and Guatemala*. Washington DC: Just Associates and Nobel Women's Initiative.

Justino, P., Brück, T. and Verwimp, P., 2013. *A micro-level perspective on the dynamics of conflict, violence, and development*. Oxford: Oxford University Press.

Lind, J. and Luckham, R., 2017. Introduction: security in the vernacular and peacebuilding at the margins; rethinking violence reduction. *Peacebuilding*, 5(2), 89–98.

Lister, R., 2003. *Citizenship: feminist perspectives*. New York: New York University Press.

Lubkemann, S., 2008. *Culture in chaos: an anthropology of the social condition in war*. Chicago: University of Chicago Press.

Luckham, R., 2017. Whose violence, whose security? Can violence reduction and security work for poor, excluded and vulnerable people? *Peacebuilding*, 5(2), 99–117.

MacGinty, R., 2014. Everyday peace: bottom-up and local agency in conflict-affected societies. *Security Dialogue*, 45(6), 548–564.

McGee, R., 2014. Power, violence, citizenship and agency. *IDS Bulletin*, 45(5), 36–47.

McGee, R., 2017. Invisible power and visible everyday resistance in the violent Colombian Pacific. *Peacebuilding*, 5(2), 170–185.

McIlwaine, C. and Moser, C., 2003. Poverty, violence and livelihood security in urban Colombia and Guatemala. *Progress in Development Studies*, 3(2), 113–130.

Miller, V., Veneklasen, L., Reilly, M. and Clark, C., 2006. *Making change happen 3: power. Concepts for revisioning power for justice, equality and peace*. Washington DC: Just Associates.

Moser, C. and Horn, P., 2012. Understanding the tipping point of urban conflict: conceptual framework paper. Working Paper no. 1 (December 2011). Urban Tipping Point (UTP) Project, University of Manchester.

Oosterom, M. and Pswarayi, L., 2014. *Being a born-free: violence, youth and agency in Zimbabwe*. IDS Research Report, 79. Brighton: Institute of Development Studies.

Oosterom, M., 2014. *'It may approach as quickly as a bushfire': gendered violence and insecurity in South Sudan*. IDS Research Report 78. Brighton: Institute of Development Studies.

Oosterom, M., 2016. The effects of violent conflict and displacement on citizen engagement: a case study from Northern Uganda. *Conflict, Security & Development*, 16(1), 75–101.

Oosterom, M., 2017. Gendered (in)security in South Sudan: masculinities and hybrid governance in Imatong state. *Peacebuilding*, 5(2), 186–202.

Oosterom, M., 2019. Youth and social navigation in Zimbabwe's informal economy: 'Don't end up on the wrong side'. *African Affairs*, 118 (June).

Pettit, J., 2016a. Civic habitus: towards a pedagogy for citizen engagement. In: A. Skinner *et al.*, eds. *Education, learning and the transformation of development*. London: Routledge, 125–142.

Pettit, J., 2016b. Why citizens don't engage: power, poverty and civic habitus. *IDS Bulletin*, 47(5), 89–102.

Prins, E., 2010. Participatory photography: a tool for empowerment or surveillance? *Action Research*, 8(4), 426–438.

Scott-Villiers, P. and Oosterom, M., 2016. Introduction: power, poverty and inequality. *IDS Bulletin*, 47(5), 1–10.

Seymour, C., 2012. Ambiguous agencies: coping and survival in eastern Democratic Republic of Congo. *Children's Geographies*, 10(4), 373–384.

Simone, A., 2005. Urban circulation and the everyday politics of African urban youth: the case of Douala, Cameroon. *International Journal of Urban and Regional Research*, 29(3), 516–532.

Thomson, S., 2011. Whispering truth to power: the everyday resistance of Rwandan peasants to post-genocide reconciliation. *African Affairs*, 110(440), 439–456.

Utas, M., 2005. West-African warscapes: victimcy, girlfriending, soldiering: tactic agency in a young woman's social navigation of the Liberian war zone. *Anthropological Quarterly*, 78 (2), 403–430.

VeneKlasen, L. and Miller, V., 2002. *A new weave of power, people and politics: the action guide for advocacy and citizen participation*. Oklahoma City: World Neighbors.

Vigh, H., 2006. *Navigating terrains of war: youth and soldiering in Guinea-Bissau*. Oxford: Berghahn.

Vigh, H., 2009. Motion squared: a second look at the concept of social navigation. *Anthropological Theory*, 9(4), 419–438.

4.2

MICRO-LEVEL ANALYSIS OF POWER AND ITS RELEVANCE FOR PRACTICE

Walter Flores

Introduction

In development work, we frequently analyse power at the macro level: power relations between government institutions and citizens, between economic and political elites and marginalised populations and between transnational corporations and southern countries. This analysis of power is important, but, depending on where one is positioned, it can seem very dense and complex.

Many intermediary organisations (those made up of professionals paid to work in the development field) implement their actions at the local or subnational level. Often, the frameworks and tools used to analyse power at the 'macro' level of national and international structures are transferred or adapted to do power analysis at the 'micro' (local or subnational) level. However, the situation is so different between the macro and the micro level that adapting methods and tools from one level to use at another may come with major limitations. This chapter will describe the approach we followed in my organisation, the challenges we faced and the learning we acquired along the way.

The Center for the Study of Equity and Governance in Health Systems (CEGSS) is a civic association of professionals founded in 2006, in Guatemala. Its purpose is to contribute to reducing social exclusion and inequality in health care, which mainly affects the rural indigenous population. The interdisciplinary team conducts participatory research, capacity building for grassroots groups and advocacy around public policies and services. Promoting citizen participation is fundamental to CEGSS's approach. For this, we provide training, basic equipment and technical assistance to a network of volunteer community-based defenders of the right to health who have been chosen by their own communities. These community defenders are organised in a grassroots network named the Network of Community Defenders of the Right to Health (*Red de Defensores y Defensoras Comunitarios por el Derecho a la Salud*, REDC-SALUD).

In its efforts to study and analyse social exclusion and marginalisation, CEGSS developed tools to analyse power and power relations among, within and between community-based organisations and government authorities in rural indigenous municipalities of Guatemala (Flores and Gómez Sánchez 2010). From those first studies and tools, we then gradually moved to develop more participatory tools (card games, categorising of actors, scoring or ranking them according to their influence by placing beans against their names), which were useful in revealing asymmetrical power relations. However, the explaining and using of the tools to generate the information was a relatively long process. We were wondering how to make the process shorter when one of our field assistants, an indigenous person who lived in a rural municipality, suggested that asking people questions directly about what we wanted to know (i.e. who and why one has influence) would be easier, and that with the help of local translators people would trust us and talk openly.

We decided to follow our field assistant's advice and conducted several individual and group interviews. To our surprise, interviewees readily understood what power and influence was about, and immediately named who had power in the community and what resources they had that gave them that level of influence. They would also identify less powerful actors and the most powerless in the community. One interviewee who participated in municipal development meetings said openly that he was not elected by his community but appointed by the local mayor, and that his job was attending community meetings and informing the authorities about what went on at them. He further explained that he did not see his role as any different from the roles that other community people play for non-governmental organisations (NGOs) or churches: they all collect information and pass it on to external organisations.

From that experience, we realised that it was wrong to assume that people in rural indigenous municipalities need frameworks and tools to understand what power is and to elicit information about it. My team and I became aware that although we meant well with our participatory tools, they might in fact be causing a disempowering effect on the community participants by undervaluing their extensive experiential knowledge about power and disempowerment.

As a result of our reflection, we ditched the tools we had been using and started generative conversations with community members and government officials.[1] From those rich conversations, we elaborated interview guides to further explore: a) specific examples of power and influence; b) what were the most relevant power resources in the locality; and c) what ideas interviewees had about how to change power relations to benefit those who were among the most excluded. From these generative conversations, we, together with communities, have developed theory and concepts that have informed our strategies and actions aimed at shifting power

1   Generative conversation is method used variously in qualitative research, organisational development and adult education. Participants are encouraged to converse freely and without judgement in order to arrive at common and deeper understandings. Also known as generative dialogue, the method has diverse origins and influences, but has mainly been inspired by the physicist David Bohm (1996).

in health care service delivery for rural indigenous populations (Flores 2018, Flores and Hernández 2018, Hernández et al. 2019).

This experience of using open generative conversations was also fed into all of our activities, including within our own organisation and among our own staff. In the next sections I will briefly explain what these micro levels of power are and how we apply such analysis to our work. I will conclude with some final reflections on why analysing and acting on micro levels of power is of relevance to improve our practice.

What is a micro level analysis of power?

In the literature, there are different academic research studies looking at power at the micro level. Several of these studies make reference to Foucault's theories, particularly the concepts he developed of a 'micro power' and 'micro physics of power' in his work *Discipline and punish: the birth of the prison* (1977/1995). For instance, Silva and Arantes (2017) use Foucault's theory to study micro-level power relations among a family medicine team in the state of São Paulo, Brazil. Other authors use political economy frameworks to analyse macro and micro levels of power. Kwami et al. (2011), in their essay about macro and micro analysis of gender, power and information and communication technology, state that while a macro-level analysis unveils power dynamics shaped by political and economic structures and processes, a micro-level approach analyses the dynamics that affect access, use and appropriation of technology and services in terms of gender, class and geographical location. The authors state that micro-level analysis is important to understand the nature of inequities.

Within CEGSS, an analysis of power at the micro level is understood as the exercise of enquiring into relationships, resources and influence among the individuals and organisations we engage with: for instance, the power resources and influence within the grassroots organisations we support; among and within the staff of our own organisation; and between ourselves and other organisations we collaborate with. The purpose of carrying out such analysis is to identify power-related challenges affecting our organisational mission and objectives, thus enabling us to strategise actions to navigate those challenges. These exercises are highly participatory, conversational and reflective. Below I discuss three examples of how micro-level analysis of power helped us identify issues and barriers affecting our work, and the strategies we implemented to either circumnavigate or resolve them.

Gender barriers to participation

As part of our approach to working with grassroots organisations, we provide subsidies for food and transport to all participants in capacity-building workshops. As an organisation, we have to produce evidence that transport and food costs are barriers to participation so that our donor will agree to such subsidies (Flores and Gómez-Sánchez 2010). Obviously, we were proud of convincing donors and providing this type of support to community leaders. However, after several months of training, we noted that many female participants who were actively participating in their municipalities were not attending the regional training workshops. After enquiring with other participants, we found that they had small children who would have had to come with them to the regional workshops. For some people, attending a regional workshop meant travelling for more than a day and staying overnight. The subsidy we were proudly providing was for one individual, so female leaders with young children were precluded from attending because the subsidy would not cover the additional food and transport for their children.

We thought of creating a differentiated subsidy for women who travel with children. This created a power struggle within our organisation. For administrators, standardised procedures are the best thing, and they do not like exceptions to rules. External auditors did not like exceptions either. The easiest approach would have been to avoid exceptions so as to maintain harmony within our personnel. But we decided that this barrier affecting female leaders was not acceptable, and so pushed for the exception, which created the conditions to convince our administrative staff and auditors. Six years after this decision, 40 per cent of all community defenders who are part of REDC-SALUD are female leaders. We cannot say this is a direct result of the support through differentiated subsidies. However, we do know that we removed a barrier that was restricting women's leadership.

From the above experience, we also assessed whether our own staff were experiencing gender barriers. By discussing it with our staff, we identified that, due to safety concerns, female field staff sometimes preferred travelling to the field in pairs rather than on their own. Also, parents of very young children needed a more flexible schedule to be able to care for their children. As result, our organisation allows team members to accompany each other during field travel when requested, and parents can request and arrange a highly flexible work schedule.

Legitimacy as a power resource

In 2013, our collaboration with communities evolved to working with citizen leaders mobilised to assume the role of Community Defenders of the Right to Health (henceforth, Defenders). There are currently over 160 Defenders (about 60 per cent male and 40 per cent female) elected by their own communities to defend them from abuses by officials and providers of health services; to act on their behalf to dialogue and engage with officials to improve the responsiveness of local services; and to inform and educate communities about their rights, entitlements and obligations. All are volunteers who receive ongoing training and technical assistance from CEGSS.

During our annual assembly at the end of that year, a group representing the majority of Defenders declared that carrying out defender roles was taking up a lot of their time. Having been trained, they said they now had the relevant knowledge and skills. In their view these factors justified that they should no longer be treated as volunteers, but be paid salaries by CEGSS to continue performing as Defenders. Although the assembly was meant to work on preparing the action plan for the year ahead, the Defenders refused to continue until we discussed and agreed upon their demands to receive payment for their work.

Under these circumstances, we started a dialogue about what power resources we as CEGSS had, what resources they as Defenders had and what resources we were able to generate once working together. During the dialogue, we identified the following:

- CEGSS's power lies in the financial resources obtained from donors.
- We had decision-making *power over* regarding the use of those resources, but at the same time had to be accountable to our donors; and, with our power, we could decide to use the resources to pay a modest income to Defenders.
- However, this would mean Defenders were no longer accountable to their communities but to us (CEGSS).
- In the case of Defenders, their power resource was the respect, trust and credibility they have in the eyes of their communities. Defenders were able to mobilise hundreds and thousands and families. This occurs because communities know Defenders represent their interests – not the priorities or interests of an NGO, political party or government authority.

We also analysed what power we would lose if we were to change our current resourcing arrangements:

- From CEGSS's perspective, the success of the Community Defenders scheme was connected to its reliance on volunteers elected by their own communities. If Defenders were no longer volunteers, that would reduce the significance of the role in CEGSS's overall work, and CEGSS would likely fail to obtain funding for this work. This would mean CEGSS would cease to exist and the Defenders would be left without the income.
- From the Defenders' perspective, they would cease to have the capacity to mobilise communities if they were to become NGO employees. Without the backup of communities, Defenders would lose the most important power resource they have. In turn, neither CEGSS nor any other NGO would be interested in employing a community-based leader who did not enjoy trust and credibility among their community.

As a result of this participatory analysis of micro levels of power, all Defenders decided that receiving a payment from CEGSS was not an option. Instead, they decided they would like to receive basic equipment that would aid their work: a jacket and ID card, a mobile phone and a small camera. CEGSS agreed that providing basic equipment was feasible, and at the same time may contribute to making their work more effective.

After an entire day of dialogue, the next day we were able to move on to planning the year ahead, building in fundraising activities to provide Defenders with this basic equipment. Since that dialogue, the issue of payment to community volunteers has never emerged again. In addition, as a norm, each annual assembly includes a discussion and planning session about what other basic equipment may be needed. For instance, last year CEGSS provided raincoats at the request of Defenders.

We transposed the learning from this dialogue to help us in convening a dialogue on power resources among ourselves as CEGSS staff. Central in that analysis was whether we as an organisation would be able to offer competitive salaries to our staff and a significant salary increase each year. Through our analysis, we identified that because CEGSS is 100 per cent dependent on grants, we do not have control in the medium and long term. However, there are non-salary resources that are very important for all the staff: for instance, an open door policy among senior management; fomenting team building activities; and supporting staff to attend professional development events at national and international level. CEGSS took these commitments seriously. In addition to a more open management and activities to strengthen the communication and relationship among our staff, both research and field staff have been supported to participate in international conferences and events.

The power of solidarity

As mentioned earlier, the network of Community Defenders that CEGSS works with and supports consists of around 160 leaders, and about 40 per cent are women (females over 18). Among the females, we noticed that while there were a few well-established middle-aged leaders, the rest were young women who did not yet have the confidence and skills of the older leaders. The CEGSS team thought up a new initiative in which established female leaders would mentor and train the young women. We envisaged that this new initiative would mostly require allocating resources for training (i.e. attendance of formal workshops and courses) and travel. We were excited about this new initiative and took the next step of sharing the idea with one of the key women leaders of REDC-SALUD – Estela, a middle-aged woman with over three decades of experience in grassroots organising.[2] Estela listened carefully to our idea and told us: 'I understand your aim and I agree it is very important for us, the experienced leaders, to support young women. However, I am already doing it.' Following Estela's comment, we assumed she meant she was mentoring others through training, and responded: 'This is great news. What kind of training are you providing to them?' To our question, Estela replied:

> There is no training at all. Young women wanting to become community leaders first need solidarity and accompaniment to survive the most difficult test. This occurs when her own family is unhappy about her attending many meetings with older females and men; when her own community is gossiping and mocking about her aspiration to learn why is there injustice and poverty

2   Estela's name has been changed to preserve her anonymity. This text is a reconstruction of a conversation held in early 2018.

in the community; gossiping because she wants to learn about the law, because she dares to speak in public; because she travels outside her community to talk to authorities, government officials and others.

Estela went on to say that her role was to talk to the families of the young women, to explain to them the work of a female community leader in terms of their daughter (or wife) wanting to help her community. She also provides comfort and emotional support to young women when they feel down as a result of community gossip and lack of family support. Estela said that she experienced this pressure herself when she started as a community leader:

> I did not have the solidarity or support of an older female leader to help me through, but I did survive that phase and became a leader recognised within and outside my community. Many young women that wanted to become leaders are not able to surpass this pressure.

Estela finished her comment thus: 'Training and similar activities may happen later. At this moment, young women need my solidarity, and the solidarity of many others.'

After the above exchange with Estela, we at CEGSS realised how wrong and naïve we were about what a young female leader needs. Instead of the new initiative that we had been imagining, we just told Estela to let us know what kind of support she needed from us to continue her solidarity and accompaniment. She did not ask for much support, only food and transport to attend a few meetings together with the young women.

About a year later, we noticed that the young female leaders that Estela had taken under her wing were more confident and assertive during the REDC-SALUD meetings. They were also more assertive and effective when engaging with authorities and implementing their roles as Community Defenders. Estela was right – solidarity is a powerful resource.

The lesson that Estela taught us is now central to our understanding and approach to supporting the development of community leaders. Instead of a predefined training or capacity-building programme, we promote exchanges in which leaders more experienced in a specific theme or skill are grouped with other leaders interested in learning about that theme or skill. Solidarity is central in the exchange, and each group decides what they want to do and how.

We are also striving to extend this learning to our own organisation's staff. We aim to show solidarity among ourselves, not only in our daily work but also in our family situation and other life events.

Final reflection

Although we should not lose track of macro determinants of power and dynamics, we should also pay attention to the micro levels of power that occur everywhere and all the time. An intermediary organisation like the one described in this chapter, without realising it, could be creating barriers to the population we support. If we develop ways to be conscious of this and reflect on it continuously, we may be able to identify and remove some of those barriers. As an intermediary organisation, we can achieve a lot more than we might imagine. We may not be able to change the macro determinants of power, but we can ensure that we are not exacerbating existing inequities of power that occur every day and everywhere.

References

Bohm, D., 1996. *On dialogue*. Brighton: Psychology Press.

Flores, W., 2018. How can evidence bolster citizen action? Learning and adapting for accountable public health in Guatemala [online]. Guatemala: Accountability Research Center, Accountability Note 2. Available from: https://www.accountabilityresearch. org/publication/how-can-evidence-bolster-citizen-action-learning-and-adapting-for-a ccountable-public-health-in-guatemala/ [Accessed 4 April 2019].

Flores, W. and Gómez-Sánchez, I., 2010. La gobernanza en los consejos municipales de desarrollo de Guatemala: análisis de actores y relaciones de poder. *Revista de Salud Pública*, 12(suppl. 1), 138–150.

Flores, W. and Hernández, A., 2018. Health accountability for indigenous populations: confronting power through adaptive action cycles. *IDS Bulletin*, 49(2), 19–34.

Foucault, M., 1977/1995. *Discipline and punish: the birth of the prison*. New York: Vintage.

Hernández, A., Ruano, A.L., Hurtig, A., Goicolea, I., San Sebastián, M. and Flores, W., 2019. Pathways to accountability in rural Guatemala: a qualitative comparative analysis of citizen-led initiatives for the right to health of indigenous populations. *World Development*, 113, 392–401.

KwamiJ., Wolf-Monteiro, B. and Steeves, L., 2011. Toward a macro-micro analysis of gender, power and ICTs: a response to Micky Lee's feminist political economic critique of the human development approach to new ICTs. *International Communication Gazette*, 73(6), 539–549.

Silva, I. and Arantes, C., 2017. Power relations in the family health team: focus on nursing. *Revista Brasileira de Enfermagem*, 70(3), 580–587.

4.3

ENVIRONMENTAL DEFENDERS: COURAGE, TERRITORY AND POWER

Fran Lambrick

Defenders of land and the environment are being killed, criminalised, attacked and threatened across the world as a result of the destruction, appropriation or invasion of territories, forests, waterways, lands and seas. Frontline Defenders (2018, p. 6) estimate that of the 312 human rights defenders killed in 27 countries in 2017, 67 per cent were defenders of land and the environment.

The killings of environmental defenders have a profound effect on entire communities and movements. Killings are the tip of the iceberg in terms of numbers of those affected by violence. In many cases, the threat of death or violence is used to stop an action or movement before it has begun. Conversely, when defenders dare to continue to speak out or take action despite the threat of violence it forces the other side (the state forces, company security guards, etc.) to use force, reveal hidden power or to concede the position or territory. For environmental defenders the physical landscape and geographic spaces where they live or work often play key roles in determining the operation of power.

In this chapter, I focus on violence against environmental defenders and how the dimensions of power shape their resistance. The chapter draws on experiences, writings and interviews with defenders from Cambodia and Honduras, including reflections on my own experiences of frontline violence and resistance in Cambodia over a ten-year period.

The next section, 'Power to scare/power to dare: violence and choice', examines fear, courage and its emergence. This is followed by 'Territory/place', which examines the spatial existence of power, how intimate knowledge of a place gives strategic and physical advantage, and how territory is also bound to identity, courage and *power within* (see Bradley, this volume). Finally, I will discuss how some defenders are challenging the negative narratives that pave the way for violent attacks, and are creating new narratives, emphasising solidarity and *power with* (ibid.).

Power to scare/power to dare: violence and choice

In 2011, five months before his murder, I was sitting next to Cambodian forest defender, Chut Wutty, at the edge of Prey Lang forest, discussing illegal logging and corruption. We were about 30m away from the Prey Lang Community Network members – several hundred of whom had come to the logging site to investigate the activities of the CRCK rubber company. Two large military trucks appeared at the edge of the field. Military police and soldiers got out of the trucks and came towards us. I knew Chut Wutty had faced assassination attempts in this forest, and I was nervous. I stood up to move back to the rest of the group. Wutty stayed seated, considering his options.[1]

'Should I run away? But where could I go?' He did not change his position, and added, 'Well, I'd like to see what they do' (Wutty, quoted in Lambrick 2012). One of the soldiers came up behind us and told Wutty, who greeted him politely, to come to the truck. 'Why would I come with you?' (pers. comm., 1 November 2011). As Wutty spoke I was taking photos, and as the exchange became heated, turned off my camera, afraid of provoking the heavyset soldier standing above us. Then he grabbed Wutty around the neck, lifted him up and wrestled him to the ground. Surrounding us were about six police and soldiers, shouting, some pointing guns.

As I jumped back, terrified, a few of the community members rushed over. They threw themselves in front of the AK47s and grabbed Wutty, pulling him out of the line of fire. Quickly there were about a hundred people surrounding us. One of the community members shouted at the soldiers: 'You have guns and we don't. So who is powerful?' In those moments, the power had shifted. The unarmed, unafraid, 100-strong community side was in control. We all surrounded Wutty's car for protection, and walked 20 kilometres out of the forest, into the night.

The next day I asked Wutty why, despite the risks, he kept doing this work. He answered, 'If I don't do this, no one will. People are too afraid. I have to keep going.' Wutty's decision to continue, knowing he could be killed, seemed to be overriding terror; and despite the physical protection of the community surrounding him the previous day, his sense of isolation was apparent. He implied he was the only person who was willing to take these risks: 'many others in the country only want to be in a senior position and to get rewards: to make more and more money no matter if it is at the expense of others' (quoted in Lambrick 2012).

The different reactions to threats – reactions that are more or less bold – can also divide a movement. My own reaction to such courage was fear: initially to pull away, to dissociate myself from the person whose presence brought armed men pointing guns. It was obvious how fear can undermine solidarity, and how the idea of being the only one able to, brave enough to, sustain the struggle was propelling Wutty into a bold and precarious trajectory.

---

1   Quotes from Chut Wutty throughout the chapter are from the documentary *I Am Chut Wutty*, directed by Lambrick and de Smet (2015), unless specified in the text as a personal communication (pers. comm.).

The threat of violence, and internalisation of experiences of violence (as examined by Oosterom in this volume), can stymie a movement, introducing psychological distortions and obstructing decision-making. When you're scared it's hard to think. The stress of being constantly at risk can reduce one's ability to make sensible decisions regarding safety – one suffers from paranoia, recklessness or a 'brain fog' clouding one's ability to process, learn from and respond to trauma. The decision-making of people who have suffered traumatic events has been shown to be less adaptive than those who have not (Ousdal et al. 2018).

While fear can be a bogeyman, clouding our choices with imagined horrors, realistic fear can also be a vital source of information. Distinguishing between realistic and imagined or exaggerated fear is easier in communication with others. If a group can stay united, there is both physical and psychological protection – *power with*. Isolation of an individual can thus reduce the collective ability to respond flexibly and adaptively to fear.

The courage Wutty showed put him in a strong position. When Wutty stayed seated, his choice was a refusal to immediately react to fear – his position: we were doing nothing wrong; his tone: polite and respectful. It was almost daring the soldiers into brutality, forcing them into the wrong rather than acting as though he *ought* to have anything to fear. This is a stance that is typical of non-violent resistance. It echoes the strategies of land defenders, social and civil rights movements and independence activists from across the world, from Mahatma Ghandi and Martin Luther King to the Waikato-Māori and Cherokee refusals to fight, and refusal to obey colonial and oppressive orders.

In those moments, when being threatened or coerced, the ability to think and choose a course of action rather than react automatically is a significant *power within* – and one that can grow and develop through experience, and in interaction with others. As one deliberately stays put or even steps forward, the looming shadows of imagined fears shrink, the ways and means to deal with realistic fears become known.

Hannah Arendt (1970) distinguishes power from force. Power she sees as an ability to act with support from and representing others, and it is the result of free and open communication between parties. Force is the means to influence the will of another, whether by coercion, persuasion, threat of sanctions or other means.

> Power corresponds to the human ability not just to act but to act in concert … When we say of somebody that he is 'in power' we actually refer to his being empowered by a certain number of people to act in their name. (Arendt 1970, p. 44)

This empowerment can be through formalised support, such as an election to a position of leadership, or the informal support and recognition of a community, such as the commitment and courage shown by the community members who rushed to Chut Wutty's aid. His power in those moments following the violent attack was entirely due to his standing with the community – and five months later, at an illegal logging site in the Cardamom Mountains, he was with just two journalists when the confrontation with the company guard, two military police and a soldier became heated and then violent as he was shot through the door of his car.

In the context of actual or threatened violence, as well as other forms of coercion and influence, offers of compensation for the loss of ancestral lands, persuasion and bribery, the attempt and often the result is to constrain the choices and bend the will of the defender. The ultimate act of force is to kill, silencing voice and denying choice. The greatest fear, for most people, is the fear of death; and thus a tool for any actor intent on enforcing his/her will on another is to make the threat of death as real and apparent as possible. After Chut Wutty's murder most people's reaction was fear: the brutality of the killing in broad daylight, in front of witnesses, was shocking. However, in the months following Chut Wutty's death, his daring and his courage started to inspire others.

It is unusual when the power to scare people is countered with daring. Daring is the ability to grasp a choice – not to react to fear or force, but to consider another response. It is not the opposite of fear but the intelligent treatment of fear and of reasons for being afraid, and a consideration of what can be gained as well as what could be lost.

When asked to explain his continued efforts to protect the forest, to investigate logging and the illegal timber business, even at high risk, Chut Wutty said: 'I understand that wealth is important, and I want to be wealthy too, but also I want to see people live with freedom, to have their culture, their traditions, to be able to pursue their own lifestyle.'

Territory/place

In Cambodia, the southwest shores are fringed with mangroves, stretching deep into the estuaries and around islands. People here live off the sea, dependent on the mangroves that form the breeding ground for fish and crabs: their food and income. Companies dredged these waterways for sand from 2008 to 2016, causing the mangroves to collapse, destroying the spawning grounds for fish and damaging community livelihoods with an 80 per cent reduction in catch (Kastl et al. 2012). Millions of tons of sand were exported every year, mainly to Singapore to be used in construction and land reclamation.

In 2015, three youth activists – San Mala, Try Sovikea and Sim Somnang – were leading a campaign with the organisation Mother Nature Cambodia to defend the mangroves. In July, along with the local communities, they boarded the sand-dredging ships, demanding that they stop their activities. Shortly afterwards the three activists were arrested and then imprisoned on trumped-up charges. In November 2017, following the success of the campaign in securing a ban on the export of sand, two other activists from the same group, Hun Vannak and Doem Kundy, were monitoring activity off the coast. They were filming container ships suspected of carrying illegally exported sand. They were arrested and accused of 'violating privacy'.[2]

2   On 26 January 2018, Koh Kong Provincial Court's Judge Keo Sokha convicted the two environmental rights defenders, Hun Vannak and Doem Kundy, on charges of 'violating privacy' (Article 302 of the Criminal Code) and 'incitement to commit a felony' (Article 495), and sentenced each of them to one year in prison, with a seven-month suspended sentence, and a 1 million riel fine (approximately 200 Euros).

Asserting that the sea is a private space where citizens cannot document the activities of ships is an extreme example of how states in collusion with the private sector attempt to control and exploit the commons, claiming power over a space that has been unenclosed and is accessible to all. The presumption of the 'privacy rights' of companies engaged in seemingly illegal activities, with severe impacts on the natural heritage of the country and the livelihoods and economic potential of communities in the area, reveals the shadow power of a kleptocratic elite, controlling both state and corporate interests (see VeneKlasen, this volume; Global Witness 2016).

The struggle over land and the environment is inherently spatial. The ways in which power is manifest in this struggle are perhaps more obviously physical and geographic in this than in other struggles for social justice. Indigenous peoples, traditional communities and all who live in and close to the forest have knowledge of paths and waterways, the species that can be eaten, stems that hold water you can drink, high ground and hiding places, which translates to power – mastery of the environment through intimacy with it.

Seasonal ceremonies relating to hunting, fishing, harvesting and spiritual beliefs have also formed a critical part of non-violent resistance and community organisation in many traditional communities. These ceremonies are often intimately linked to the natural world, to lands and forests, sowing, transplanting, changes in seasons, harvesting. The passing down of ancestral knowledge and ritual practices relating to natural processes is important in building unity, *power with*, and strengthening identity, *power within*.

When Chut Wutty was killed in 2012 he was on an investigation trip accompanying two journalists to the Cardamom Mountains. It was a region he knew well, where he had been working in the early 2000s; but there he wasn't organising a community forest protection movement as he was in Prey Lang. He didn't hold the initiative – the trip was quickly organised, not part of a sustained community-based effort. At the attack in Prey Lang the 10–20 military and police who aggressively targeted Wutty in a planned attack could do nothing against nearly 100 Prey Lang Network members who had set out a week before, well organised and prepared, marching through the forest, patrolling, with food, water and cooking equipment, and meeting by pre-arrangement at the entrance to the CRCK rubber concession. They were ready for a confrontation, and when it happened they responded as a unit, in tune with the place and its risks. They knew what to do.

Wutty spoke about the forest as a protector: 'The forest is like the skin protecting our bodies, and without it we couldn't survive.' He compared the forest as protector with himself, saying that the communities see him the same way. As a defender he was motivated by the cause of meeting their needs for sustenance and survival, as the forest gives sustenance and survival also. In many indigenous traditions nature is seen as the protector and patron of human beings. In Cambodia's mangrove forests the trees, with their branches and roots growing into each other, cannot even be distinguished as separate organisms. Their physical interconnection reflects the ecological and cultural interconnection of people with each other and with the place.

Understanding ourselves as separate from the natural world rather than as part of it is inherent to the worldview and way of life that bulldozes, controls, mines, cuts and displaces. It is a simplistic dichotomy that leads to the erasure of the other, embodied, way of seeing the world: with humans as a part of nature, where our survival is not separate from the survival of the forest, or the river or the land around us.

During the appeal trial for Sim Somnang, Try Sovikea and San Mala in Phnom Penh, a group of activists went to demonstrate, calling for their release. We took large photographs of the mangroves, with the idea that we would talk to people about the activists' work to protect the environment, and simply show the green beauty and abundance of that place. Minutes later the police started grabbing the pictures, pulling them out of our hands, aggressively pushing us. It was as if even the representation of a forest, beautiful, intact and worth defending, was a provocation to violence. One of the activists, Ratha, turned to the cameras and said, 'Actually we're glad they took them. Maybe they will look at them in the police station, and slowly learn to love the forests and the estuaries that we are fighting for' (pers. comm., 15 February 2017).

This identification of ourselves as nature, as experiencing *power with* not only other people but also the ecosystem, is at the root of environmental defenders' courage. The physical existence of a landscape and territory is part of the resistance to protect it. In the attempt to gain power over a situation or territory individuals are targeted with violence and even death, but their courage to face attacks asserts their greater existence as part of a community and of the environment.

Narrative

Defenders of the environment are often cast as anti-progress, anti-development agitators, dissidents or even separatists, criminals or terrorists. A dominant narrative of 'progress' surrounds large-scale development projects, the consolidation and mono-cropping of agricultural land and other interventions of the state and corporations, which are portrayed as both beneficial and inevitable. The power of this narrative is also its implicit assumption of a shared value: economic growth, and of cultural homogeneity in pursuing gain.

In this story of progress toward the common good, environmentalists can be easily attacked as dangerous dissidents. The narrative that casts activists as dangerous, people who should be avoided, and the threat it carries is blatant. After San Mala's release from jail he explained his resolution had been formed when he first started environmental activism, years before being branded a criminal:

> Before we became Mother Nature activists, we had already prepared ourselves to face the fear – and all these obstacles. We understood that if we were threatened or sent to jail, it would be for only one reason: to try to stop our activism. So we must ask ourselves if we should stop and give in to their

wishes, or should we fight for what is right, in order to liberate our country? (pers. comm., unpublished interview, 17 January 2017)

The power to choose differently from most people is strange and inspiring, and presents an alternative story: one that is not founded on the narrative trajectory of economic growth and personal gain but, as Mala said, on 'what is right'.

Laura Zúñiga Cáceres is the youngest daughter of Berta Cáceres – the indigenous peoples' leader, co-founder of the Civic Council of Popular and Indigenous Organisations of Honduras (COPINH), women's rights defender and organiser – who was murdered in 2016. Laura wrote a letter for her mother following her murder, in which she overturns the narratives of 'progress' and 'development' in Honduras. In doing so she dignifies the shouldering of oppression, a word that is absent from the narrative of progress that portrays all people as being on a path toward economic betterment.

Bertha Cáceres,[3] my mother, my mommy, she was struggle in action, with oppression piled atop her, carrying on her back all the pains that this system imposes on the poor, the poor indigenous, the poor indigenous women. (Zúñiga Cáceres 2017)

The image of an indigenous woman carrying pains imposed by the system is a potent contradiction to the 'development' narrative that presents indigenous people and women as among the poorest of the 'poor' – people that are lifted up by development – and the economic system as a saviour, not an oppressive force. In response to resistance, the narrative goes further: indigenous people are labelled as 'terrorists' and 'opponents to development' in the media and in the courts in Honduras (Ardón and Flores 2017).

Laura casts indignation on the 'new forms of colonialism' – sold as development – that beset Honduras:

This country is so battered, with US military bases, with 30 percent of the territory granted to transnational corporations, companies that take over ancestral territories, with projects like the free trade zones, which are new forms of colonialism … with high rates of poverty, violence, femicide. In this country, the pain turns to rage, because they have stolen Bertha's arms, they have robbed me of my mom's arms. This country, which is humanity itself, refuses to resign itself to this assassination. (Zúñiga Cáceres 2017)

Laura refers to the wave of anger and hope that followed Berta's assassination, with demonstrations of thousands of people bearing slogans such as *Berta Vive!, Berta Cáceres no murió, se multiplicó!* ('Berta Lives!', 'Berta Cáceres did not die, she

3   Laura Zúñiga Cáceres uses the correct spelling, 'Bertha', while commonly her mother's name is written as 'Berta' (see Zúñiga Cáceres 2017).

multiplied!'). These slogans and Laura's reflection reject the portrayal of her mother as a victim and of Berta's struggle as a losing battle. 'She, the mother, the lady, the commander, my mommy, Bertha Cáceres with oppression piled atop her, she rebels against death, she climbs inside the heart of a people that have no borders. Bertha has multiplied and there is not an assassin who can kill her.' (Zúñiga Cáceres 2017).

The work of overturning the subtle and flagrant narratives that create a cultural licence to oppress activists, indigenous peoples, defenders, women, all those who dare to resist, is in itself a key tool of non-violent resistance. In this effort, articulating their own stories, puncturing dominating narratives, many defenders are offering hope and the chance for a different kind of ending – not a tragedy and not a happily ever after, but the continuing opportunity to choose how to respond: as Chut Wutty said, 'to live with freedom'.

Conclusion

The power to scare someone, to force them, with the threat of death or violence is countered by some individuals who choose to dare. This choice, *power within*, is deeply connected to *power with*, detectable in how fear is handled, the affirmation of a community, physical protection that creates a space for courage. It is also the invisible power of a narrative relayed through action – an old narrative showing human beings as an interconnected part of the natural world.

Before his death, Chut Wutty told his son that he would either die or be sent to jail in the end, and that this should not be treated as something extraordinary – 'birth and death are normal' (pers. comm. with R.O. Chhuey, 1 September 2012). Wutty's courage is a rejection of the invisible power of dominant narratives of individualism. His freedom to choose a more difficult, more terrifying path was also the exercise of *power within* – to dare.

Laura compares her mother to a seed: 'Bertha the planted', her 'movement-building prowess' continuing after death as a source of new life. In *power with*, which is deeply connected to the land she fought for, 'where her Lenca people are', even her death becomes a rebellion against the narrative of the killers (Zúñiga Cáceres 2017). The powerful refusal to accept a narrative of victimhood or of defeat is also an assertion that we are animals who give birth and die, and are part of families, communities, generations of ideas – that as living beings we are not discrete. Like the forest, rivers, plants and animals, an activist is regenerative. Her existence was never so contained, so atomic that the bullets could hit their mark.

References

Ardón, P. and Flores, D., 2017. Berta lives! COPINH continues. *International Journal of Human Rights*, 14(25), 109–117. Available from: https://sur.conectas.org/en/berta-lives-copinh-continues/ [Accessed 15 April 2019].
Arendt, H., 1970. *On violence*. New York: Harcourt, Brace & World.

Frontline Defenders, 2018. *Annual report on human rights defenders at risk in 2017*. Blackrock, Ireland: Front Line. Available from: https://www.frontlinedefenders.org/sites/default/files/annual_report_digital.pdf [Accessed 5 February 2019].

Global Witness, 2016. *Hostile takeover: the corporate empire of Cambodia's ruling family*. London: Global Witness. Available from: https://www.globalwitness.org/en/reports/hostile-ta keover/ [Accessed 16 March 2019].

Kastl, B.*et al.*, 2012. *Coastal mangrove forest devastation and channel sedimentation in Koh Kong Province, Cambodia*. Gland, Switzerland: International Union for Conservation of Nature. Available from: https://cmsdata.iucn.org/downloads/mangrove_devastation_koh_kong_report.pdf [Accessed 16 March 2019].

Lambrick, F., 2012. Who is responsible for the death of Cambodia's foremost forest activist? *The Guardian* [online], 1 May 2012. Available from: https://www.theguardian.com/environment/blog/2012/may/01/death-cambodian-forest-activist-chut-wutty [Accessed 10 April 2019].

Lambrick, F. and de Smet, V., dir., 2015. *I am Chut Wutty*. Oxford: Last Line Productions. Available from: https://itunes.apple.com/gb/movie/i-am-chut-wutty/id1281567462 [Accessed 18 March, 2018].

Ousdal, O.T.*et al.*, 2018. The impact of traumatic stress on Pavlovian biases. *Psychological Medicine*, 48(2), 327–336. Available from: https://quentinhuys.com/pub/OusdalEa17-Tra umaPavlovianBiases.pdf [Accessed 5 February 2019].

Zúñiga Cáceres, L.Y., 2017. We are going to triumph (M. Cox, trans.) [online]. Available from: https://www.commondreams.org/views/2017/03/05/we-are-going-triumph [Accessed 16 March 2019].

4.4

THE DECOLONISING ZAPATISTA REVOLUTION

Raúl Zibechi

Introduction

Zapatismo, or neo–Zapatismo, is a political movement with strong roots in the indigenous communities of Chiapas, Mexico, and in particular among the Tzeltal, Tzotzil, Tojolabal, Chol and Mam communities. The *Ejército Zapatista de Liberación Nacional* (Zapatista Army of National Liberation, or EZLN) was created in 1983, but first came to public attention on 1 January 1994, when thousands of armed indigenous people took control of the principal towns in Chiapas. They sought recognition among civil society actors and a response from government to their demands – centred on autonomy for the indigenous peoples and self-government for the lands they had taken back from landowners. Following a brief period of armed confrontation, lasting less than two weeks, they entered into dialogue with the authorities.

In 2013 I participated in the *escuelita zapatista*, or 'Zapatista school', in the Morelia *caracol*.[1] In this chapter, I seek to use this experience to illustrate some of the characteristics of the movement, drawing on my day-to-day involvement at the three levels of Zapatista autonomy: the community, the municipality and the region. I do this by tying together my daily experiences and my life with families, in their work and in their debates, in an attempt to understand the ways in which the movement is organised, how it functions and how it portrays itself. The voices represented here are, almost entirely, those of the men, women and children of the community, making it possible to understand better what the construction of a new world means in the 5 regions, 30 municipalities and more than 1000 communities involved in the Zapatista process. Fundamentally, this involves self-government, without any reliance on state or federal government.

---

1   *Caracoles* ('snails') are regional units of organisation within the Autonomous Zapatista Communities.

Zapatismo is a fusion, or mixture, of two currents: indigenous land struggles and the fight for survival as peoples. It is rooted in five centuries of history, and has more recent origins in a group of armed militants that emerged in the wake of the Massacre of Tlatelolco on 2 October 1968 as part of a broad, armed, student-based pro-democracy movement known as the *Frente de Liberación Nacional*, or National Liberation Front (FLN). The FLN made contact with the indigenous communities of Chiapas, learning from them new forms of political engagement that differed from those predominating in the cities, and in turn describing their organisation and sharing their experiences as militants of the armed movement. The EZLN was born of this encounter between equal, but different, experiences, following a decade of intense, quiet activity. Their history has been marked by periods of intense participation on the political stage, combined with long periods of silence. They made a powerful reappearance on 21 December 2012 when 40,000 well-organised, but this time unarmed, people once again occupied the principal towns of Chiapas.

The main focus of the Zapatistas has been to demonstrate the operational logic of their new political culture, which they call *mandar obedeciendo*, or 'lead by obeying'. This means that their leaders (in the communities, autonomous municipalities or good governance boards) are guided in their activities by principles such as *bajar y no subir* ('work from below, not seek to rise up'), which demonstrate the vocation of their members to serve their communities and not to seek personal advantage from them, as occurred in the past. In general, the Zapatistas do not participate in elections and do not participate in official elections for representatives or office; but in the 2018 elections they did present a candidate, María de Jesús Patricio Martínez, known as Marichuy, who travelled the country engaging in dialogue with villages, *colonias* and *barrios* (urban neighbourhoods) and communities in remote areas of the country. The aim of these activities is to create conditions for the self-organisation of all sectors of Mexican society, whether or not they share the aims of Zapatismo.

Simultaneously the *escuelitas*, or immersion experiences, confirm the division of society into *los de arriba y los de abajo*, or the haves and the have-nots. This social division is not based on class; nor is it scientific – but it has the virtue of cutting across all other categories: gender, ethnicity, class, sexuality, race and nationality. It combines with the desire to construct spaces that echo the characteristics of the world of the have-nots: 'rebellious, heretical, rude, irreverent, annoying, uncomfortable' (EZLN 2013a). Furthermore, the *escuelitas* reject the concept of citizenship, which they consider to be the 'the most dishonest identity', as it extinguishes social differences. In adopting this position, the Zapatista discourse revives the tradition of anticolonial resistance defended by Frantz Fanon (1952), who stressed the existence of 'two zones' – that of the oppressor (the 'zone of being') and that of the oppressed ('the zone of non-being') – which do not meet because for the exploited 'there is no compromise, no possible coming to terms' (Fanon 1967, p. 47). While in the 'zone of being' violence against the oppressed is the exception, in the 'zone of non-being' it is the rule, a factor that leads to a fundamental modification of emancipatory thinking and practice because it is impossible for a revolutionary theory born in the 'zone of being' to have universal pretensions.

The EZLN is committed to transforming reality from below, bypassing the state and official institutions. The latest series of EZLN statements may be summarised in a single phrase: 'We don't want only to change the government, we want to change the world.'

The community from within

The Zapatistas suggest that those who sympathise with their way of doing things should dedicate their time to understanding directly what the movement has done since its inception. They invited a group of sympathisers, including me, to take part in a six-day long *escuelita*, or immersion experience, in the five *caracoles*, during which we became students of the grassroots of the movement, learning from indigenous Zapatistas. In other words, we did not hear from the *comandantes* and *subcomandantes*, but from the ordinary people who make up the grassroots of the EZLN. It was an intense process of listening, a kind of ritual, which started with three days of fiestas, followed by six more of immersion in the *escuelita*.

The Zapatistas opened their hearts and their inner landscapes to activists from all over the world, but always according to their distinct indigenous–Zapatista approach: emphasising the *how* rather than the *why*. This is not a question of gaining access to a revealed, rational body of knowledge, because they do not possess such a thing in an available form 'that can be closed up or filed away, and even less a knowledge alienated from a subject. Rather, it demands the commitment of the subject who handles or manipulates it' (Kusch et al 2010, p. 32). While it is true that we are witnessing the birth of a new political culture, it is a culture that cannot be explained but must be lived; it is a knowledge that cannot be transmitted, but that can be accessed only through a ritual of commitment: by being present and by sharing.

As Kusch and a wide range of indigenous thinkers have commented,[2] this political culture cannot be transmitted using traditional methods, by establishing a political stance supported by leaflets, books, conferences and lectures. It is, furthermore, 'a knowledge for living' that can be 'grown', 'multiplied' and – of particular importance – 'brought into existence' (Kusch et al. 2010, p. 39). It is far from being a codified form of knowledge that focuses principally – in the words of Fanon's critique of revolutionary parties – on 'the most politically conscious' (Fanon 1967, p. 86). It operates in a different way, as it tends, in Kusch's well-known formulation, to 'multiply like sown land' (2010, p. 33): that is, sow without reaping, sow as part of a ritual of life, trusting that time, too, will do its work.

I stayed in the '8 March' community, in the '17 November' municipality Morelia *caracol* – one of more than 200 communities in the Zapatista region. The community has more than 1000 hectares of high-quality land, so its members no longer need to work the dry, stony hillsides. They grow traditional crops and also,

---

2   Silvia Rivera Cusicanqui, Luis Macas, Sabino Romero, Felipe Quispe, Simón Yampara, Félix Patzi, Floriberto Díaz, for example.

at the recommendation of the leadership, fruit and vegetables. Not only did the *comuneros*, or community members, free themselves from the yoke of the landlords, but also their diet was improved and they are able to save some money. Each family keeps a sack of the coffee it produces and sells the rest. Depending on market prices they are generally able to buy two or three cows with the proceeds, which act as a 'bank' and are sold when the need arises – for example in the event of health problems or if a water filter fails.

The costs of the health centre and the *escuelita* are covered in the same way, as are all the transport and accommodation expenses of the *comuneros* who have responsibilities in the three levels of self-government: at local (or communal) level, or in the autonomous municipalities or regional good governance boards. The few things that are not produced by the families themselves (salt, sugar, oil and soap) are bought in the urban centres of the municipalities in Zapatista shops, established in properties that were occupied following the 1994 uprising. The communities are therefore linked to but not dependent on the market, and are not obliged to resort to it, their entire economy being contained within a self-sufficient circuit that they control.

The shops are staffed by different community members every month, following a rota. During the month *comuneros* are staffing the shop, their crops are looked after by the community. Similarly, when they are participating in the good governance boards, their duties are met according to the same reciprocal arrangement.

A rebel health care system, controlled by women

Every community, however small, has a primary school and a health centre. The assembly chooses their board members (half male and half female), the teachers and the health care workers. Nobody can be denied access, because these are community services. In the case of health care, several things are apparent: the power of women, who take control of these spaces and make them their own; the Zapatista integration of different approaches to health care without excluding any; and the levels of autonomy enjoyed by the various levels (community, municipality and region), each of which has its own health centre.

Medicines produced by the pharmaceutical industry sit on the shelves of the health centres side by side with a large supply of medicinal plants, which, in the community I stayed in, are processed by a very young girl into medicines and ointments. In common with all the basic Zapatista health centres, this one also has a bonesetter and a midwife. A young man is responsible for administering Western medicine. In general, the centres deal with relatively simple cases, while individuals with more serious problems are sent to the clinic in the *caracol*, and, if this is unable to resolve the problem, to the state hospital in Altamirano.

The activities of the Zapatistas in the field of health are organised around resistance to the domination inherent in state health practice. They assert this by affirming their own identity, providing health to all communities and struggling against patriarchy: in sum, strengthening community and female autonomy. For this reason, the health model involves health promoters (*promotoras*) who rely on traditional knowledge (herbalists, bonesetters, midwives), not in pursuit of an essentialist indigenous practice but as techniques that are complementary to Western medicine. The starting point is the rejection of the humiliation and mistreatment that indigenous people – and especially indigenous women – suffer at the hands of the state hospital system. Community-based and constructed on the foundations of the culture and experience of the communities, it does not rely on state health provision, either because this does not reach them or because it humiliates them.

To understand fully the process of constructing a rebel health system in Zapatista communities, one must view it through the eyes of women – its principal beneficiaries – and of those who receive its services. Despite maternal mortality in the region being the highest in Mexico, health care represents an empowering space for women: 'working on health has given Zapatista women the confidence and capability to confront and renegotiate gender, ethnic and class relations in their families, communities and regions' (Forbis 2011, p. 372).[3] The women feel comfortable because it is they who take responsibility for childcare, and because they are the repositories of knowledge about how to look after the body.

Work on health care began before the 1994 uprising, in the 1980s. Men and women elected by the community assemblies as health promoters were trained, and initiated the process of recovering medical knowledge in each area of operation. Reviving the knowledge of herbalists, bonesetters and midwives was not an attempt to develop an 'alternative' health system, but part of working towards community self-sufficiency. This obliged them to rely on their own efforts, knowledge and capabilities. But this knowledge had been progressively lost as a result of emigration to areas with different plants and crops, government programmes that imposed state medical models, and a lack of self-esteem and loss of faith in their own traditions.

In 1997, 91 health promoters met in the Zapatista community of Moisés Gandhi, in the *Primer Foro Encuentro de Promotor@s de Salud* (First Forum of Men and Women Health Promoters),[4] producing the 'Declaration of Moisés Gandhi':

> Health is living without humiliation; being able to develop ourselves as women and men; it is being able to struggle for a new country [*patria*] where the poor and particularly the indigenous peoples can make decisions autonomously. Poverty, militarization and war destroy health. (Speed et al. 2013, p. 187)[5]

---

3 All quotations from Forbis are rendered into English by the translator.
4 The symbol '@' is used by some writers in Spanish as a useful way to achieve gender-neutral spelling, in this case to refer to both male and female health promoters.
5 Translator's note: This English translation of part of the Declaration has been taken from *Dissident Women: Gender and Cultural Politics in Chiapas*, by Speed et al. (2013). Subsequent excerpts have been rendered into English by the translator, based on the original Declaration of Moisés Gandhi in Spanish, which can be found at http://www.cedoz.org/site/content.php?doc=500&cat=83.

In an effort to recover traditional knowledge, they built herbalist laboratories and trained more than 1000 women in ancestral practices. They called on existing practitioners to provide training, but this proved a difficult process as 'at the beginning, many comrades were unwilling to share their knowledge, the men and women saying it was a gift that cannot be transferred, because it is something that you carry within you' (Muñoz Ramírez 2004). Through debate and the intervention of the Zapatista health authorities, it was possible to overcome resistance. These practitioners became teachers of traditional health, multiplying the numbers of midwives, bonesetters and herbalists.

Becoming a health promoter provides an opportunity to gain recognition in the community, as promoters are both office-holders and assume a role that is also 'a means for women to organise publicly and dispute gender hierarchies; demanding their right to work for the good of the community through health, just as men have in the past' (Forbis 2011, p. 389).

As students of the Zapatista *escuelita* we were able to witness how women have their own collective projects, administered by the group, through which they cover travel costs when participating in training events and other organisational activities. Women's collective productive projects are the bedrock of their material autonomy, freeing them from dependence on men. According to one commentator, the work of women in health 'has changed gender power relations', which have become complementary as a result of their efforts (Forbis 2011, p. 394).

Nevertheless, difficulties remain. The *promotor@s*' communities and families have not always showed understanding of their role, though this is subject to continuous debate. They no longer have to ask permission to leave their communities alone to participate in training events or fulfil their representational duties; but rumours, gossip and criticisms are still heard, and at times problems need to be resolved in community assemblies. When women gain knowledge and acquire new skills in their health work, it can be disconcerting for men, especially because for many women promoters this is just a first step towards appointment to regional-level positions of authority.

For the Zapatistas, breaking dependency on state hospitals and the power of the medical profession, valuing traditional medicines and overcoming domestic violence are necessary steps if oppression is to be ended and autonomy fortified. Health is collective, not individual, and should be neutral in the sense that it attends to everyone, regardless of skin colour, language, age, beliefs, gender, party or wealth. According to the Declaration of Moisés Gandhi, it should be 'in the hands of the people'. This means that health care should be built collectively, using different methods of healing, 'sharing this knowledge with the entire community in order to rediscover our health and friendship, and the confidence of our elders, so that their knowledge is not lost'. As in all aspects of life, ranging from travel to power, the promoters 'seek communitarian solutions to needs for medical attention, rather than individual ones, at the same time as they actively create new kinds of social connection' (Forbis 2011, p. 403).

The Zapatista autonomous health system has hospitals, clinical and herbal laboratories, health posts, ambulances and pharmacies distributed across the three levels of Zapatista autonomous power: community, municipality and region. The clinics in the *caracoles* tend to be very advanced: one of them even has an operating theatre.

A final aspect of health provision relates to men and their changing roles. Membership of the good governance boards is generally shared equally between men and women, as in the Morelia *caracol*. Families represent the opposite extreme: they are characterised by a marked division of labour. Men cultivate coffee and tend cattle, helped by older boys, while the women carry out domestic duties, helped by girls. But the women leave their communities to train as midwives or represent their municipalities in the good governance boards, and while they are away the men look after the children for days on end. At times, too, the men share housework, though this is not common. The Declaration of Moisés Gandhi states that women demand freedom and equality, the right to enjoy free time, to decide on the number of children they will have, to participate in decision-making and the management of family, community and organisational finances. It argues that a great deal of progress has been made, but that 'we men must reassess our attitudes towards women and learn to live in equality'. It also indicates that 'health promoters [of both sexes] must set an example in our homes, men and women living together in equality'.

The material underpinnings of autonomy

Since the uprising of 1 January 1994, some 200,000–250,000 hectares of good land, previously in the hands of large cattle farmers, have been occupied by the Zapatistas and members of peasant organisations. Having taken control of the land, the Zapatistas were able to build communities, municipalities and autonomous regions that differed from those not in Zapatista hands, with 'productive autonomy' and governance institutions that were not of the state.

Key to this endeavour is collective work, which from the Zapatista viewpoint constitutes 'the engine of autonomy'. To understand the functioning of the Zapatista economy one has to discard habitual ways of understanding the economy including, even, 'alternative' economics. To them the economy is not an autonomous sphere; nor is it governed by laws. Instead, it is subordinated to the communities that are themselves permanently under threat from the Mexican state, their productive activities responding to the need to resist the militaristic actions of the government.

The conceptual tools of political economy analysis, developed in a different historical context to analyse a different reality, would not help explain what is happening in the autonomous territories of Chiapas. Academic common sense maintains that the economic basis of the Zapatista communities is:

> the model of the *milpa* [cornfield], principally [involving] family-level production for the domestic consumption of maize, beans and a variety of vegetables and fruit; with limited commercialisation of the surplus … but rather

occasional sales ... of animals, coffee, and occasional paid work. (Stahler-Sholk 2011, p. 433)[6]

To this 'model' are added sheep and rabbit farming, market gardening, artisan production, collective marketing initiatives, and the provision of social services in areas including health, education and the provision of drinking water. Stahler-Sholk's analysis continues: 'this array of different projects does not constitute a comprehensive alternative model', which would be politically important for sustaining autonomy, but does 'represent the seeds of an alternative development strategy' (2011, p. 434).

This analysis, though one of the most rigorous and committed available, concludes that 'the development model followed in the Zapatista communities could be scaled up if it were not for the relative absence of productive projects', and that yields of crops such as maize could be doubled or tripled if tractors were used (Stahler-Sholk 2011, p. 435). The preoccupation with 'economic sustainability' and with the search for an 'alternative model' presupposes dealing with Zapatista reality using concepts inherited from political economy. I maintain that, instead, the analysis should focus on the organising principle of the Zapatista communities: resistance.

In effect, 'productive projects' are all about economic resistance, at three levels or areas – the communitarian, municipal and zonal economy – spanning the family to the good governance boards (EZLN 2013b). At each level, the same logic of collective labour applies. It is not a 'subsistence economy' because survival is structured around resistance – a collective resistance, community-based, organised according to the principle of autonomy. Resistance is not an end in itself: the aim is to maintain autonomy. In everyday life, this tends to take the form of scraping together 'the fare' – the transport costs of travelling from one's own community to go and work alongside other communities, in other municipalities and zones – because individuals must travel to fulfil their responsibilities.[7]

Collective labour underpins the commons, and is the true material base that produces and reproduces living communities, based on relations of reciprocity and mutual help rather than the hierarchical and individualised relations at the core of state institutions. The community lives not because of common property, but because of collective labour that is creative, and is re-created and affirmed in everyday life. This collective work is the means through which the *comuneros* and *comuneras* make a community, expressed in social relations that differ from the hegemonic ones (Zibechi 2018).

Collective labour is part of all community activities. It enables both the reproduction of material goods and the community as such, from the assembly and feasts

---

6   All quotations from Stahler-Sholk are rendered into English by the translator.
7   The following two paragraphs are reproduced from my essay 'People in defence of life and territory: counter-power and self-defence in Latin America', published in the Transnational Institute's annual *State of Power* report (pp. 152–3), with kind permission of the editors, Nick Buxton and Deborah Eade (Zibechi 2018).

to funerals and wakes, as well as alliances with other communities. Resistance struggles that ensure the reproduction of community life are also anchored in collective labour. Emphasising the multiple forms of collective labour allows us to see power and counter-power from a different perspective. First, collective labour is not an institution but a set of social relations. Second, because they are social relations, they can be produced by any collective subject in any space. As they are distinct from the community's property relations and authorities, they can reappear wherever the subjects or movements engage in community-inspired practices.

A new world

All communal education activities, too, are carried out collectively. Commissions with rotating membership bring together school pupils, promoters and members of the Education Committee – itself made up of *comuneros* elected by the assembly – who do not necessarily have children in school. To make the learning experience as complete as possible, pupils participate in school governing boards so that secondary schools actually form new educators. The school is a space where communal practices are reproduced and re-signified, including collective work, 'leading by obeying' (*mandar obedeciendo*), autonomy and respect for the decisions of young people – among these the aim to keep distance between teachers and pupils to a minimum, and that pupils take ownership of their own learning and of the physical space of the school – all based on a powerful, permanent and profound communication between all. This echoes Paulo Freire's views on education:

> In fact, there is a tacit consensus concerning the pedagogical method: everything should start with a continuous questioning, or 'problematisation,' of reality – not only of the immediate socio-cultural reality of each pupil but also of the global context. The themes, activities or values – that is the contents – to be worked on in the classroom should emerge from this continual questioning of reality. These questionings should be 'appropriated' by the group, which, together, should work to find ways to resolve the problematic and uncover answers to the questions that have been raised – or come close to these answers – whether through collective reflection, documentary or social research, experimentation, etcetera. (Gutiérrez Narváez 2011, p. 259)

In his polemic against Marxist anthropologists Clastres (1978) criticised them for applying concepts such as 'relations of production', 'infrastructure' and 'superstructure' to any reality they encounter in any part of the world, without taking into account – as for example with indigenous communities – that the principal objective is to continue functioning as communities rather than to increase production. In the case of the Zapatistas, these communities are defined as autonomous and in resistance. Their movement should not be analysed in terms of what it 'lacks' in comparison with the erstwhile Western revolutionary project represented by communist parties and others. Nor should it be assumed that Zapatismo belongs to the political project of the Latin American left. Instead, its contributions to these projects should be recognised, along with its points of divergence and its distinctive features. I prefer to interpret the movement from a different perspective: Zapatismo is neither a 'social movement' nor a revolutionary process with a clear, established project to transform the world or effect a revolution. It is hard to know what it is: existing categories – such as the trade union, national liberation, feminist, indigenous or environmental movements – do not apply.

The Zapatistas tend not to project their activities into the future. They do not speak of socialism or give a name to the society they are struggling to create; nor do they design a revolutionary project which they then try to apply.

> We do not know why they say socialism. We want land, health, housing, education, freedom, peace, justice. We don't know if that is called socialism or paradise. The name does not matter to us; what does matter is that we have 13 demands. (EZLN 2013b, p. 29)

For hegemonic political culture, statements like this are a symptom of de-politicisation or theoretical poverty; it fails to recognise that the Zapatistas live as they think and think as they live – a practice that is unusual among organisations of the left.

Zapatismo is a new kind of movement, which should not be labelled using outdated concepts, including 'social movement', a term that itself needs de-colonising. Zapatismo is one of a clutch of new movements that has emerged during the last two or three decades (Zibechi 2003): many of its characteristics are found in other Latin American movements, whether they represent indigenous peoples (in particular the Nasa in Colombia and the Mapuche in Chile), landless peasants or collectives from the urban peripheries. The two principal ways in which it differs from the other movements are its comprehensive autonomy, involving a rejection of government subsidies and social policies, and the fact it has created its own decision-making bodies, operating on three levels of governance distinct from state forms of power and rooted in the community. It is a movement focused on young people and women, and is profoundly anti-capitalist. Taken together, these two principles (autonomy and separate institutions) and the three focuses of the movement (young people, women and anti-capitalism) constitute five salient characteristics, which I briefly examine below.

First, the *autonomy* of the Zapatista communities – illustrated above through the examples of health, education and economy – covers all areas of life. The Mexican government's social policies are not intended to combat poverty, as the official discourse claims, but to destroy the autonomous Zapatista communities. Wherever EZLN grassroots communities build an *escuelita*, the government installs a state-funded alternative, offering food and construction materials to the families who send their children there. The same happens with health and housing. For this reason, I call these 'counterinsurgent' social policies (Zibechi 2010).

Second, Zapatista autonomy differs from all other processes that seek to build autonomy for poor social groups, because of its comprehensive nature and the

Zapatistas' refusal to receive anything from the state (though they do accept support from Mexican and international solidarity groups). One of the reasons many communities and families have abandoned Zapatismo is precisely its decision to reject government programmes on the grounds that they undermine and annul autonomy. Autonomy is the least negotiable of all the Zapatistas' demands, as it affects the very nature of the movement. Just as capitalist society focuses on the economy, Zapatismo focuses on autonomy. Autonomy must be present in all aspects of life, but particularly in relation to food security, in which the poor are most vulnerable.

Third, the Zapatistas have built *non-state power structures*, that is, structures inspired by the communities: assemblies in which all decisions are taken by consensus following long processes of discussion; rotation of representatives in order to ensure that hierarchies (present in any form of power) do not become frozen into a separate bureaucracy sitting above the community. The concept of *mandar obedeciendo*, or 'leading by obeying', summarises the way in which the Zapatistas understand power. It is not a *power over* but a collective *power to* and a *power between*: respectively, 'the unique potential of every person to shape his or her life and world' and '[find] common ground among different interests in order to build collective strength' (Miller et al. 2006, p. 6). The leaders do not have power: they are a kind of unpaid official who takes on the desire of society to appear as a single whole, where power is not separate from society – which implies that while power exists in all societies, it is not always coercive in form (Clastres 1981).

Fourth, Zapatismo is *a movement of women and young people*, though adult and old men are present too. Half of all Zapatistas are under 20, and men and women are represented equally at the three levels of government. There are many more women than men engaged in the area of health, and they have a significant presence in education as well as participating in all aspects of Zapatista life, from the community assemblies to demonstrations. Very slowly, men are beginning to take on domestic tasks and to look after their children. In a demonstration at which I was present, some men carried their children – a role that in the indigenous world has always corresponded to women.

Fifth, Zapatismo is *an anti-capitalist movement*: not content merely to declare itself against the current system – though such denunciations are helpful – it battles capitalism, and does not reproduce it in its territories. Zapatistas do not engage in capitalism in the fields of health, education, production or distribution, or when playing community governance roles. There is no paid work, but the communities engage in collective activities in order to provide material support to teachers, health workers and anyone who is elected to 'work' for the community. Fundamentally, Zapatismo can be viewed as a way of doing – a practice associated with a particular political culture: 'The essential nature of the movement is the construction – based on the principle of 'mandar obedeciendo' – of a practice that generates a collective sense and confers legitimacy to the processes and structures of self-government' (Stahler-Sholk 2011, p. 444).

Conclusions[8]

As a general rule, social movements are counter-powers that seek to bring balance or present a counterweight to the large global powers, such as multinational corporations and the states that work with them. Often, these counter-powers act in a way that imitates state power, with similar hierarchies, even if they are made up of individuals from different social sectors, ethnicities and skin colours, genders and generations.

Counter-power is usually defined as seeking to displace hegemonic power, but is often constituted in a similar manner to state power as we know and endure it, at least in Western societies. In Latin America we can't use an essentialist understanding of the community as an institution, but rather one based on strong, direct, face-to-face relationships between people whose daily life is closely intertwined.

The proposals of the left for 'counter-power' are always marked by an underlying temptation to become a new power, constructed in the image of the state. In the reality of communities that resist, constructed power comes from an entirely different source from those that dominate the great revolutions or within social movements. In hegemonic political culture, the image of the pyramid inspired by the state and the Catholic Church is constantly reproduced in political parties and unions, with amazing regularity. Controlling power happens at the apex of the pyramid, and all political action channels collective energy in that direction.

There are, however, distinct traditions in which communities channel all their energy into avoiding having powerful leaders, and that reject state-types of power. A community is certainly a form of organisation that includes power relations, but its character differs from that of state power. Elders' councils or appointed and rotating positions are transparent powers, under constant collective control. This means they are not autonomous forms of power; they cannot exercise power over the community, which is a characteristic of the state with its non-electable community, separated from society and standing above it.

In discussing such types of power, we need to differentiate them from other forms of exercising power – which is why I refer to them as non-state-powers. Perhaps the best-known cases are the good governance boards in the five Zapatista regions or *caracoles*.

Women and men are equally represented and are elected from among hundreds of members in the autonomous municipalities. The entire government team – up to 24 people in some *caracoles* – changes each week. This rotating system, as the Zapatista community members explain, gradually enables everyone to learn how to govern. More than 1000 communities, 29 autonomous municipalities and some 300,000 people govern themselves through this system. Zapatista autonomy does not create bureaucracies because the rotation system disperses them, avoiding the formation of a separate, specialised body.

---

8   The following section is reproduced, lightly edited, from Zibechi, (2018, pp. 160–162), with kind permission of the editors, Buxton and Eade.

Movements of poor young rural people and women of colour are criminalised all around the world by states. They are made up of people who have nothing to lose because they cannot and do not wish to take part in institutional politics. They do not have a place in representative democracies, which seek to homogenise those who are different in order subordinate them. They do not have a place in political parties, not even in those of the left, which as a rule seek to present their demands without involving them – a practice that is unacceptable to communities that, as a core part of their identity, champion a new political culture that is neither institutional nor representative.

Throughout human history, transitions from one society to another have involved long processes during which one form of life slowly imposes itself over another, until all society's pores have been saturated by the new. It would seem that the Zapatistas believe that the transformation to a new society will take a long time, that they will not lead it and that it will not be a planned process, as revolutions have been up till now.

The Zapatistas' vision of social transformation, which includes periods of systemic chaos, is close to indigenous worldviews, which see and feel changes as a new cosmic time or a new cycle, where what lies invisible or hidden underground comes to play an important role, displacing whatever prevailed before. The concept and the practice of the revolution are being de-colonised from below.

References

Clastres, P., 1987. *Society against the state: essays in political anthropology* (R. Hurley, trans., in collaboration with A. Stein). New York: Zone Books.

EZLN, 2013a. Ellos y Nosotros. V. La Sexta. Enlace Zapatista, México, January. Available from: http://enlacezapatista.ezln.org.mx/2013/01/26/ellos-y-nosotros-v-la-sexta-2/ [Accessed 2 November 2013].

EZLN, 2013b. Resistencia Autónoma: Cuaderno de texto del primer grado del curso. La Libertad según l@s Zapatistas. Available from: http://media.espora.org/mgoblin_media/media_entries/317/EscuelitaEZLN-Resistencia_Autonoma.pdf [Accessed 15 January 2019].

Fanon, F., 1952. *Peau noire, masques blanc*. Paris: Seuil; this translation, *Black skin, white masks* (C.L. Markmann, trans.). London: Pluto, 1986.

Fanon, F., 1967. *The wretched of the earth*. London: Penguin.

Forbis, M., 2011. Autonomía y un puñado de hierbas. In: B. Baronnet *et al.*, eds. *Luchas 'muy otras': Zapatismo y autonomía en las comunidades indígenas de Chiapas*. México: Universidad Autónoma Metropolitana, 371–409.

Gutiérrez Narváez, R., 2011. Dos proyectos de sociedad en Los Altos de Chiapas. In: B. Baronnet *et al.*, eds. *Luchas 'muy otras': Zapatismo y autonomía en las comunidades indígenas de Chiapas*. México: Universidad Autónoma Metropolitana, 237–267.

Kusch, R. *et al.*, 2010. *Indigenous and popular thinking in America*. Durham, NC: Duke University Press.

Miller, V., VeneKlasen, L., Reilly, M. and Clark, C., 2006. *Making change happen 3: power: Concepts for revisioning power for justice, equality and peace*. Washington DC: Just Associates.

Muñoz Ramírez, G., 2004. Chiapas la resistencia. *La Jornada*, 19 September. Available from: https://www.jornada.com.mx/2004/09/19/chiprincipal.html. [Accessed 15 January 2019].

Speed, S., Aída Hernández Castillo, R. and Stephen, L.M., 2013. *Dissident women: gender and cultural politics in Chiapas*. Austin: University of Texas Press.

Stahler-Sholk, R., 2011. Autonomía y economía política de resistencia en Las Cañadas de Ocosingo. In: B. Baronnet *et al.*, eds. *Luchas muy 'otras': Zapatismo y autonomía en las comunidades indígenas de Chiapas*. México: Universidad Autónoma Metropolitana, 409–447.

Zibechi, R., 2003. Los movimientos sociales latinoamericanos: tendencias y desafíos. *Observatorio social de América Latina*, 9 (January), 185–188.

Zibechi, R., 2010. *América Latina: contrainsurgencia y pobreza*. Bogotá: Desdeabajo.

Zibechi, R., 2018. People in defence of life and territory: counter-power and self-defence in Latin America. In: N. Buxton and D. Eade, eds. *State of power*. Amsterdam: Transnational Institute, 139–157.

PART 5

Unlearning and learning power for reflective social change

5.1

LEARNING ABOUT POWER IN A MASTER'S FOR REFLECTIVE SOCIAL CHANGE PRACTITIONERS

Rosemary McGee, Jethro Pettit and Fiammetta Wegner[1]

Introduction

In the early 2000s, a group of us at the Institute of Development Studies (IDS) at the University of Sussex, UK, decided to create a new Master's programme for social change practitioners from around the world, grounded in methods of critical reflexivity, action research and power analysis.[2] The idea for the MA in Power, Participation and Social Change (MAP)[3] was partly in response to the lack of applied, experiential and reflective learning opportunities for activists and development workers. We had also identified a need for more critical, power-conscious approaches to practices of civic and political participation, given the growing interest in participatory and accountable governance – change processes which were in danger of being instrumentalised and watered down.

While strong traditions of political participation had prevailed in social movements and liberation struggles during the 1960s and 1970s, and participatory methods of community-driven development had flourished during the 1980s (Chambers 1983, Chambers 1993), the rapid mainstreaming of participation by aid

1 The chapter draws in places on the unpublished PhD thesis of Jethro Pettit (2012) and the unpublished scholarly piece submitted by Rosemary McGee in part-fulfilment of the Postgraduate Certificate in Higher Education (McGee 2014). Fiammetta Wegner, herself a MAP alumna, collaborated with us in producing this chapter by conducting the interviews we draw on and some of the material in the chapter comes from her reports. Jethro Pettit contributed to the section on the origins of MAP, discussed the interview findings and reviewed drafts.
2 MAP was initially designed by John Gaventa, Peter Taylor, Jethro Pettit and Darcy Ashman, and further developed and improved by Rosalind Eyben, Mariz Tadros, Patta Scott-Villiers, Rosemary McGee, Alex Shankland, Katy Oswald, Marjoke Oosterom and Jo Howard.
3 Formerly MA Participation, Power and Social Change (2006–18), and originally MA Participation, Development and Social Change (2004–05).

and government agencies that ensued had led to concerns. Processes that had been devised for social emancipation and shifting hierarchies of knowledge and power were being simplified into tool kits for aid projects, service delivery and data collection. Participation was being re-cast in neo-liberal language as a way of gaining efficiencies, of turning civil society actors into service providers, and of rubber-stamping plans that complied with dominant development narratives rather than being used as a democratic force for transforming power relations in favour of the poor and marginalised (Cornwall 2000, Cooke and Kothari 2001).

MAP was conceived to address these issues, both as a critical and reflexive approach to learning for change-makers and as a way to help reposition participation as civic and political empowerment (Gaventa and Pettit 2010). Initial design costs were covered from a grant from bilateral aid donors strongly committed to promoting participation and a rights-based approach to development.[4] The programme was designed to support experienced activists and development workers to carry out critical enquiry using methods of action research, reflective practice and power analysis. We recruited practitioners who had relevant work experience in communities, civil society organisations (CSOs), social movements, governments and businesses, and who were interested in reflecting deeply on power in social change practices. The first group of 19 joined the programme in May 2004, and as of this writing there have been 13 MAP cohorts and some 140 graduates.

In this chapter we reflect on the experience of MAP. As befits the constructivist approach of MAP and our positions as people with strong professional and personal stakes in this programme, our stance is deliberately experiential and situated. We first sketch out the context of higher education in the UK since the turn of the century, noting tendencies and trends relevant to MAP as well as significant differences between IDS and most University Schools. Against that backdrop we tell the story of how MAP has developed over time. There follows the main body of the chapter, 'Unlearning and learning power,' in which we present MAP curriculum content and pedagogy and what alumni have got from MAP, drawing on a set of interviews conducted for this purpose by a MAP alumna with other MAP alumni and staff. From this multiply situated account we home in and reflect on a number of challenges faced by teaching staff and MAP students arising from aspects of the programme itself and of its institutional context.[5] Noting aspects of the current global context which render all the more urgent the critical analysis of power and the capacity to transform it, we conclude that MAP and its kin need to resist tendencies of dilution or standardisation and continue in their role of forming critical, reflective, reflexive practitioners.

---

4   The UK's Department for International Development, the Swedish International Development Agency (Sida) and Swiss Development Cooperation.
5   It would be consistent with transformative learning theory to call them 'learners' rather than 'students'; but as the whole body of learners at IDS and other UK higher educational establishments are referred to as 'students' we use that term in this chapter, or 'alumni' when referring specifically to those already graduated from the programme.

A changing context: the UK higher education and development aid sectors

From 2010 onwards, the UK university sector entered a stage of fiscal emergency. Drastic changes to funding mechanisms were introduced, including radical cuts to teaching budgets. The far-reaching effects were operational, political and pedagogical in nature. Operationally speaking, a highly managed programme of marketisation, corporatisation and privatisation ensued, entailing stimulation of entrepreneurship; the subsidisation of science, technology, engineering and medicine; and a corresponding devaluing of social sciences and humanities, considered to be oversubscribed in relation to employment market demand. Universities were to become corporate enterprises operating in an increasingly competitive and globalised market for both degrees and research contracts.

Politically and pedagogically speaking, this turn transformed universities from 'centres of critique' into 'servants of the status quo' (Eagleton 2010). Critics of the UK government's higher education policy direction note 'a pervasive sense of fraud and disappointment in the pedagogical process – you pretend to teach me and I'll pretend to learn' (Wernick 2011). For programmes deploying alternative pedagogical approaches, including enquiry-based learning and action research, there were particular implications. In Tosey and Marshall's (2017) account of the demise of enquiry- and action research-based human resource development programmes in the UK university sector over this period, they note: a decline in employer funding for programme fees, which deters mid-career practitioners and professionals from university study; university departments under growing pressure to maintain financially viable student numbers on all programmes; and 'institutional moves towards larger cohorts, shared module timetable slots, and room allocations based on recurrent, short teaching sessions'. In this situation such programmes 'fall prey to criticisms of being too demanding, too costly, too risky, too different, and perhaps not willing to fit in' (Tosey and Marshall 2017, p. 397).

As an applied research and teaching institution, IDS has a different funding model from normal university departments, developed in response to earlier UK government austerity measures in the early 1990s when core funding was removed in favour of competitive tendering. Its income comes from three streams – research grants, development consultancy and advisory contracts, and postgraduate student tuition fees. Like normal university departments, IDS has felt keenly these more recent shifts in the higher education sector, coupled with other stresses of its own: similarly radical shifts in the development aid funding environment over the same period; changes in government research funding mechanisms; a growth in competitiveness in the market for development consultancy and advisory services; and rising operating costs. Combined, these factors have led to rapid expansion and a more business-like approach in IDS's teaching programmes. Among its seven Master's programmes, MAP falls into the category of 'multi-disciplinary and social change-oriented programmes using action research' identified by Boden et al. (2015, p. 10), whose distinctive nature, they argue, could be at risk in this UK higher education climate. Moreover, donor funding priorities shifted away from the areas of participation and rights in the late 2000s and 2010s, and the development aid industry took an 'unreflective turn'.[6] This made it harder for IDS staff working in these fields to win funding for their work overall, and lowered the profile of these issues and the availability of related capacity-development support among international non-governmental organisations (NGOs) from which MAP drew a lot of its students.

A changing course: MAP's evolution over time

Designed over 2001–04, MAP started as a 15-month programme with a 'sandwich' structure: an initial three months at IDS; nine months of practice back in the student's workplace or a different host organisation, with a week's intensive mid-year 'progress seminar' at IDS; and a final three months at IDS. In 2006 we adjusted it to an 18-month cycle to align it with IDS terms and respond to students' aspiration to be more embedded and aligned with other IDS students. In 2011 we redesigned it further into a more conventional 12-month MA format, with two terms of taught modules at IDS followed by a field-based period of action research or action learning and the production of a final, cumulative and significant, 'Synthesis Paper', equivalent to the dissertation requirement on IDS's other Master's programmes. The main rationale for this redesign was low student numbers. MAP's original length and structure excluded applicants from some scholarships they could otherwise have applied for, making it financially prohibitive for some of the applicants we most wanted to attract; it also made it harder for some to take leave of their jobs and homes than a conventional 12-month MA structure might.

MAP's design was shaped by our research team's interest and experience in methods of critical and transformative adult learning. While the structure and content have evolved, the MAP approach remains one of linking theory and practice by combining academic study with action research within a change-oriented professional practice, organisation or movement. Students design their own Critical Enquiry into Practice (CEP), focused on an issue or process that interests them and their host organisation. While at IDS they build close relationships with their peers, faculty and a supervisor to support their learning through the 12-month programme. They are encouraged to reflect on their position as action researchers and change agents, and track their journey through research designs, presentations, progress reports (shared with peers and staff, in class and in distance webinars) and a synthesis paper. Reflective journaling and submission of key artefacts from students' practice are encouraged. The changes in MAP's name over time reflect changes in emphasis: from an original focus on theories and practice of participation in the context of development aid projects, to a later emphasis on critiques of instrumentalist participatory practice and on applied understandings of power framed by a deliberately universalist conception of development and social change.

6   To borrow and adapt a phrase from educational theorist Donald Schön (1991), who writes of a 'reflective turn' in educational practice.

A growing network of MAP alumni continues to radiate out from IDS, spreading and thickening as it goes, with 'Mappers' popping up in influential practical, facilitative and decision-making roles around the globe, as well as collaborating with us and each other as co-researchers or co-facilitators of inspiring initiatives based on action research and power analysis. While we maintain contact with many individual alumni, we have long wished to take stock of MAP and its effects in a more systematic way. We were keen to understand better how far it fulfils its aim of supporting change-makers to unlearn and learn critically and reflexively about power and of repositioning participatory approaches as civic and political empowerment.

To this end we conducted a series of semi-structured interviews with purposive samples of MAP faculty drawn from various points in MAP's history, and of MAP alumni from a range of cohorts who now occupy a range of roles in different organisational settings around the world. Eleven alumni were invited to reflect on: their current understandings of power and social change and how these are reflected in their current practice; the factors that have influenced in their learning and unlearning on these themes; the MAP experience itself; and how their understandings and practices have evolved since taking the programme.[7] Four staff who have been highly engaged in MAP over its lifetime were invited to reflect on: which aspects of it mattered most to them; their aspirations for learners; how power dynamics are handled; their experience of teaching on an unusual programme within a relatively normal institutional environment; the effects their teaching role has had on them; and the extent to which they think MAP has been successful in enabling students to become critical, reflective practitioners.

Findings processed initially into a written report underwent a series of iterations consisting of rounds of feedback from us and analytical, deliberative discussion between the three of us, leading to some co-constructed conclusions which we have then honed and reflected on further as we drafted the chapter.[8] The next section presents these, clustered into themes which we have defined inductively through this iterative analytical process.

Unlearning and learning power

The 'raw material': student and staff experience

MAP students are, of course, not empty containers or blank slates to be filled, as in the 'banking method' of education that Paulo Freire critiques – and neither are the staff. In

7   Had we been attempting a representative sample, these 11 would have constituted a skewed sample due to the disproportionate number of 'stellar' or exemplary MAP alumni among those with whom we are still in active contact or who responded to our initial 16 requests for interviews. Purposive sampling was more suitable for our purposes and our limited funding, as a limited number of deeper, richer interviews would tell us more of use than a larger number of shorter, shallower interviews.

8   The interview data was summarised and analysed by Fiammetta Wenger in her internal unpublished report titled 'MAP's contribution in learning and unlearning power for reflective social action: reflections and analysis by a MAP alumnus in conversation with other alumni and teaching staff' (2018).

fact, the MAP pedagogy starts from quite the opposite premise. But who comes to MAP, as both students and facilitators of learning, is important in shaping what can happen there and whether and how MAP's pedagogy and content take root, so in this sense they and the experience they bring are the programme's 'raw material'.

Over its 15 years there has been remarkable consistency in the MAP teaching team, with members only leaving it when they leave IDS for retirement, another job or a new lifestyle option. Several of these have retained some involvement with MAP for some years from their new positions. All MAP teaching staff were historically members of IDS's Participation, Power and Social Change team (later renamed the Power and Popular Politics team), and more recently some came from the Participation, Inclusion and Social Change team. Nearly all the staff have interdisciplinary social science and humanities qualifications, and all combine academic backgrounds with considerable practical experience in various social change occupations and a lifelong commitment to working with change agents. Relatedly, these individuals have a history of advocating for progressive change within IDS, including in the teaching programme. Through their involvement with MAP they seek fulfilment of their own professional theories of change and permanent exploration of their own practice.

When MAP began, students were largely mid-career professionals and practitioners playing various roles in development aid in settings in Latin America, Africa or Asia, or in community development in Europe or North America. Over time, reflecting changes in the UK higher education context and in the place and nature of postgraduate education as well as in response to the changing design of MAP, the student intake has shifted. Mid-career practitioners continue to apply and thrive in the programme; but on average students come younger and earlier in their careers, with fewer years of professional or voluntary experience, and a higher proportion have undergraduate degrees in relevant subjects. There is no discernible change in the geographic origins and focuses of the students, who come from the UK, Europe, North America, Oceania, Central Europe, Asia, Latin America and Africa.

Students come to MAP already aware of power dynamics at some level. Corresponding to the changes in MAP's name over time, there have been slight shifts in who it attracts and what they are seeking. Whereas earlier students often sought a solid grounding in participatory methods for use in development and aid contexts, the aspiration of seeking to better understand, explain or tackle power dynamics has been increasingly prominent among recruits since 2004. When 'power' was further emphasised in the title in 2018 several students, especially from countries and regions where power has been dramatically contested in recent times, report specifically choosing the programme for this reason.

The pedagogy: how MAP facilitates unlearning and learning

MAP teaching happens in the form of relatively informal and highly interactive workshop sessions of several hours' duration. The teaching team act as facilitators rather than instructors. The group size for core modules is generally 8–20 students, varying year by year. We use a combination of short lecture-style inputs (often with PowerPoint or flipchart presentations); reflection in class as individuals, pairs or small discussion groups; and larger, more structured and extensive task-focused processes of group work. Throughout every MAP cohort we actively encourage the formation or organic emergence of 'learning pairs' or groups of students with affinities related to their interests, experiences or learning needs. Extracurricular student-led learning sessions are also actively encouraged, although response to this encouragement differs across cohorts. The pedagogical approach is:

- **Experiential:** MAP assumes that students' understanding and learning are based on the forming and reforming of experiences, rather than understanding being fixed and immutable. MAP entry criteria required a minimum of three years' relevant employment or voluntary experience until 2016, and now two. Many classroom activities and some assessments call on students to retrieve experiences and critically analyse them. In the first session of the year a 'Rivers of Life' exercise brings each individual's background and experience into the collective and sets the scene for subsequent learning process based on mutually valuing that experience and continually applying new lenses to it.[9]
- **Reflective:** We use critical and creative methods to develop self-awareness of our own power, identities and worldviews, and how these shape our perceptions and actions. Time is spent making sense of learning process itself, with a series of 'reflective learning sessions' focusing on cross-cultural communication, critical and experiential learning, and positionality and reflexivity in participatory and action research. The notion of reflection–action cycles is introduced early on and put into practice in the programme's various assessment and review mechanisms.
- **Reflexive:** Students are taught how to 'make aspects of the self strange' (Bolton and Delderfield 2018, p. 10) by questioning their own attitudes, habits, values, assumptions and thought processes. They are enabled to recognise resonances or dissonances between their values and the social or professional structures that frame their lives, and to recognise their power, the limits to their knowledge and the risks these bring – particularly of marginalising people or groups from processes.
- **Critical and empowering:** Rather than adopting predetermined conclusions and approaches, students are invited to develop their own interpretations and

9   In the 'Rivers of Life' exercise, a common technique in reflective learning, participants create a visual image of their life as a river, showing what and who influenced their values and interests and their coming to that point in their lives (e.g. what led them to take the programme). Points on the river are illustrated with tributaries, branches, beds, rapids, waterfalls, stagnant (or reflective) pools, bridges – and influences on the shore with images of people, schools, key life experiences, barriers, turning points. Images and colours are encouraged, and a minimum of words. After drawing, participants share their pictures and tell their story in small groups or all together if time allows. The exercise can be used to look forward at where the river is going, and adapted using other metaphors for other cultural settings, e.g. as pathways in a dry landscape.

evaluations of course material, both theoretical and practical, with a critical-constructivist approach to claims of truth and validity. We encourage them to ask continually 'why should things be thought or done the way they usually are?' and 'what are the possible alternatives?'

- **Substantive:** The content is conceptual, epistemological and methodological. Students get grounded in concepts, theories and practices of power and participation useful for understanding and shaping social change, influencing development policy and practice, and deepening personal and collective reflective learning. They are introduced to the epistemological terrain of social constructivism and critical realism, and supported to put into practice associated methodological approaches of action research, action learning and critical enquiry – all situated in relation to the MA's key concepts and to relevant criteria of validity and ethics.

- **In a safe space:** Each MAP cohort is supported to build a strong, well-grounded group dynamic which, when successful, is key to a positive, transformative MAP learning experience. From the outset, efforts are made to ensure the classroom and relationships within class group and with staff are experienced as safe spaces by all members. This entails discussing norms of confidentiality that will be adopted at times, and negotiating how the 'lecture capture' video technology in use in all IDS classrooms will be governed by the group so as to respect this.

- **Mentored:** The MAP model differs from other MA academic supervision models in establishing and maintaining a year-long mentoring relationship between one MAP teaching team member and one student. Individual supervision/mentoring sessions are routinely offered twice per term, and students are encouraged to approach their supervisor in between these as necessary. The mentoring relationship often outlives the student's time at IDS.

- **Formatively assessed:** Assessment is formative as well as summative. Ongoing engagement is encouraged by students in their own assessment, generating information they and staff can use constantly to improve learning while it is going on. Students write individual reflective submissions on assessed group work, collectively debate and set their own presentation criteria, and give and receive peer feedback and critique. Periodic pauses are undertaken to reflect together critically and holistically on the programme, appraising the ways and extent to which its aim are being translated into all its aspects. Substantial formative, non-anonymous feedback is given on written work. The fact that the relatively small number of MAP assessments are all marked by a small teaching team who know the students helps ensure that assessment is formative and feedback gets followed through and acted on in supervisory and teaching relationships.

The content: conceptual, theoretical, epistemological and methodological

MAP is about power-aware, participatory approaches to social change processes, both those supported by international development aid and those involving social activists in the global North or South. It offers three core modules, the first two conceptual (term 1) and the second methodological and epistemological (term 2). In their second term students choose one long or two short elective modules from a wide range offered across the IDS MAs.

The first term provides conceptual and theoretical grounding and exposure to key academic and practitioner-generated literature. It starts by introducing the key concepts of power and empowerment, participation and social change using a range of material from diverse perspectives, and then returns to these concepts to analyse them critically. Students turn their own experiences into case studies, subjecting them to dialogical critical reflection with their peers and faculty, using the concepts and theory covered. A small group project involves students in visiting and observing local citizen engagement initiatives, and applying key concepts from the programme.

The methodological module is focused directly on providing students with the epistemological and methodological bearings and orientation they need to position themselves and set up and design their own 'Critical Enquiry into Practice'. It offers a range of social research methods and general aspects of social research design, as well as a highly power-aware perspective on the specifics of action research design, process and quality, including covering ethics and positionality in depth. Action research projects are conceived, designed, undertaken and presented for assessment in groups of 4–8 students. Over this second term, students' own emerging plans for their critical enquiries are built up incrementally, enriched by class content, peer critique and a growing habit of journalling.

After the two taught terms each student undertakes a 'Critical Enquiry into Practice' over a 3–4 month period. For this work-based action learning or action research initiative they each attach themselves to a host organisation, professional practice or social process, critically exploring their own practice and that of the host, and seeking to apply their learning to the benefit of the host. Following this, the student writes an extended 'Synthesis paper' in which they synthesise their learning over the year. They are actively encouraged to include in it diverse forms of evidence and sources relating to the questions, ideas and inspirations they have engaged with.

The learning: how alumni describe what they got from MAP

MAP students learn and practise a critical awareness of power on four levels: individual, collective, at the broader organisational and structural level, and at the post-structural level of power rooted in norms, discourses and ideology.

The majority of the participants in alumni interviews mentioned perceiving, feeling, seeing or addressing dynamics of power before MAP but not being able to fully understand, explain or tackle them. MAP provided them with a framework to address, name, organise, articulate, explore and practise power in a generative way. Most alumni interviewed mentioned that they had later expanded their understanding and practices beyond the ones presented in MAP and in diverse directions, according to their interests, needs and contexts – more intentionally addressing inner power in their work, enabling inner power to emerge and enabling people to become aware of their power.

Those whose work involves facilitation, community work and activism do this in a range of ways:

- facilitating spaces in communities or the workplace;
- organising activities such as community theatre;
- integrating approaches specifically focusing on power (like embodied or silence practices and sentient methods which allow for a deeper and more emotional way of learning);
- supporting people to unlearn socialised norms of disempowerment and develop inner power; and
- coaching individuals to recognise when they are using power in a degenerative or self-serving fashion.

Those engaged in research integrate power perspectives by, for example, looking at how economic inequalities are buttressed by invisible power.

On an individual level, as well as learning to articulate their lived understandings of power, alumni have developed critical reflexivity – the capacity to critically reflect on themselves, their positionality and behaviour. MAP offered a safe space to reflect and clarify personal assumptions, emotions, behaviours and positions in relation to power. Some retain habits for personal reflective and reflexive enquiry acquired on MAP by continuing to journal, continuously connecting the professional with the personal, and systematically integrating personal reflection into their working practices.

On a collective level, they experienced MAP as a community of learning in a safe space founded on trust, which facilitated their learning. The importance of having a safe collective space for analysing power, both in MAP and in subsequent work experience, has stayed with them. They continue to apply methods encountered in MAP in their collective facilitation work: from relationship building to creating spaces for critical and collective learning, strengthening of community spaces and assets, and social healing practices. To achieve this they employ a diverse range of tools and methodologies, such as experiential learning, power analysis, creative practices (storytelling, theatre, embodiment) and participatory research methods. The way MAP alumni approach their work on power in their contexts seem to be in many respects a recreation of the dynamics of collaborative questioning, analysing and sense-making experienced in MAP, which allowed them to learn directly from their own experience while accessing new concepts, methodologies, skills and lenses.

The majority of alumni interviewees reflected that, while their understanding and practice of dealing with power has changed significantly at the individual and collective levels, they have also become more aware of power on other levels. Some have become more committed to addressing power of a structural nature and at the post-structural level of discourses, norms and ideology. They identified in themselves a heightened awareness of the influence of development jargon and western approaches in contexts where such approaches are not relevant or contribute to exacerbating poverty, dependency and negative power dynamics. In their current engagement with campaigning, advocacy, research or claiming accountability, they routinely tackle knowledge inequalities, dominant information and narratives; and even when not addressing structural power directly, they are aware of how those dynamics affect people at collective or community and individual levels. Their ways of acting on this increased awareness include using the power-cube to undertake multi-level analysis, doing power mapping, and adopting action research and aid ethnography as methodologies that permit them to understand and engage with power embedded in organisational or social structures and in social norms, discourses and knowledge hierarchies.

Challenges

For the students interviewed, the journey of MAP is recalled as full of excitement, stimulus, satisfaction and delight – even while some of them experienced phases of confusion or doubt during their Master's connected to the deep processes of unlearning they went through. In interviews with staff, many challenges surfaced. Some of these relate to their experiences with other students who took to MAP less readily or wrestled, sometimes painfully, with ontological or epistemological aspects of it, while others arise from dissonances between the programme's form and substance and the institutional context in which it is taught.

The staff reflected on supporting students struggling psychologically with insecurities, crises of self-confidence and internal tensions that they confronted as a consequence of deep engagement with power or surfaced in themselves through reflective practice and reflexivity. These struggles are not unusual in deep and experiential approaches to learning, which use moments of 'dissonance' or 'disjuncture' to shift perception and understanding (Jarvis 2006, p. 7). While the staff often felt fairly well-equipped on an instinctive and interpersonal level to accompany supervisees through these 'cycles of depression, challenge, learning, struggle and revelation' (in the words of one staff member), these demands stretched their capacity to the utmost at times, and some cases lay beyond their disciplinary domain and professional roles and competences, requiring physical health and mental health interventions. In this, MAP staff are far from alone among their IDS colleagues or more broadly: University staff across the UK have experienced a marked increase in mental health needs among their students since the early 2000s, attested to by extensive media coverage. Yet the highly reflective nature of some MAP core sessions and optional modules does lead students to dig deeper within themselves than most university programmes do; and while this practice can be supported relatively solidly in small groups and suitably safe spaces, it raises the question of how to provide safe enough spaces in this rapidly changing university environment.

Inevitably, the shifts in context, together with the design adjustments MAP has undergone, have had pedagogical implications as well as impacts on the student and staff experience. Since the programme format has become more standardised, marketing and student recruitment processes scaled up, and the entry requirement of three years' relevant prior experience reduced to two, staff occasionally encounter students who are not initially well-attuned to the highly intentional and well-publicised differences in pedagogical approach between MAP and other Master's programmes. While in most cases they embrace these, in some instances they find them a source of confusion, disappointment or tension, which can affect dynamics in their student cohort.

MAP teaching faculty find there is now less room for doing things differently than when MAP started out, and experience incentives to conform in their pedagogical practice as a result. More positively, since the last redesign MAP student numbers are safer than before – although still not consistently meeting the target of at least 15 per year, and considerably lower than any other IDS Master's. While MAP students and staff are fortunate to still enjoy relatively small group sizes, staff are aware that this can be sustained thanks to other MAs' higher recruitment and larger class numbers – partly driven by the current ranking of IDS and the University of Sussex as first in the world for Development Studies in the QS University Rankings – and may prove less tenable in the long term.[10]

All staff interviewed, including ourselves, reflected on the process of 'normalisation' which MAP has undergone through its various restructurings, as well as the challenge of creating suitable spaces for staff's collective reflection and continual refreshing of the programme amid increasing institutional pressures of financial targets plus numerous project, administrative and management responsibilities. Alumni interviews highlighting staff energy and passion showed that staff generally balance these tensions to the students' satisfaction; yet staff wondered how various sector-wide and internal structural factors might affect the programme's distinctive identity, ethos and pedagogical approach. Continued growth in student numbers could affect the quality of relationships between students and teaching staff and among students themselves, as well as 'pressing in on' the spaces available for MAP to enable inner, mutual and deep learning.

In sum, a number of features of the current UK university context, and to some extent of the development aid arena, tend to militate against experiential, collaborative and constructivist learning and complicate the endeavour of instituting empowering, reflective practices and processes in the classroom and beyond. Yet despite the challenges, the learning experience for the alumni interviewed has been rewarding, rich and transformative, as has the experience of teaching on MAP for the staff involved.

---

10 See https://www.topuniversities.com/universities/university-sussex/postgrad.

Conclusion

Writing on the contemporary challenges of teaching action research (AR) in universities the world over, Boden et al. (2015, pp. 10–11) conclude by asking:

> Do we live in a world of limitations on AR, or a world of unrealised possibilities? [...] It is hard to ignore that Western universities are increasingly colonized and organized by neo-liberal schemes of administration, commoditization of research and teaching, and command-and-control management and that this pushes them away from their potential to act as sources of community and citizen development and the promotion of a better and fairer society. This process [...] appears non-negotiable and irreversible. But the lessons [...] are that possibilities to steer universities to a more pro-social focus and to enable them to become more humane places in which to study and work continue to exist. How do we actualize the unrealized possibilities?

To run an MA programme like MAP certainly goes against the current. But our experience is that there are prospective learners out there who are looking for precisely this, because they are counter-current practitioners. They continue to seek and find in MAP a transformative experience of questioning dominant norms and assumptions, learning new ways of seeing and doing things, and re-evaluating their life and working experiences as well as their engagement in struggles for social justice.

Given current global trends (see VeneKlasen, Scott-Villiers, Bradley this volume), we might view these counter-current practitioners as a dwindling and threatened species, requiring us to nurture the individuals and conserve the species from extinction. Taking an alternative view, we look forward to welcoming more and more of them at IDS, spawned by the growing global scandal of inequality and power abuse and the endless human capacity for resisting oppression and injustice. We will need to stand ready to support them in actualising their unrealised possibilities.

References

Boden, R., Greenwood, D.J., Hall, B., Levin, M., Marshall, J. and Wright, S., 2015. Action research in universities and higher education worldwide. In: H. Bradbury, ed. *The Sage handbook of action research*. 3rd ed. London: Sage, 281–290.

Chambers, R., 1983. *Rural development: putting the last first*. Harlow: Longman Scientific and Technical.

Chambers, R., 1993. *Challenging the professions: frontiers for rural development*. Rugby: Intermediate Technology.

Cooke, B. and Kothari, U., eds, 2001. *Participation: the new tyranny?* London: Zed Books.

Cornwall, A., 2000. *Beneficiary, consumer, citizen: perspectives on participation for poverty reduction*. Sida Studies 2. Stockholm: Swedish Agency for International Development.

Bolton, G. and Delderfield, R., 2018. *Reflective practice: writing and professional development*. 5th ed. London: Sage.

Eagleton, T., 2010. The death of universities. *The Guardian*, 17 December. Available at: http://www.theguardian.com/commentisfree/2010/dec/17/death-universities-malaise-tuition-fees [Accessed 3 June 2019].

Gaventa, J. and Pettit, J., 2010. Power and participation. In: R.A. Couto, ed. *Political and civic leadership: a Sage reference handbook*. Thousand Oaks, CA and London: Sage, 513–522.

Jarvis, P., 2006. *Towards a comprehensive theory of human leaning*. London: Routledge.

McGee, R., 2014, Enabling students to become critical, reflective practitioners: is MA participation, power and social change contributing as much as it can? Unpublished essay. PGCertHE, University of Sussex.

Pettit, J., 2012. Facilitating reflective learning: a pedagogy for the embodied mind. Unpublished PhD thesis, University of Bath School of Management.

Schön, D., ed., 1991. *The reflective turn: case studies in and on educational practice*. New York: Teachers College Press.

Tosey, P. and Marshall, J., 2017. The demise of inquiry-based HRD programmes in the UK: implications for the field. *Human Resource Development International* 20(5), 393–402.

Wernick, A., 2011. Will there be universities after the revolution? Campaign for the Public University, 9 November. Available at: http://publicuniversity.org.uk/2011/11/09/will-there-still-be-universities-after-the-revolution/ [Accessed 3 June 2019].

5.2

REFLEXIVE AID PRACTICE: NAMING AND DEALING WITH POWER

Rosalind Eyben

Often used synonymously with 'critical reflection', reflexivity, as I understand it, means deliberately becoming unsettled about what I have taken to be normal. Reflexivity requires recognising that my 'normal' is shaped by power. Power is the socialisation process that shapes what I believe, what I say, what I do – and who I make friends with. Reflexive practitioners working in the field of international development cooperation scrutinise their beliefs, words, actions and relationships, as shaped by power, and enquire whether and how these are supporting or undermining social justice. Step 1: give power its name. Step 2: deal with it. This can be hard. It helps to do it with others. We can practise this in workshops. But, for me at least, it is always work in progress – as I learnt when participating in a development practitioners' reflexive immersion visit to a West African village.[1]

Naming 'power'

When employed by a government aid agency in the 1990s, my policy responsibility was gender, racial and other inequalities; yet, when speaking with my superiors I found it almost impossible to utter the word 'power'. My heart raced, my bowels fluttered and my mouth dried. Contentious, even threatening, 'power' is a word that some development organisations, such as the World Bank, prefer not to use – other than in reference to formal political power. Giving power its name challenges the 'self-evident and natural order which goes without saying and therefore goes unquestioned' (Bourdieu and Nice 1977, p. 166). Power resists its naming.

By the turn of the century aid agencies began to promote poor people's 'empowerment', and it became easier to insert 'power' into the conversation (Eyben et al. 2008). When facilitating workshops, I encouraged participants to become comfortable

1 This chapter is adapted from Chapter 8 in Eyben (2014).

in naming 'power'. As a collective effort, it was easier for them to articulate fears and reflect on experience than it had been for me ten years earlier, when I was a solitary, scared individual trying to name 'power'. *Power with* others can release the *power within* each of us to recognise and start dealing with *power everywhere* – taken-for-granted practices and beliefs.

At a two-day workshop on empowerment for staff in a multilateral agency, I divided participants into small breakout groups to recount to each other personal experiences of power in their work – deliberately avoiding greater specificity – and requested them to draw a picture of one of these experiences to share in plenary with the other groups. Without exception, the stories they chose to portray were of projects their agency funded in Africa, projects that had poor people's empowerment as an explicit goal. Extraordinarily, bearing in mind that workshop participants came from all parts of a large organisation working all over the world, several groups had chosen the self-same project for their story – including two breakout groups where none of its members had had any direct involvement with that particular project. At the end of the first day, the workshop ended on a self-congratulatory note: 'Look how good our organisation is at doing empowerment.' Yet, overnight, many participants came to realise that these stories they had shared in plenary were their agency's 'fables', already familiar to most participants.

Talking this over at the start of the second day, they discussed how these fables glossed over inequitable power relations. For example, those with direct knowledge of the projects concerned mentioned how women had stayed silent in the village organisations established by the agency. Why, participants wondered, had they avoided the opportunity offered them by the workshop to move out of their comfort zone? Looking afresh at the previous day's illustrations of their sanitised fables, it dawned on them that not only had they failed to portray power dynamics in the communities their projects were supporting, but also, as one workshop participant put it, they had 'removed themselves from the picture'. Indeed, when we took a second look we saw that no agency staff were represented in any of the pictures. It was then that they remembered the other stories about power – those recounted by individuals in their small breakout groups but not selected for presentation in plenary. Some of these had been about agency staff in projects, and others about individual experiences of power within the organisation itself. They asked themselves why and how had they had initially chosen not to bring these accounts into plenary. What did this tell them about naming and dealing with power?

Putting ourselves into the picture

The first element in thinking critically about post-colonial geopolitics, suggests David Slater, is to analyse presence and absence (2004, p. 26). Just as hidden and invisible power resists its naming, so it allows aid organisations and their staff to decide when and how they want to be visible or to appear absent from the scene. At the workshop I have just described, agency staff realised that the only people present in their empowerment pictures were some happy beneficiaries whose lives had been improved by an omnipotent but absent benefactor – the aid agency – whose staff had created the picture. Giving themselves permission to name 'power' had been the first step to be visibly present, and thus to reflect critically on their aid relationships. It allowed them to talk about how power worked within their organisation and within the wider aid system. Rather than re-tell organisational fables, they began recounting their own experience.

The following year, I supported a working group of an international network of aid agencies seeking to produce guidance for its members about the empowerment of people in poverty. The guidance was to include case studies of empowerment submitted by the member agencies. Some in the network saw these case studies as a vehicle for donor staff to learn about how and when to support local empowerment processes, while others – focusing on the self-evident truth that donors often play a minor role in such processes – argued that the case studies could be about any empowerment (not necessarily supported by donors), and should concentrate on the positive outcomes for poor people rather than being concerned with the processes and relationships that led to these outcomes. The case studies this latter group offered for inclusion in the guidance note were remarkably similar to the 'fables' at the agency workshop discussed earlier: even when the donor agencies had been involved, they were mentioned in the case studies. To put their agencies into the picture, they argued, would be narcissistic, impervious to my counter-argument that by lurking in the shadows they were exercising hidden power and that putting themselves into the picture would require aid agencies to be alert to how they related to others. How can donors learn to support a process of empowerment without examining their own behaviour in that process?

On the other hand, particularly when communicating with their domestic constituents, many agencies make themselves over-present: they are donors as saviours, filling the whole frame, painting out the many other actors who are contributing to a successful outcome. Thus, in 2011 the UK government aid agency Department for International Development (DFID 2011) committed itself to having secured by 2015 'schooling for 11 million children – more than we educate in the UK but at 2.5% of the cost'. Everyone else (recipient country governments, local community organisations, teachers and parents) – all involved in helping those 11 million children get to school – had disappeared from the narrative. The harder it is to secure the budget allocation for development aid the greater the tendency to exaggerate reports to domestic constituencies (like the British public) about the positive effect of international aid money, rendering invisible the multiplicity of all those other people and organisations whose dedicated action and commitment, along with international aid, had secured the desired outcome. The practical consequence of these exaggerations and omissions are projects and programmes designed in accordance with a false reality, and thus likely to fail. 'All power deceives' (Chambers 1994, p. 14).

Painting myself into the busy and dynamic picture of international aid locates me in relation to everyone else within the picture. And, importantly, this picture is without a frame: much of what is happening in my picture is shaped by what is going on in other pictures – as I was to learn in my immersion visit of international aid practitioners to the village in West Africa.

Power is everywhere: an immersion visit

At the time of my arrival at the Institute of Development Studies (IDS), the group I joined was designing a Master's programme on Participation, Power and Social Change that emphasised reflexive practice, irrespective of whether one was a recipient government official, a non-governmental organisation (NGO) worker, a development consultant or donor agency staff member (see McGee et al., this volume). We were interested in developing collective reflexive practice methods, for example through staff workshops, of the kind I have just discussed. I learnt, however, that even such methods are not free from power, including in training programmes designed to encourage aid agency staff to reflect critically on their work, as I now discuss.

In an immersion visit staff from aid agencies spend a few days living and working with host families in a local community (Irvine et al. 2004). Importantly, this is preceded by a day of collective enquiry about what they expect and hope to learn from the experience; and at the end they come back together to share what they have learnt and the changes they intend to make to their practice. An international NGO volunteered to pilot this reflexive immersion approach, and one of its West African country offices helped organise a visit of about a dozen people to a Sahelian village where a local partner organisation ran community development programmes. In addition to head office staff from the NGO, the NGO's country director joined the immersion along with a staff member of a bilateral agency that funded some of the NGO's work and me from IDS.[2] James, the NGO's local area director, and a national of the country we were visiting, was in charge of arranging the immersion.

On the last evening of our stay in the village with my interpreter, Susan, I was wandering around the village when an elderly woman called out to us from over a thorn fence, requesting we enter her compound. Inside was a young woman crouching beside the mud-bricked wall of the house, trying to remain invisible to passers-by. Her name was Rachel and an acquaintance of Susan. Through Susan I learnt that Rachel had been living away from the village, with a job in town, and that she was on a visit home to her family. The previous week Rachel had gone to the home of a married sister in the neighbouring village, and a young man there had kidnapped Rachel and held her against her will. As is the custom, Susan explained, he refused to release Rachel until her parents came to fetch her and agreed to a marriage – already, through force, a fait accompli. Distraught and betrayed by her parents, Rachel had run away to hide with this elderly woman, an aunt. Rachel did not want to marry her kidnapper. She wanted to return to town and live her own life. She was staying in hiding in the hope that her kidnapper and his kinsmen who were hunting for her would give up the chase and she could sneak onto a bus or lorry passing through the village at night. But she was worried

2   All the names in this story are pseudonyms.

that, even then, she might be spotted trying to escape and that she would be dragged off the bus. Could I help?

I wondered to myself whether Susan already knew of her friend's situation, and that I had been encouraged to wander in the direction of the old woman's compound. We were leaving early the next day in the NGO's fleet of vehicles. We could pick Rachel up directly from her aunt's compound and take her with us to the town where we were due to stay for our post-immersion reflection. What to do? By now it was dark and I did not know where to find James. I decided to catch him the next morning when we immersion visitors were due to meet for a collective session with our host families. The following day, as I had planned, I took James aside, explained the situation and requested that we take Rachel away with us. He refused. The girl might be feigning distress, he said – just part of the courtship ritual. I disagreed. From the fear Rachel had shown, her aunt's anxiety and my interpreter's concern, I was sure Rachel was being forced into a marriage against her will. James sighed and said flatly we could not take her away with us. Both the NGO and its local partner, the community-based organisation that had organised our visit, would be blamed by the village elders for helping Rachel flout parental authority and for breaking with tradition. All the development work in that and neighbouring villages risked being undermined and the NGO would get a bad name, he said. There was no time left to argue. The Land Rovers were revving their engines. And did I have the right to insist? It was not *my* organisation's work that would be undone. We left without Rachel. On the journey to town I continued to fret with myself. Should I have argued more with James? Pointed out to him that the NGO prided itself on its international reputation for its support for women's rights, and yet here in this village Rachel's fate was less important than maintaining good relations with the powerful people in the community? Should I have overridden his authority and taken the matter to his country director who was with us on the immersion?

Once back in town, we immersion visitors met, as planned, to reflect on our experience. We talked about some difficult topics. For example, despite apparently having received strict instructions in advance from the local organisation not to do so, the village elders could not resist making a bid for aid. The village chief had spoken about the role of white men in the village – from the colonial officer who had overseen the construction of the road 60 years earlier to the Mission that white men had built and that still provided health and educational services to the village. Now a new group of white people had come to the village, he said, 'to take care of them'. We also discovered that all our host families had talked about race. By participating in their daily lives and working alongside them we seemed to have reinforced the community's widely held view that white people are good and their own black rulers bad. One child even asked one of the black visitors why he was not white, 'because he behaved like one'. I commented in the group that even in an immersion visit – a reflective learning process – it was as easy for us donors, as it was for the village elders, to fall back into bad old habits. For example, on our last full day in the village, in a meeting with the local government official I noticed we were offering him unsolicited advice about how to do his job.

We spoke frankly of these things, but I stayed silent about Rachel. None of the others knew about her story or of James turning down my request to help her escape. I did not wish to be seen criticising James, on whose interest and enthusiasm our immersion visit had depended. I believed I understood his dilemma, but remembered also how initially he had made light of Rachel's staying hidden, as if it were just a game. I wondered whether, had James been more sensitive to gendered power relations he might have made a different decision. Above all, I regretted that during this day of reflection I felt unable to talk with him and the others about the episode. I felt that to do so could be interpreted as privileging my voice and authority over his in an aid system where I was structurally located in a more powerful position than he. I now realised that in the preparatory session before going to the village we had not collectively reflected about the power relations at work within our own group. Thus, James and I were now unable to talk frankly about the dilemma he faced when I requested that he protect the girl. We had brushed the matter under the carpet.

The power of the way we do things around here

The international aid system is sometimes portrayed as a hierarchical system of power: a vertical aid chain of official aid agencies at the top; international NGOs and recipient governments in the middle; and local NGOs and community organisations at the bottom. In reality, it is both more complex and more fluid. In this immersion visit, power was variously at work within the village and between the NGO and its local partner, as well as between James and me. I think of the aid system as an unfenced field within which certain emotions, values and behaviours become set in a pattern that from one generation to the next define what is do-able and say-able. This is invisible power at work (see VeneKlasen, McGee, Pettit, Bradley, Gaventa, Rowlands this volume). At the same time, the aid field is open to other fields where the pattern of established ways of thinking and doing may differ – in this particular case with respect to gender norms. Having left the village and found work in town, Rachel was able to distance herself from and reject the habits and customs of her home community.[3] She had acquired different ideas and values about how she wanted to live. But, because there were not enough people in the village who shared Rachel's new perspective on the unacceptability of forced marriage, she had no choice but to try to leave and return to that other field – and this she was stopped from doing. Shortly afterwards women's rights campaigners in this West African country had successfully lobbied their parliament to legislate against forced marriage – by which time James might have been sufficiently emboldened to tell the village elders that 'times they are a-changin'.

---

3 The theoretical argument here derives from Bourdieu's concepts of *habitus* and *fields*. See Jenkins 1992, Chapter 4) for an introduction to these.

Conclusion

For me, this immersion visit encapsulated how power operates in aid relationships. When complex power dynamics are at work, I learnt how easier it is to be reflexive about *past* action than to be reflexive *in* action. This was not a workshop with role play, but a real live crisis in which Rachel's future was at stake, and James and I had to make decisions very fast without time to think through and talk over the matter. I learnt that organised reflection of the kind we had in our immersion visit does not necessarily make it a deep reflection, or necessarily make it easy to speak with colleagues about issues of power and position that influence our actions, even when we have put ourselves in the picture and realise what is happening. I learnt that I cannot choose when to think and respond to the complexities of power. It is not just for talking about in workshops. Power is everywhere all the time, and in all relationships. To name and deal with power in moments of crisis thus requires continuous reflexive practice.

Power becomes visible when a sufficient number of people start talking about it. As they recognise that power has been constructed through social interaction, so they can change their interaction – in the moment rather than reflecting after the fact – to make power operate more fairly. Thus, we need to learn together with others to deal with power. The more we talk frankly with each other about it when in safe spaces (such as workshops) and the more we develop skills of reflexivity related to power, the greater the chance we give ourselves to deal with power when a crisis (opportunity) occurs.

References

Bourdieu, P. and Nice, R., 1977. *Outline of a theory of practice*. Cambridge: Cambridge University Press.

Chambers, R., 1994. All power deceives. *IDS Bulletin*, 25(2), 14–26.

DFID, 2011. The future of UK aid [online]. Department for International Development. Available from: https://www.gov.uk/government/news/the-future-of-uk-aid [Accessed 29 July 2019].

Eyben, R., 2014. *International aid and the making of a better world: reflexive practice*. London: Routledge.

Eyben, R., Kabeer, N. and Cornwall, A., 2008. Conceptualising empowerment and the implications for pro-poor growth. Paper for the DAC Poverty Network. Brighton: Institute for Development Studies.

Irvine, R., Chambers, R. and Eyben, R., 2004. *Learning from poor people's experience: immersions*. Lessons for Change in Policy and Organisations 13. Brighton: Institute for Development Studies.

Jenkins, R., 1992. *Pierre Bourdieu*. London: Routledge.

Slater, R. 2004. *Geopolitics and the post-colonial: rethinking north–south relations*. Oxford: Blackwell.

5.3

CONSCIOUSNESS-RAISING, INTERSECTIONALITY AND MOVEMENT-BUILDING FOR SOCIAL TRANSFORMATION

Mariela Arce Andrade and Valerie Miller

Background

This chapter's ideas and reflections emerge from our personal experiences as long-time activists committed to challenging the oppression and violent inequities of power across the Americas. Having met in the midst of liberation movements, we belong to an early generation of popular educators formed by our political activism – from organising village cooperatives to supporting revolutionary struggles to coordinating solidarity networks, advocacy campaigns and women's movements. It has been in these contexts where we encountered popular education as an organising and social transformation strategy and, along the way, faced the painful and maddening contradictions of patriarchy. From these experiences, we developed our feminist consciousness, including a set of ethics and an awareness of the multiple intersections of power affecting people of different identities and contexts beyond just gender. Since the 1970s, we have been privileged to be part of the evolution of popular education – collaborating in the exciting and challenging processes that have woven together some of its dynamic threads of pedagogy, power and feminism. Continually inspired by courageous colleagues and companerxs around the world,[1] we remain fiercely hopeful and passionate as we seek new paradigms and practices of power, community, justice and love.

Introduction: popular education for social transformation

In this chapter we explore a series of questions:

1   In contemporary Spanish, especially Latin American Spanish, some choose to use 'x' at the end of a noun to indicate either masculine or feminine, rather than using 'o' for masculine and 'a' for feminine.

How has popular education with its consciousness-raising approach evolved over time?

What are some practical examples of its methods and processes?

How do they contribute to a deeper understanding and creation of personal and collective power geared toward concrete action and social transformation?

We draw both on our past histories and recent collaborations as members of Just Associates (JASS) – an international network of activists, feminist popular educators and academics committed to movement-building and social justice. Recognising the different roots and pathways of popular education, we present the following reflections as one part of an ongoing dialogue with colleagues to deepen our synergy, solidarity and action across borders, with all the contradictions and challenges such an exploration implies.

The evolution of popular education has been marked by passionate debates and creative tensions that continue today in the ever-changing political contexts of our lives and societies. The idea of popular education, usually attributed to the Brazilian educator Paulo Freire, was given life by his consciousness-raising literacy methods designed to challenge oppressive systems of power and strengthen peasant and worker awareness, analysis and movements (see Freire 1970a, Freire 1970b, Freire 1994, Freire and Coutinho 1970; see also Horton and Freire 1990, Freire and Freire 1994). Recognising how certain forms of power caused poor people to internalise their own sense of inferiority and paralyse their capacity to act, his programmes began with a dialogue process that allowed people to reflect on their realities, name those dynamics and nurture their own self-worth as thoughtful, creative human beings capable of changing their worlds. Based initially on an analysis of class and a development of critical consciousness, this approach – which he called *cultural action for freedom* – helped marginalised peoples reinforce and increase their individual and collective power and break out of what he called the *culture of silence* that kept them submissive and powerless.

Feminist popular education: consciousness-raising, power and intersectionality

For us, the soul of our work as feminist popular educators is consciousness-raising and movement-building – building *power within* ourselves and *power with* others to develop our *power to* be and to act – to become caring, compassionate makers and shapers of change (see McGee and Pettit's introduction to this volume, Miller 2002). Feminist popular education is a transformative process not just for women but for everyone, whatever gender, race, class, sexuality or age. Focused on individual and collective reflection, knowledge and action, it draws on synergies created by a new appreciation of our identities and the connections between our hearts, minds and bodies. It's about challenging what we have been taught about ourselves and our world so we can overcome what the African-American poet Maya Angelou (1978) calls the 'hatefulness' of 'bitter twisted lies'. It's about unlearning these destructive internalised beliefs and ideologies that silence and shame us or make us feel superior and blameless. It's about decolonising our souls, challenging and disrupting hateful ways of knowing and being; about questioning dominant narratives and twisted assumptions about society and people's places within it; about what is considered normal and therefore left unquestioned. But, most importantly, it's about freedom, love and creativity – about a critical awareness and appreciation of ourselves and communities. Ultimately, it's about learning how to tap into our different sources of hope and power to become stronger and more loving voices of integrity and change so that together we can create new relationships with ourselves and our earth to support worlds of dignity, respect and justice.

In the face of the 'twisted lies' of oppression and patriarchy, women have engaged in countless resistance strategies over the years challenging male dominance and other forms of subjugation and discrimination. Whether during suffrage or abolition movements or present-day struggles against violence and racism, women have developed educational processes not only to understand the forces shaping their worlds but also to mobilise energy and action that affirm the fullness of all humanity and the common good. Drawing lessons from their political organising, feminist educators from the 1970s onward engaged with Freire and other popular educators to challenge and enrich the original conception and application of popular education.[2] Different terms emerged to describe this work – including feminist popular education (FPE), feminist pedagogy and liberatory feminist education, among others.

As women named the real-life power dynamics and socialised norms of patriarchy that kept them silent and submissive, they also developed a clearer appreciation of their own wisdom and worth, and the need for developing *individual power within themselves* and *collective power with others* (see Bradley, this volume). Not surprisingly, in contexts like Mesoamerica with a rich history in popular education, work with male colleagues became difficult since most men still operated under the dominant paradigm of power and patriarchy, complicated by loyalty to narrow class-based and revolutionary ideologies of the time. Women popular educators found they needed to form special spaces of analysis and creativity to develop their own ideas and methodologies, free from the paternalistic put-downs of some male counterparts. In this ongoing evolution, feminist educators and activists emphasised the multiple ways of knowing that came from women's life experience, and offered a more holistic vision and practice of knowing and action. They went beyond reliance on rational thought or rigid theoretical frameworks to incorporate the wisdom gained from emotions and feelings as well as the brain and body. Sometimes known as a

---

2   To mention a few: Magali Pineda (Dominican Republic), Rosa Paredes (Venezuela), Anne Hope (South Africa), Hope Chigudu (Zimbabwe), Nani Zulminarni and Dina Lumbantobing (Indonesia), Deborah Barndt (Canada), Girlie Villariba (Philippines), Andrea Cornwall (UK), Lisa VeneKlasen (USA), bell hooks (USA), Malena de Montis (Nicaragua) and this chapter's authors, Mariela Arce Andrade (Panama) and Valerie Miller (USA).

heart–mind–body approach, it recognised these elements as places of pain and oppression as well as sources of inspiration, knowledge and transformation.

African-American women scholars and others saw that gender was not the only place of discrimination and violence, and thus enriched the approach by highlighting the intersecting ways that power and identity operate (see for example Crenshaw 1989, Davis 2011, de Montis and Maessick 1989, hooks 2014, among others). *Intersectionality* combines an analysis of identities as complex places of subjugation, transformation and meaning, recognising the interactions between gender, race, sexuality, class, ability and age (among others) in people's intimate, family, community and wider societal relationships. Contextual analyses further reveal interactions between systems – from economic and political to social and cultural. We also incorporate discussion of other interacting mechanisms of power that reinforce prejudice and privilege and limit people's participation in public decision-making, from elections to policy formation. These range from *visible* forces (governments that set and enforce discriminatory rules) to *shadow* powers (corporate and other actors that control politics and silence opposition with money and intimidation) to *invisible* forces – ideology and belief systems such as patriarchy, racism, colonialism and imperialism that crush people's self-worth and threaten their capacity to participate (see Bradley, this volume, Miller et al. 2006, Gaventa 2006). Women are at the forefront of confronting these destructive dynamics in their lives, families, communities and world – dynamics that devastate the social fabric, the health of the planet, and possibilities for more egalitarian and democratic societies. Their activism and leadership trigger violent backlash and repression, resulting in dangerous realities that place further demands on our education and organising work today.

Over the years, popular education has been widely embraced by activists, scholars and development practitioners. It has inspired the creation of a host of participatory and interactive learning methods; but in many cases, these have been separated from the explicit *political* objectives and organising strategies that are vital to popular education's practice and processes of social transformation. In some instances, popular education has been reduced to a set of fun and dynamic teaching and personal development techniques. In others, it has been interpreted as an approach for making complex information simple and easy to learn, assuming – incorrectly – that information alone will change attitudes or motivate action. This has led to confusion in some circles about what, precisely, popular education is, and how it relates to social justice work.[3]

Meanwhile, recent years have spurred a renewed interest in more effective ways to build the voice and power of marginalised communities. In the face of ever-more unequal and unjust global dynamics, social justice actors are rediscovering popular education for its potential to effect transformative, people-centred change and movement-building. Amidst all of this, women's everyday

3   This paragraph is drawn from VeneKlasen and Miller (2012).

acts of resistance, including the drive to seek connection and community with others, have kept popular education alive – if not in name, then in practice.

Grounded in a commitment to intersectionality, we and our colleagues around the world highlight key features of the approach that help distinguish it from traditional non-governmental organisation (NGO) advocacy and conventional apolitical technical methodologies (see VeneKlasen in this volume) and emphasise its radical potential for building power, movements and social change processes

Deepening knowledge, self-awareness and critical consciousness

Informed by a vision of dignity, solidarity and intersectionality, feminist popular education is for everyone confronting injustice. It begins with people's day-to-day lives and realities that serve both as sources of knowledge creation and as primary sites for transformation. In a spiral process of inquiry and action, people examine their experience and generate their own knowledge – which they then question, enrich and apply to transformative actions, building relationships and power together. In our work with women, the process affirms their worth and wisdom while challenging the particular forces that silence and abuse them in their intimate, personal and public lives. As the foundation of critical consciousness, this process inspires and sustains people's liberation, connection, active engagement and capacity to self-organise in response to injustice.

Yet, awareness also can foster anger, pain and loss as people realise the impact of oppression and its consequences. Key elements of political awareness involve inspiration, integration of healing and heart–mind–body intelligence as well as a commitment to mutual support, dignity and fairness, and a recognition of how power operates in everyday life.

Understanding and navigating power

Deepening activists' ability to see and analyse how power operates across differences (see Bradley, this volume) helps them understand and challenge the structural drivers of inequality and violence against women and other marginalised groups, and anticipate and manage conflict both among organisations and in relation to inevitable backlash. Naming how power operates, both to oppress and to liberate, bolsters activists' confidence in the possibility of change, and better equips them to analyse and address its complexities. This is especially true as people connect power's transformative dimensions – *power within* themselves and *power with* others to build the crucial *power to* make change. Developing a common framework for understanding all the dimensions, mechanisms and intersections of power, oppression and transformation – including the ways that we perpetuate and reproduce inequality in our own lives – enables people to work together more collaboratively and respectfully.

Validating and energising people's knowledge, agency and spirit

Feminist popular educators recognise that people are energised and transformed in safe and challenging spaces of trust and creativity and by experiences that inspire and tap into how they feel, think and move. This holistic heart–mind–body approach reinforces our multiple forms of intelligence, our sense of self and desire to take action. Yet patriarchy operates to denigrate how women view their own mental capacities, relationships, feelings and bodies, invalidating women's knowledge and privileging male-centred norms and expertise.[4] For example, age-old strategies for harvesting seeds developed by indigenous women over centuries were not considered 'knowledge' until formally trained scientists (usually men) documented and structured that information. In contrast, feminist popular educators recognise the richness of people's knowledge, and support them in challenging and deepening their understanding, questioning and adding new analysis as needed. They also promote the hope, joy and spirit of wholeness that strengthens people's integrity, community and legitimacy. Drawing on powers of dreaming, laughing, physical movement, relaxation and all forms of artistic expression is crucial for our creativity, inspiration, well-being and activism. This is one of the reasons why songs, drawing, poetry, skits and personal sharing are so vital. However, to avoid becoming solely a 'feel-good' personal experience, it is critical that these forms of learning and connecting are combined with political analysis, strategising and organising since feminist pedagogy integrates conceptual, affective and embodied learning with power and politics.

Recognising and addressing trauma and violence

For many women, joining social movements or becoming outspoken brings stigma and isolation, even retaliation, from their own communities, organisations and sometimes families – not to mention violence from corporate or government powers. Women's multiple workloads exacerbate stress. Over many years, and especially in violent or threatening contexts, physical and emotional trauma can leave deep scars that, if unattended, undermine women's sense of self and agency. Processes such as healing, self-care and community-building help revitalise women's spirits and faith in people's potential for love and generosity. Calling forth creativity, solidarity and courage, they sustain movements in the face of fear, despair, exhaustion, loneliness, sexual abuse and violence that such backlash provokes. As fundamentalists attempt to roll back rights and state and non-state actors use violent repression, feminist educators and organisers incorporate risk assessment, security strategies and practical tips for women and their communities to safeguard their lives and work and to renew their energies, imagination and hope.

---

4   And other prejudicial beliefs based on race, sexuality, ethnicity, age and religion (among others) interact to further silence women.

Valuing feminist popular educators

Never neutral, feminist educators serve as catalysts, facilitators, prodders, probers, cheerleaders, coaches, resources and honest brokers. Key to creating, leading and sustaining transformational education/action processes, their roles are often invisible and overlooked. Yet their commitment, knowledge and talents are the lynchpin in developing empowering spaces and processes where people can strengthen and nurture themselves and their movements. Over the past several decades, the de-politicisation of popular education and donor devaluation of deeper training processes have resulted in a severe decline of skilled, politically savvy popular educators.

Self-diagnosis of reality: an example of feminist popular education[5]

One of the tenets of popular education rests on the idea that any transformative learning-action process starts with people's reality. Among the different methods available, we find one from Mesoamerica of particular value because of its multi-dimensional and transformational qualities. Popular educators there developed an approach called the 'Self-Diagnosis of Reality': a carefully facilitated participatory process where communities marginalised by poverty did their own diagnosis – reflecting on different aspects of their lives and circumstances as a way to both develop and deepen critical consciousness and contribute to planning popular education and action initiatives. Feminist educators added a gender and sharper power lens, and eventually an intersectional analysis to the process. They incorporated reflections on how dimensions of reality and power play out not only from a class perspective in peasants' and workers' lives but also in women's experience – in their hearts, minds and bodies, and in their intimate relationships as well as in the family, organisation, community and wider world. The approach focuses on three dimensions of reality and areas of change – context, concepts and practices – and is a diagnosis as well as a first step in the education process. Originally called the *Triple Autodiagnóstico de la Realidad* (Triple Self-Diagnosis of Reality), it focuses on three dimensions: context (the surroundings that shape people's lives); concepts (the ideas, beliefs and cosmovisions that shape their thinking, feeling and action); and practices (the actions people take in their lives).

The Self Diagnosis of Reality method underpins and guides learning and action by having people themselves reflect on their circumstances, worldviews, feelings, knowledge and behaviours in dialogue with facilitators who also contribute their own ideas. The dialogue provides space for creating and refining programme content, and can be a baseline for evaluations and learning self-assessments. It also

5   While some of the examples of feminist popular education we present – such as the Self-Diagnosis of Reality – have emerged from diverse groups, most have been designed and defined with women's groups in particular who are confronting sexism, racism, poverty, and government and corporate discrimination. Whatever the issue or intersections, these principles and processes can be applied across differences.

serves as a touchstone for deepening reflections throughout the entire experience. From the dialogue, organisers adjust and enrich initial programme plans – allowing facilitators to choose activities and learning opportunities that best respond to participant realities as they explore, question and work to reimagine themselves and transform their worlds.

Moments and examples: from drawings to mapping

So how does this process actually proceed? One example comes from *Alquimia*, a multi-year Mesoamerican women's leadership school offered by JASS from 2014 to 2016 that brought together activists from seven countries.[6] To launch the process, facilitators first created a warm, supportive, engaging environment. Passing a candle around in a ritual of welcome, the 30 rural and indigenous participants and facilitators explained what light they would like to share with others and what light they would like to gain from their time together. For many participants it was a first moment of personal and political connection with women from different contexts and struggles. Each morning began with a similar ritual of inspiration and meditation led by participants.

As part of the initial self-diagnosis, facilitators asked participants to draw an image illustrating their leadership. Each drawing was given a number so the images could be displayed anonymously. After a gallery walk, people discussed – *what do the images say about leadership?* Facilitators then posed a series of specific questions as a way to decode the drawings further, for example:

How big is the woman leader in relation to other community members?
What is the leader doing?
What attitudes about leadership does the image convey?
And, to wrap up – What do the drawings say about our vision and exercise of leadership and the challenges we face?

Questions were deliberately non-judgemental. Since drawings were posted anonymously, the reflections were not personalised. The group noted that the images illustrated different approaches to leadership, from very directive to more participatory and egalitarian. As a follow-up, facilitators led a simple circle dance accompanied by words and themes about important leadership qualities and challenges.[7] People moved together in swaying harmony, feeling the power and joy of their bodies and connections. Music and dance were integral to the process,

6   Regional and national *Alquimia* Leadership Schools are grounded in a transformative, empowering process of learning, action and solidarity to create new paradigms and practices of power in which participants share their histories, struggles, ideas and the challenges of difficult and changing contexts – surfacing and processing the pain of personal and political violence, and drawing on the energy and joy of dance and art.
7   Facilitators for the dance aspects of *Alquimia* came from *Cantera*, the Centre for Popular Communication and Education in Managua, Nicaragua (http://canteranicaragua.org).

inspiring energy, connections, self-awareness and joy – reflected in part by processes of *Biodanza* ('dance of life').

Participants also drew maps of positive and negative contextual forces affecting their lives and leadership. In these analyses, they examined how context impacts each of them personally – in their emotions, spirits and bodies, as well as in their families, communities and work. Here, women recognised some of the costs and stigmas as well as some of their joys and rewards, and began naming specific forces and power dynamics shaping their relationships and struggles – from 'diva' leadership styles to sexual abuse within their movements to spaces of solidarity.

In the closing sessions of the self-diagnosis, participants generated and prioritised a list of skills, knowledge, tools and values that they felt were critical for improving their leadership and advancing social justice struggles, emphasising the need for self-care, renewal and healing. A participant–facilitator dialogue followed on the programme content and design. In country groups, people reviewed and refined the proposed curriculum outline presented by the design team, each country providing its own particular feedback and recommendations to shape the programme. In a concluding moment, country teams wrote down their goals and commitments according to the different realms of their activist lives – personal, family and organisation/movement. They read them aloud and noted some common themes. Facilitators then incorporated the information into the design.

Building on the self-diagnosis

During the second gathering, after participants reflected more on questions of context, power and collaboration, facilitators reintroduced the leadership drawings done during the diagnostic phase. Participants greeted the images with shouts of laughter, surprise and a bit of chagrin, but with an openness that generated an animated dialogue. Being together in a trusting and caring environment encouraged honesty with themselves and others. Many went up to their drawings immediately and carried out their own personal self-critiques:

> Oh dear, look at me, I am standing on a podium – huge and tall – all the other women are tiny sitting at my feet.
> Hmmm, that's me on the stage, talking down to everyone. Can you imagine? [She begins to chuckle] I even drew some of the women with small heads, nothing else. I cut off their bodies. Sometimes I chopped off their heads. What was I thinking?
> But look at Rosa's, she put people in a circle. Relationships are more equal there, everyone seems to be participating and engaged.

Developing alternative leadership approaches was seen as both a form of resistance and transformation. The participants themselves deepened their understanding of leadership as the facilitator probed with a range of other questions:

How do these drawings reflect the realities of our organisation's leadership?
How are they different or not from traditional male models?
What needs to go into leadership approaches that challenge oppression and promote women's voice, solidarity and collective power?
What obstacles do we face; how are we working to overcome them?
What qualities, skills, attitudes and styles are necessary?

Reviewing the comments, the facilitator added anything important that seemed to be missing, and closed with a wrap-up and summary of major insights which were then incorporated into further activities on leadership

Other processes and examples of feminist popular education

Power of safe, supportive, creative spaces of solidarity, inquiry and transformation

Another foundational process of feminist popular education involves the formation of safe, supportive and creative spaces of inquiry and transformation where people's health, spirits and relationships can be replenished, and their awareness, analysis and actions energised. JASS defines these as *political spaces for challenging and changing power, building common ground among diverse activists and renewing their strategies and energies*. When activists come together, they come with histories of trauma, stigma and isolation that are more severe when confronting multiple discriminations of gender, race, class and sexuality, among others. To build solidarity and collectively strategise about the risks and violence they face, people need safe spaces to break silences, analyse power dynamics and find shared purpose. Such spaces are critical for generating political awareness, connection, new organising strategies, and the resilience and healing that comes with feeling safe and supported. Given the nature of oppression and trauma, groups often form their own separate spaces of reflection in response to the types of discrimination they face, as was seen when women popular educators developed their special creative space apart from male colleagues.

Deep trust and solidarity are fundamental to these environments: places where people feel free to challenge themselves and others in a constructive, loving and productive way, something Mesoamerican activists termed *crítica amorosa* – loving critique. The drawing process, described above, is one concrete example of learning and unlearning where people reflected critically on their own practice and ideas of leadership without defensiveness or fear and, as a result, experienced major transformation. This unusual openness to critique emerged from the facilitators' commitment to inclusion and building loving respect across all differences, and in part, from the region's history and politics. Years of intense, sometimes vicious infighting among different Mesoamerican women's organisations, indigenous groups and revolutionary movements have led to a greater awareness about the destructive and abusive nature of power, prejudice and rigid ideologies, and to a search for ethics to guide their interactions. Women have felt the profound pain, paralysis and setbacks caused by such power dynamics within themselves and their movements.

A loving climate contributes to healing some of these historic wounds, building bridges between people and movements, and ensuring that in the telling of women's personal stories they will not be judged or disrespected, and their struggles and pain acknowledged and addressed no matter their race, class, sexuality or age. Yet, the challenge of creating such a space is complex and not easy, especially given women's stories that are marked by a mix of dynamics and contradictions – of violence and resilience, of hope and fear, of sadness and joy. Feeling increasingly safe, women reveal intimate and sometimes traumatic experiences which may require special psychological support in order to respond to their deep pain and suffering.

Power of symbol and metaphor: alchemy and cooking pots

Alquimia participants came from seven countries with different cultural and political contexts and backgrounds – *mestiza*, indigenous and women of African ancestry – from diverse schooling and movement experiences, views of feminism, religion, language and leadership. Yet, common threads united everyone – being defenders of human rights, survivors of violence and open to learning from one another. Amidst this rich and challenging diversity, we found symbols and metaphors powerful for engaging participants creatively and collaboratively. Tapping into a non-analytical, more aesthetic level of knowledge and meaning reinforced important connections and ideas in fresh new ways that conceptual rational processes cannot.

The symbolism of the school's name, *Alquimia* (alchemy), gave meaning to the process and participants. It affirmed women as alchemists of life and knowledge: transforming products of the earth into life-giving food and medicine, transforming inferiorities into self-esteem, relationships into collective power, despair into hope. *Alquimia* symbolised our methodology – the sharing, transforming and producing of collective knowledge and strategy in a safe magical place where women create power together. To enrich the symbolism, facilitators put a big clay cooking pot in the centre of the room – a simple container crafted by unknown hands and baked in Nicaragua's fierce sun to give it strength. With a huge wooden spoon, we stirred and mixed our thoughts and began to produce an alchemy of collective wisdom and questions. The pot was surround by flowers and candles that provided added beauty to the room.

To begin, facilitators gave participants coloured cards and asked them to write down any experience, feeling, knowledge, story or example of a craft that they wanted to share. Music accompanied the process. After reading and depositing their cards, participants joined facilitators in swaying to the rhythms separately and then together, holding hands, creating a living moving circle that fostered another sense of bonding and power. A set of questions guided the subsequent discussion:

What did I feel?
What does this moment mean to me?
What does it say about our own power relations in the group?

What value does this type of exercise have in our work?

What are the ways we create alchemy in our organisations?

Throughout the workshop facilitators repeated this process with different questions to stimulate reflection on other topics. For example: What lessons do I take away from this experience? What questions does it raise for me? What else do we need to think about? In their wrap-up, facilitators added new information to challenge and enrich people's knowledge. One participant summed up the learning:

> What's most beautiful about all of this is that we are defining and enriching the concepts and ideas based on our own different visions and perspectives – ideas from all of us.

However, symbols can also be problematic and need to be chosen well. Another *Alquimia* symbol – the simple outlines of a lovely woman's face with flowing hair – was used on tote bags for the group and on the large welcome sign hanging in the meeting room. Yet the image looked to many of the participants like a representation of an urban middle-class figure not embodying the features or spirit of the indigenous and rural participants.

The mural of mentors and ancestors: a history of our struggles and transgressions[8]

The mural process engages participants in creating a visual tribute to ancestors and mentors who have helped shape them as activists and feminists. This exercise can be used at different moments for personal introductions, building a sense of community, and for beginning dialogues on leadership qualities and human rights struggles over time. People bring in a photo or symbol of a person who has inspired them in their growth as an activist and share why. Placing these images on a coloured square, participants create a vivid mural/quilt that serves as a meaningful backdrop – bringing in ancestors' energy, qualities and history of struggle – which increases appreciation for their transgressions and can encourage cross-generation dialogues important for movement-building. Indigenous women found this exercise especially meaningful. By revering women ancestors, it opened up community dialogues on women's roles and power without fear of traditional backlash.

> I met with women in my village to do this activity. We identified our mothers and grandmothers who had worked courageously for the community, who were not afraid to speak up. The women loved it. I could do it with no trouble since our authorities teach us to respect our ancestors and that's what

8   Developed by Alda Facio in conjunction with JASS colleagues.

we were doing – remembering and revering our women ancestors. (Panamanian participant, *Alquimia* Leadership School)

The house of multiple oppressions: the master's house

Developed by JASS colleagues in Southern Africa and inspired by Audre Lorde's 'The master's tools will never dismantle the master's house' (1978), this exercise was adapted for the *Alquimia* school to illustrate the power dynamics of patriarchy and the house's multiple pillars of oppression where people learn to dominate and discriminate against others (De Montis 2015). In a multi-stage process, participants construct an image of the house, naming patriarchy's basic columns and support structures – such as family, education, religion, media, civil society, corporations and state – and then examining how each institution interacts and impacts gender, race and class. Deconstructing the house, people develop a more complex understanding of power, intersectionality and strategy. Facilitators ask: what does each structure say to us about how men and women should act in society; about poor people; about indigenous, white or mestizo persons? Personal and organisational questions follow:

How does living in the house affect me?
How do I and all of us (whatever gender, race, class or sexuality) maintain and reinforce it?
How can each of us and our organisations become forces for liberation?
What effective strategies are transforming these structures?

Virtual feminist dialogues

In conjunction with its *Alquimia* school, JASS opened a series of lively online dialogues and debates on issues of important concern to Latin American activists. Through these, women exchanged ideas and experiences and probed different perspectives. Using a simple list-serve format, topics included feminism, power, fear, violence and safety, among others. The role of facilitator was key in catalysing and motivating dialogue and in presenting occasional summaries and questions to deepen conversations. Having a respected feminist legal scholar and activist in this role was critical in providing legitimacy to the process and ensuring that the subsequent publication of the dialogues had a useful coherence and flow (Facio 2014). Given the contexts and technologies, safer formats and platforms are needed to ensure basic protection and security.

Conclusion

Recognising that people are capable of great generosity and creativity, feminist popular education helps us affirm the best in each other, and challenge and change the intersecting power dynamics that diminish and demean all of us. Through reflection and action, we deepen our vision, values, strategies and solidarity necessary for transforming oppression and fear into movements for justice and liberation.

As activists and educators, we are engaged in the never-ending quest for freedom, dignity and community that is embodied in these efforts. With all our questions, imperfections and contradictions, we bring with us our hopes and dreams and stubborn commitment to creating a better world. Feminist popular education gives life and meaning to our quest.

References

Angelou, M., 1978. *And still I rise*. New York: Random House.

Crenshaw, K., 1989. Demarginalizing the intersection of race and sex: a black feminist critique of antidiscrimination doctrine, feminist theory and antiracist politics. *University of Chicago Legal Forum*, 1989(1), 139–168.

Davis, A.Y., 2011. *Women, race and class*. New York: Knopf and Doubleday.

De Montis, M., 2015. *Casa de los múltiples opresiones*. Managua: Escuela Feminista de Alquimia and Just Associates.

De Montis, M. and Maessick, M., 1989. *A panorama of Nicaraguan women*. New York and Managua: Women's International Resource Exchange and Cenzontle.

Facio, A., 2014. *Dialogos virtuales feministas*. Washington DC: Just Associates.

Freire, P., 1970a. *Pedagogy of the oppressed*. New York: Herder & Herder.

Freire, P., 1970b. Cultural action and conscientization. *Harvard Educational Review*, 40(3), 452–477.

Freire, P., 1994. *Pedagogy of hope: reliving pedagogy of the oppressed*. London and New York: Bloomsbury.

Freire, P. and Coutinho, J.d.V., 1970. Cultural action for freedom. *Harvard Educational Review*, 476–521.

Freire, P. and Freire, A.M.A., 1994. *Pedagogy of hope: reliving pedagogy of the oppressed*. New York: Continuum.

Gaventa, J., 2006. Finding the spaces for change: a power analysis. *IDS Bulletin*, 37(5), 23–33.

hooks, b., 2014. *Feminist theory: from margin to center*. 3rd ed. London: Routledge.

Horton, M. and Freire, P., 1990. *We make the road by walking: conversations on education and social change*. Philadelphia: Temple University Press.

Lorde, A., 1984. The master's tools will never dismantle the master's house. In *Sister outsider: essays and speeches*. Berkeley, CA: Crossing Press.

Miller, V., 2002. Political consciousness: a perpetual quest. Washington DC: Just Associates, 31 May. Available from: https://justassociates.org/sites/justassociates.org/files/political-consciousness-perpetual-quest-valarie-miller.pdf [Accessed 20 December 2018].

Miller, V., VeneKlasen, L., Reilly, M. and Clark, C., 2006. *Making change happen 3: power. Concepts for revisioning power for justice, equality and peace*. Washington DC: Just Associates.

VeneKlasen, L. and Miller, V., 2012. Feminist popular education and movement building. Draft Discussion Paper, April, Washington DC: Just Associates. Available from: https://justassociates.org/sites/justassociates.org/files/feminist-popular-education-movement-building-miller-veneklasen.pdf [Accessed 20 December 2018].

INDEX

A page reference in *italics* indicates a figure and tables are shown by a page reference in **bold**.